The Grace of Friendship

Some cry up Gunnersbury,
For Sion some declare;
And some say that with Chiswick House
No villa can compare;
But ask the beaux of Middlesex,
Who know the country well,
If Strawb'ry Hill, if Strawb'ry Hill
Don't bear away the bell?

The Grace of Friendship

HORACE WALPOLE
AND THE MISSES BERRY

Edited by Virginia Surtees

MICHAEL RUSSELL

Editorial matter © Virginia Surtees 1995

First published in Great Britain 1995
by Michael Russell (Publishing) Ltd
Wilby Hall, Wilby, Norwich NR16 2JP

Typeset by The Typesetting Bureau
Wimborne, Dorset
Printed and bound in Great Britain
by Biddles Ltd, Guildford and King's Lynn

ISBN 0 85955 216 0

Contents

List of Illustrations

Strawberry Hill from the south east, as seen in late eighteenth century.

Library at Strawberry Hill.

Little Strawberry Hill, early nineteenth century, from an engraving after a drawing by H. S. Storr.

Mary and Agnes Berry, by Zoffany, *c.* 1771-2. Probably made at Chiswick. Private collection.

Mary and Agnes Berry, 1791-2. Miniatures by Miss Foldsone. Private collection.

The Misses Berry, watercolour by Paul Sandby. The Royal Collection. 1994. Her Majesty the Queen.

Mary Berry, *c.* 1793. Bronze portrait bust by the Hon. Mrs Damer. Private collection. Photograph Courtauld Institute of Art.

Horace Walpole, Earl of Orford, 1793. Pencil drawing by George Dance. Permission National Portrait Gallery, London.

Horace Walpole, 1788. Three caricatures by John Carter. Permission The Huntington, San Marino, California.

Horace Walpole, Earl of Orford, 1795. Pencil drawing by Sir Thomas Lawrence. Permission National Portrait Gallery, London.

Acknowledgements

My thanks are due to Her Majesty the Queen for gracious permission to reproduce the drawing from the Royal Collection of Mary and Agnes Berry by Paul Sandby.

I should like to thank Mr John Ingamells for making available to me material in the Brinsley Ford Archive, The Paul Mellon Centre for Studies in British Art. Miss Sarah Wimbush, Courtauld Institute of Art, has helped me in various ways and I should like to extend my thanks to her and to Miss Elizabeth Powis, The Paul Mellon Centre for Studies in British Art; to Miss Christine Turfitt, Local Studies Library, Richmond, and to Miss Penny Ward, Margate Library.

Author's Note

The letters of Horace Walpole included in this volume are a selection from those in volumes 11 and 12 of the Yale edition edited by W.S. Lewis, 1944, as are those of Mary Berry, though few of hers survive. Unless indicated otherwise all letters are from Horace Walpole to Mary Berry. The letters between Mary Berry and General O'Hara published in *The Berry Papers* conform to the originals in the British Library except for an occasional difference of punctuation and the rare omission of an unessential phrase.

Spelling has not been adjusted and points of omission have not been introduced.

Introduction

The Berry sisters, the 'Berrinos', or more accurately Mary, the elder of the two, and Agnes her junior by a year, represent to posterity the image of two exceptional young women who brought sunshine and interest to the Honourable Horace Walpole, 4th Earl of Orford, in his last years.

Strawberry Hill, Twickenham, his Gothic 'castle' on the banks of the River Thames, is still there to attract and seduce. It remains an abiding indication of the eclectic taste of one of the most celebrated personages of the eighteenth century. His voluminous correspondence, which embraces all of sixty years, is a celebration of the art of letter-writing. Witty, erudite, urbane and informed, it conveys to each correspondent the sense of being personally engaged with the author in the telling of whatever tale Walpole was at pains to communicate – never mind that the same information in nearly the identical phrase was offered to others of his friends.

Not only through the lustre of his parentage (his father, Sir Robert Walpole, George II's powerful Prime Minister, had been created 1st Earl of Orford in 1742), but also by connection of blood or friendship he was on familiar terms with the distinguished names of his time in artistic, literary and social circles and could be a sharp commentator or an amused conveyor of gossip which added spice to his communications – though this ingredient was tempered and mostly free from malice by the time he knew the Berrys.

A man of some wealth, a politician with twenty-five energetic years in Parliament behind him, he had led a varied life of travel, a fashionable and favourite pursuit in which both Italy and France stood high in his affections. As an accomplished author he had a printing press installed in a cottage beside his house, his 'Officina Arbuteana'; its final use in 1789 was the printing of his *Reminiscences of the Courts of George I and George II* for the Berry sisters; an antiquary and collector he would always be, and Strawberry Hill his constant love.

When in late 1787 he first saw the sisters at an evening assembly he shrank from an introduction for, as so often in life, having heard too ample an account of their varied accomplishments he assumed that their pretensions were in like degree. However, finding himself next to Mary at a small gathering the following year, he was delighted to discover the reverse. He was enchanted by his new friend whom he recognized as a model of propriety, 'an angel inside and out', fluent in French, acquainted with Latin, well read, and seemingly endowed with every excellence including that of unaffected modesty. Agnes, in turn, measured up to her sister, though gentler and more retiring, allowing the lead to the elder, yet her superior perhaps with her pencil and in the modest skill of her sketches in watercolour.

At this meeting in 1788 Walpole, born in 1717, was nearly seventy-one years old (considered an old man for those times), of delicate health and often ravaged by painful arracks of gout, slender of figure, as he had always been (though rather bent with age), the pallor of his face contrasting sharply with his dark eyes.[1] Yet he was still elegant, with manners most polished, intelligence undimmed, his enjoyment of the contemporary scene as rich as ever – even if a strong element of 'fuss' intruded where the sisters' well-being was concerned, particularly while they were abroad; since for Walpole, dependent on their proximity to Strawberry Hill, as his letters testify by their unremitting demands for Berry companionship, their welfare was, perforce, of lasting importance. This and his deep affection for the young women took place beside his love for Strawberry Hill as the overriding absorption of his last years, though this devotion towards both sisters can more precisely be distilled.

It was Mary who claimed the larger share of his thought and heart and it seems likely that he might have sought a marital companionship had not his fear of the ridiculous prevented him – a lifelong bachelor in his seventies and a regular martyr to gout would be open to derision for contemplating marriage with a young woman in her early twenties, only recently introduced. But that he loved her, letters testify – though subterfuge and self-ridicule play their part.

Horace Walpole was a survivor. He had lost most of his friends of his youth and middle age and those who had lived as neighbours along the Middlesex river shore. 'Dowagers as plenty as flanders inhabit all around me,' he had once said. Newer friends helped to take their place, none more so than Mary and Agnes Berry.

Winters were partly spent at his London house, No. 11 Berkeley Square, but Strawberry Hill was always able to entice him back. This was the home where he lived simply. Rising at nine he would follow the daily ritual in the bow-windowed breakfast room on the first floor, facing eastwards to the river, the Ham meadows beyond, a favourite prospect: two or three cups of tea from the finest of porcelain cups, followed by slices of bread and butter, attended by his elderly spaniel, the portly Tonton, placed comfortably by his side. He would not eat again till dinner at four o'clock where no wine accompanied his light meal of game or a sliver of venison pie. Coffee would be brought to him upstairs at five and there he would remain until an early hour of the morning, conversing with friends by candlelight on the transient gaieties of his youth and the rewards of a notable life relegated now to memory or immortalized in the letters by which he hoped to ensure a lasting recognition.

The small box-like building on a slightly raised piece of land that he had bought in 1747 for £1,350 had been of no architectural merit whatsoever. It was its incomparable setting on a peaceful reach of the river below Hampton Court, with a prospect of Richmond Hill and its wooded park standing sentinel against the open sky, which had so beguiled him.

His father had spent thirteen years building the majestic Houghton Hall on his Norfolk estate on the site of a more humble dwelling. When it was completed in 1736, Walpole, then nearly twenty, had made his first visit there and had been immediately attracted by the splendour of the house and landscape. So it was of no small preoccupation to him as the owner of his new acreage at Twickenham to do likewise on a miniature scale and in a very different style; for whereas his father's great mansion was a monument to the classical order, his was to be a truly Gothic 'rural bijou'. To alter, rebuild, to add to and to purchase more land as his taste dictated – these were his intentions. The beginnings were slow. The little house as it stood was cramped, leading his friend Lady Etheldreda Townsend to exclaim at her first visit, 'Lord God! Jesus, what a house!' By degrees, and planned in much detail in association with two friends self-styled the Committee of Taste, such a house as had never before graced the banks of the Thames emerged. Battlemented and pinnacled, with a tower at one end and bow windows at the other, it gave small indication of what Walpole had achieved indoors. 'The gloom of Abbeys and Cathedrals' was what he eagerly sought and this 'gloomth' informed the many rooms, mostly small, of this extraordinary house.[2] The characteristics of his Gothic requirements were firmly upheld in the shape of cloisters, narrow arched windows 'fattened with rich saints in painted glass', chimneypieces copied from sixteenth-century cathedral tombs, while that of the Holbein Chamber (itself a room of Gothic imagination run riot) was partly derived from Rouen's high altar and the tomb of Archbishop Warham at Canterbury; that of the Round Drawing Room, though later, was still more distinguished, being a dredged-up version by Robert Adam of Edward the Confessor's tomb in Westminster Abbey. In the Library on the first floor, which looked to the river, the bookcases placed on four sides of the room were modelled from an illustration by Hollar of the choir-screen side doors in Dugdale's *St Paul's*; the decoration of the ceiling was Walpole's own. Tapered columns supported the arches of the staircase landing, repository of the armoury. The Gallery, where his pictures mostly hung, the Great Parlour, the Blue and Red Bedchambers, the Green Closet, the Tribune with its dome of sultry yellow glass, all these were redolent of their creator's taste and claimed the contents of his varied collections of coins, prints, manuscripts, precious objects, sculpture and curiosities.

A dusty road ran past the main door but the garden front where once lay meadow-land was now transformed into a lawn with a graceful avenue of lime trees extending from the house to the river, then far closer to the house than it is now. Flowering shrubs and blossom trees were introduced, a terrace laid out and a small secluded Prior's Garden was formed carrying on from the cloisters, giving something of a like effect. Many large trees were planted, Walpole lamenting the length of time for growth. To crown all, not caring for a Twickenham address shared by too many, when coming upon an ancient deed with the name of Strawberry Hill inscribed, he declared 'Never call it Twickenham again.'

Installing the Berrys nearby at Little Strawberry Hill was not only an act of generosity to an impoverished family but it focused their availability and established a pattern of visits. What is never revealed is how the family responded among themselves to the claims on their unfailing acquiescence to call, to write, to entertain, as Walpole desired. Did the father tease his daughter with regard to the septuagenarian's affection? Most surely not. Imagination recoils at so well-mannered a family jesting at his expense. But was Mr Berry obliged, in conformity with the observances of the day, to chaperone his daughters on each and every visit to Strawberry Hill and Berkeley Square? From one letter we learn that he fell asleep – perhaps the only person ever to have done so in Walpole's company.

This then was the man who succumbed to Mary Berry's charms. Owing to the devotion she inspired in him, we have an almost daily account when they were apart of the occurrences, sometimes trivial but never dull, which informed the last eight years of Walpole's life.

Mary and Agnes Berry

To read of Mary and Agnes Berry is to picture them as orphans, but this was not the case. Mr Robert Berry, their father, a shadowy figure (though 'a little merry man with a round face'), rarely makes an appearance in the following letters, for Mary, the strongest personality of the three, takes charge. A weak man, he had been wholly dependent on his wealthy maternal uncle, Robert Ferguson, of Raith in Fife, a city merchant of Broad Street, London, who made his nephew an allowance of £300 a year. Robert Berry had married a Miss Seton, a distant cousin, but she had died within a few weeks of the birth of her youngest daughter, Agnes, who, born on 29 May 1764, was fourteen months younger than her sister Mary, born on 26 March 1763.

Ferguson had urged his nephew to marry a second time, on the chance of producing a male heir who with Robert would inherit his large fortune. To this Robert Berry would not consent and he remained a widower until his death in 1817. Meanwhile his younger brother, William, had ingratiated himself in no mean way so that on the death of Ferguson in 1781 it was he who inherited the bulk of his uncle's estate. Ten thousand pounds was the capital sum Robert received, to which his brother added £1,000 a year.

Mary and Agnes were born at their maternal grandmother's house, Kirkbridge, near Stanwick, Askham, Yorkshire and remained there with their father until 1770. Still living on the meagre allowance of £300, the family moved to a rented property at Chiswick, College House, and here a governess was in charge. On her departure, however, a few years later, the girls' education relied solely on self-instruction and one can only be astonished at their wide accomplishments. In French they were well-nigh bilingual and according to Lord Houghton they had 'a sufficient command of the Latin classics to give a scholarly turn to their knowledge without a taint of pedantry, a thorough understanding of their own language and literature which shone in all their conversations';[3] and all this with much modesty of bearing. To Mary it was a source of bitterness for many years that her father had been cheated of his proper inheritance. But how, one wonders, would she have welcomed a stepmother, even if an inheritance had been the consequence? She was to say that 'nobody ever suffered insignificance more unwillingly' than herself; 'nobody ever took more pains by every honourable means compatible with a proud mind to avoid it', and endeavoured to forget the 'inevitable circumstances while making others remember how little she deserved it'.

With Ferguson's death the Berrys, father and daughters, now in possession of their small inheritance, were able to travel on their first journey abroad in 1783, to Holland, Switzerland and Italy, the sisters' intelligence and winning manner gaining them friends and acquaintances. A year earlier they had made a short tour of England with Weymouth, then a resort of royalty, as their objective, but foreign travel, as well as being cheaper than staying at home, afforded them the long-held desire to see countries of which they had read and to become familiar with the landscapes and masterpieces of art and architecture.

Mary's journals of this first adventurous enterprise were written in three small calf-bound books measuring some seven inches by three; two others of a later journey, bound in vellum and marbled paper, were of a similar size. Occasional sketches in pen and brown ink and pencil are glanced within the pages. The text reads like a guidebook and yields little in evoking a more intimate response to the people with whom she became acquainted. She had been 'monstrously sick' when crossing to Holland; from Rotterdam they had made their way to Liège (some twenty miles south of Maastricht), stopping at Brussels and attending a performance of Molière's *Les Femmes Savantes*. Liège proved a town of 'booksellers' shops filled with nothing but libertine and profligate tales and novels and where every priest openly keeps a mistress'. Coblenz followed Bonn, then Strasbourg, Basle and Geneva. At Bonneville the inn was only a 'comfortable habitation for vermin'. However, the scenes presented to the eye at Chamonix were 'the most sublime that imagination could form'. Mary was absorbed in such a confusion of ideas that she had to sit down and could neither speak of the magnificence which presented itself to her eyes 'nor wish to hear others speak on the subject'. Arrived in Italy she familiarized herself with beds which would perhaps have 'turned our stomachs in England'. At Bologna they watched Marlow's *Tamerlane* performed in the 'new theatre' built in 1756 from original designs by Bibiano. Here she was told that all Italian actors were very bad; but these were called superlatively bad. Sightseeing in Florence and Rome began in earnest as well as the meeting and introduction of acquaintances, including Sir Horace Mann, Bt, British envoy at Florence and a friend of Horace Walpole for many years; Thomas Pitt (in 1784 Lord Camelford), nephew of William Pitt; Sir James Graham, Bt, of Netherby, father of the future statesman; and the painters Gavin Hamilton and Philip Hackert. Another artist whose paintings they went to see were those of Angelica Kauffmann soon to be engaged on her portrait of the fascinating Lady Elizabeth Foster in her broad shady hat, whose sojourn in Italy was in consequence of her acting as governess and guardian to a little by-blow of the Duke of Devonshire and a pretty milliner.[4] Cardinal de Bernis, Archbishop of Albi and now French Ambassador to Rome and one of her most celebrated personages, entertained royally in the Palazzo Carolis on the Corso facing the Piazza di San Marcello. To him the Berrys were introduced on New Year's Day 1784; they were likewise presented to Pope Pius VI.

From such eminence the Court of Naples seemed but a step and there the Berrys were received by Queen Caroline, wife of Ferdinand IV and daughter of Empress Maria Theresa. Mary had already made a marked impression on Gustavus III, King of Sweden, whom she met again in Naples. One evening in Rome he had appeared in all his jewels – 'his star, his epaulettes and his watch chain of diamonds had not lost their magic power,' observed an onlooker. He played some Swedish game with Mary 'and lost twenty sequins to her'. Another Englishman reported that there were 'two very pretty English girls, Miss Berrys. I don't know how it is but in the conversations I always find myself close to them in preference to the Roman Dames. The King of Sweden is of the same mind for he always goes to their box at the Opera, this makes the Roman ladies very jealous.'[5] In Naples the sisters were often again in the company of the Swedish king, going with him on an expedition to Baiae, taking supper with him after the opera, invited to his opera box. Of Caserta, Mary's opinion was that the architecture was not in good taste and she was surprised to find that in the royal apartments the floors were all covered with English carpets.

[8]

It was in March 1784, on their return to Rome, that Mary first met General Charles O'Hara. Eleven years would pass and then, deeply in love, she would agree to marry him, but within a few months he proved a faithless lover and their engagement was at an end. Now, in Rome, he was travelling with his friend, General the Hon. Seymour Conway, a cousin and dear friend of Walpole, who lived at Park Place, Henley-on-Thames, and in London at 4 Little Warwick Street, Pall Mall.

Conway had married as her second husband the widowed Caroline Countess of Ailesbury (she retained her nomenclature in the manner of the day), daughter of the 4th Duke of Argyll. Their daughter, Anne, born in 1748, was a sculptress of some note; as a young child she had lived at Strawberry Hill under Walpole's care. Her marriage to the Hon. John Damer had ended in disaster and had left her a widow. More particularly in this account, her lesbian tendencies were recognized, though her love for Mary Berry went unnoticed by Horace Walpole. This emotional undercurrent was apparent in Mrs Damer's irritated reaction to Walpole's occasional possessiveness of Mary.

In Rome in the early spring of 1784, on first making the acquaintance of Conway and O'Hara, the Berrys spent five hours with them at St Peter's 'in the examination of this wonderful building'. As the Berrys prepared a leisurely removal to France, on driving from Rome to Florence they fell in again with their military acquaintances on the Terni road, sharing an early breakfast soon after four in the morning and riding out in two *calèches* to see the cascades. When they left for Spoleto the two men took the direction of Foligno.

The Berrys were at Lausanne in early August where Mary made the acquaintance of the precocious Germaine Necker (later de Staël) and remarked on the boldness of manner of this girl of eighteen. After wintering at the famous health resort of Montpelier, the family were in Paris in spring 1785 where Mary became fairly intimate with Gustavus III's newly appointed Ambassador to France, Monsieur de Staël, who spoke of his projected marriage to Mlle Necker. This took place the following year, bringing with it the hoped-for 650,000 livres. Thereafter the family returned to England, passing the next three years in London and visiting friends in the country.

Of a graver disposition than her sister, Mary carried the responsibilities of the family; hers was the mind that determined and directed. She became later a very forceful character – as well as an insatiable lion-hunter – but at the time of their meeting Walpole in 1788 she had many attractions of youth; her chief beauty lay in her dark glancing eyes, 'such a pair of eyes never were in another head'. Walpole himself observed that the elder of the sisters had a face 'formed for a sentimental novel, but ten times fitter for a fifty times better thing – genteel comedy'.[6] Her lively manner, if assured, gained her friends, though in later life her overbearing style was less pleasing. Lord Dudley was surprised that 'she should have lived so much with people of fashion without acquiring better manners'. He recognized her 'good talents, and [she] is besides friendly, honest and sincere; but she has a loud harsh voice and is unacquainted with grammar'.[7]

But in 1788 Walpole could see no fault in his new, attractive friends and if Mary's letters, few as have survived, inclined to the humdrum and were devoid of wit, he would not have cared, so eager was he for the next instalment.

The Letters

The year 1788 was the start of this noted friendship, when the Berrys were living in a partly thatched house on Twickenham Common, rented for the season. The month was October. Writing to his friend, the Countess of Upper Ossory, Walpole told her of the Berrys' forthcoming visit to see his printing press at Strawberry Hill. Remembering his gallantry of former days, he improvised and had ready set these stanzas for their arrival.

> To Mary's lips has ancient Rome
> Her purest language taught,
> And from the modern city home
> Agnes its pencil brought.
>
> Rome's ancient Horace sweetly chants
> Such maids with lyric fire;
> Albion's old Horace sings nor paints –
> He only can admire.
>
> Still would his press their fame record,
> So amiable the pair is!
> But, ah! how vain to think his word
> Can add a straw to Berrys!

> [Oct. 13, 1788]

The next morning the Latian nymph sent me these lines:

> Had Rome's famed Horace thus addresst
> His Lydia or his Lyce,
> He had ne'er so soft complain'd their breast
> To him was cold and icy.
>
> But had they sought their joy to explain,
> Or praise their generous bard,

Perhaps, like me, they had tried in vain,
And found the task too hard.

[Oct. 14, 1788]

To which Walpole replied with a play on words, using 'foil' and 'clinquant' to express the same meaning.

[Strawberry Hill
Tuesday, Oct.14, 1788]
To Miss Mary Berry
on her stanzas in answer
to his from the press at Strawberry Hill.

I will certainly not contend when I am so glad to be *foiled*, as I am in every sense of the word; for you perceive my great ambition is to *set you off*; and since *clinquant* is of no other use, and as Strawberry *Hill* is the lowest in all the parish of Parnassus, I hope you will allow me the honour of being your *Phébus en titre d'office*; though I shall be the reverse of all deputies, for my charge will be a sinecure, as my principal, the true inspirer, will, I am persuaded, always execute his office himself, and leave on the superannuated list

Your devoted servant
Hor. Walpole

[From Mary Berry]   Twickenham Common
Saturday morning, [Nov. 1, 1788]

As an apology for the enclosed, I must tell you that your verses to us have occasioned half a dozen others (some of them by people whom we never saw), in which our *name* and praises have been played upon a thousand different ways. Our sentiments upon them I have ventured to express to you in the following lines. Rhyming seems to be quite catching, but I fear I have got the disorder of a bad sort.

I have the honour to be much yours,
M. Berry

TO THE HONOURABLE HORACE WALPOLE
Far in a wood not much exposed to view
With other forest fruit, two berries grew;

[12]

Unheeded in their native shade they lay,
Nor courting much, not too much shunning day.
A wand'ring sage, whose footsteps oft had roam'd
Out of the beaten track that fashion own'd,
Observ'd these berries half concealed from sight,
And or from chance, or whim, or his delight
Of bringing unregarded worth to light,
Tasted the fruit, and in a lucky hour
Finding it neither vapid yet, nor sour,
A sort of lively, rather pleasant taste,
A flavour, which he thought he lik'd at last,
Something perhaps upon the strawberry cast;
The new-found fruit with partial care he prais'd,
And so the berries' reputation raised. . .
The berries, conscious all this sudden name
Prov'd not their value, but their patron's fame,
Conscious they only could aspire to please
Some simple palates, satisfied with ease,
But if with nobler, finer fruit compar'd,
They many faults and few perfections shar'd,
Wisely determin'd still to court the shade,
To those that *sought* them, only pleasing made;
No greater honours anxious to obtain,
But still, *your* fav'rite berries to remain.

*In London for the winter months the Berrys were now at their house
in Somerset Street, which ran between Orchard Street and Duke
Street, parallel with Oxford Street, probably on the site now occupied by Selfridges. This had been their home since 1786. In consequence of their removal to London and so as not to be deprived of
their company, Walpole was mostly at his house, 11 Berkeley Square,
on the east side.*

[Berkeley Square]
Feb. 2, [1789]

I am afraid of protesting how much I delight in your society, lest I
should seem to affect being *galant* – but if two negatives make an

affirmative, why may not two ridicules compose one piece of sense? And therefore, as I am in love with you both, I trust it is a proof of the good sense of

> Your devoted
> H. Walpole

In the winter of 1783 while in Rome, the Berrys had been presented to Cardinal de Bernis, one of the most distinguished personages in the capital of the time, notable for combining his spiritual devoirs with those of ambassadorial magnificence. Since 1769 he had been France's envoy to Rome where his popularity was parallel to his prodigality.

[From Mary Berry]   Somersett St
                                          Wednesday night, [Feb. 4, 1789]
You will oblige us by honouring this portrait of Cardinal de Bernis with a place among your prints. We happen to have two or three impressions of it. Could I borrow for a moment the lively language, elegant expression, and polished wit, which in conversation animates these vulgar, heavy features, I would thank you in such terms as the subject deserves for your company last night, and the many pleasant hours we have passed in your society; but as there is no borrowing abilities, even upon usury, I must content myself with reminding you that as, in this portrait, a most heavy unpromising countenance conceals an active, intelligent mind, so the homeliest expression of thanks often accompanies the truest sense of obligation.

> M. Berry

[Berkeley Square]
March 25, 1789
You have not half the quickness that I thought you had – or, which is much more probable, I suspect that I am a little in love, and you are not, for I think I should have understood *you* in two syllables, which has not been your case. I had sealed my note and was going to send it when yours arrived with the invitation for Saturday. I was to dine abroad and had not time to break open my note or write it again, and so lifted up a corner and squeezed in *I will* – what could those

syllables mean, but that I will do whatever you please? Yes, you may keep them as a note of hand always payable at sight of your commands – or your sister's, for I am not less in love with my wife Rachel, than with my wife Leah; and though I had a little forgotten my matrimonial vows at the beginning of this note, and was awkward and haggled a little about owning my passion; now I recollect that I have taken a double dose, I am mighty proud of it; and being more in the right than ever lover was, and twice as much in the right too, I avow my sentiments *hardiment*, and am,

Hymen, O Hymenaee!

Throughout their friendship the Berrys invariably spent Sunday evening with Walpole but on the following occasion, despite poor Mr Berry's inopportune torpor or perhaps because of it (Walpole kept late hours), he and his daughters were summoned for the next morning to be instructed, in the most considerate manner, how to find themselves a house for the summer within the confines of Twickenham parish. Their previous one on the Common was available but at an unaffordably exorbitant rent.

Mrs Damer, to whom Walpole was devoted having known her since childhood, became an adoring friend of Mary. This did not quite please Walpole. The slight jealousy was returned when he seemed to Mrs Damer to be too possessive of her friend. Mary Berry accepted her affection and loyalty and years after Anne Damer's death wrote of her with sincere feeling as having given her 'the truest, the most faithful and most generous friendship that ever animated two human beings'. Mrs Damer's marriage to a spendthrift who shot himself and left his widow crippled with debts was a calamity. However, by living frugally and helped by her sister, the Duchess of Richmond, and her parents, and making a successful profession as a sculptress for which she had worked seriously and had studied anatomy, she made a life for herself in her small house in Sackville Street.

[Berkeley Square]
Saturday, [? April 11, 1789]

Mes très chères Fraises,

As the honeymoon is not over, I hope you will come and see me again tomorrow evening, and that our papa will not be sleepy so very early.

> Your most affectionate
> and *doubly* constant husband
> H.W.

[From Mary Berry]   [Somerset Street]
> Sunday evening, [April 12, 1789]

A thousand thanks, my good Sir, for your *earnestness* last night and your kind attention this morning about a house for us. My father goes to Twickenham tomorrow or next day and carries with him our best wishes to find a place in that neighbourhood but be assured a short distance from Strawberry Hill will be one of the first recommendations to us.

I fear we shall not meet often this week. Allow us, therefore, to lay a plan already for next week, and to beg the favour of seeing you tomorrow sennight, which will be the 21st. Without a little arrangement and consideration beforehand, I find one's time passes away in London *nec recte suaviter*, while we insure both when we are lucky enough to spend the evening with you.

> M. Berry

PS. Do tell us where Mrs Damer lives. Though we are not to have the pleasure of being admitted till next week, we wish no longer to delay leaving our name at her door.

Until age crept upon him Walpole had been an enthusiastic theatre-goer, numbering many actors of the day among his friends. On the evening of 13 April he had been to Drury Lane Theatre to see Elizabeth Farren and John Philip Kemble in Congreve's Love for Love. *His hour for dining was four o'clock, while in the metropolis fashion dictated the later hour of six or thereabouts.*

> [Berkeley Square]
> April 14, 1789

Suavissima Maria,

I could not answer your note yesterday, for I was at dinner, as I do not wait till the Great Mogul Fashion, gives me leave to sit down to table – besides I was to go [to] the play and like to see the beginning as well as the end.

I pray that our papa may find a house at Twickenham – Hampton Court is half way to Swisserland.

In the middle of the last act last night there was an interlude of a boxing match, but it was in the front boxes. The folks in the pit, who could not see behind them better than they generally can before them through domes and pyramids of muslin, hinted to the combatants to retire, which they did into the lobby, where a circle was made, and there the champions pulled one another's hair, and a great deluge of – powder ensued; but being well greased like Grecian pugilists, not many curls were shed. Adieu!

Tickets for the trial of Warren Hastings were gratefully acknowledged. Having resigned his successful administration as first Governor General of British India, Warren Hastings returned to England in 1785. A few years later he was made the scapegoat for the sins of the East India Company and was impeached on grounds of corruption. His trial at the High Court of Parliament was a lengthy one but he was finally acquitted after seven years.

[From Mary Berry]   [Somerset Street]
                                    Saturday afternoon, [April 18, 1789]
Was I to begin thanking you, when should I have done? And what is three tickets or three dozen of tickets for any show upon earth in comparison to my other obligations to you, in comparison of the flattering regard, that lively interest, that real friendship with which upon every occasion you act towards us? Believe me, and it is all I feel able to say, it is not lost upon us. We feel it all, and the impossibility of ever thanking you for such obligations. For tickets to the trial, to anybody else I could write a fine note; to you it is impossible.
                                                                    M.B.

[To Mary and Agnes Berry]   [Berkeley Square]
                                              April 28, at night, 1789
My not saying *no* to Thursday, you I trust understand that I meant

yes, and so I do. In the meantime I send you the most delicious poem upon earth. If you don't know what it is all about, or why, at least you will find glorious similies about everything in the world, and I defy you to discover three bad verses in the whole stack. Dryden was but the prototype of *The Botanic Garden** in his charming 'Flower and Leaf'; and if he had less meaning, it is true he had more plan, and I must own that his white velvets and green velvets and rubies and emeralds were much more virtuous gentlefolks, than most of the flowers of the creation, who seem to have no fear of Doctors' Commons before their eyes. This is only the second part, the first part is not born yet – no matter; I can read this over and over again forever, for all is the most lovely poetry – then one sighs, that such profusion of poetry, magnificent and tender, should be thrown away on what neither interests nor instructs, and with all the pains the notes take to explain, is scarce intelligible.

How strange it is that a man should have been inspired with such enthusiasm of poetry by poring through a microscope, and peeping through the keyholes of all the seraglios of all the flowers in the universe! – I hope his discoveries may leave any impression but of the universal polygamy going on in the vegetable world, where however it is more *galant* than amongst human race, for you will find that they are the botanic *ladies* who keep harems and not the gentlemen – Still, *I* will maintain that it is much better that we should have *two* wives than your sex two husbands.

Your doubly constant

Telypthorus†

Daniel Charles Solander, botanist of Swedish birth, came to England as a young man, working at the British Museum, first in cataloguing its natural history collection and later as Keeper of the Department of Natural History. A box made in a form for holding botanical specimen papers adopted his name and before long its usage for works on paper became universal.

*Part II, by Erasmus Darwin, 1789. Botanist and poet and grandfather of Charles Darwin.
†Here the signature was altered to 'Thelyphthora' by Mary Berry.

[From Mary Berry]   Somerset Street
                              Wednesday morning, [April 29, 1789]
A thousand thanks for *The Botanic Garden*. The first thirty lines,
which I have just read, are delicious, and make me quite anxious to go
on, for I must at last own with blushes what I have hitherto concealed,
perhaps improperly, from my husband; but as I *am* married it must at
last come out that I was early initiated into all the amours and loose
manners of the plants by that very guilty character, Dr Solander, and
passed too much time in the society and observance of some of the
most abandoned vegetable coquettes. I hope my having long entirely
forsaken all such odd company and lived a very regular life will in
some degree apologize to you for my having been early led astray.
    We rejoice in the hopes of seeing you tomorrow evening.
                                                        M. Berry

*The Berrys were on a round of visits in Yorkshire and it was now that
Walpole's 'fuss and fidgets' began – and were never to leave him while
the sisters were beyond his reach.*

*A new Tonton enters the stage, a young dog of the Berrys, called
Tonton to please Walpole and left with him while the Berrys were on
their journeyings. The old Tonton, vastly spoilt, stone deaf and nearly
blind, who had been Walpole's companion for nine years, had died in
February at the age of sixteen, having been bequeathed by his old
friend the Marquise du Deffand at her death in 1780. Too old himself
to acquire another dog, he was delighted to have the companionship of
the new Tonton in the owners' absence.*

*Walpole's friendship with George Selwyn was lifelong and through
his sister's marriage to a Walpole cousin the kinship drew them even
closer. Vanbrugh's early-eighteenth-century King's Theatre, facing the
Little Theatre in the Haymarket, was burnt down on 18 June but with
its rebuilding Walpole's humorous, if extravagant, proposal of a green
room evaporated.*

[To Mary and Agnes Berry]   Strawberry Hill
                                              Tuesday, June 23, 1789
I am not a little disappointed and mortified at the post bringing me no
letter from you today; you promised to write on the road.

I am not at all consoled for my double loss: my only comfort is, that I flatter myself the journey and air will be of service to you both. Tonton does not miss you as much as I do, not having so good a taste, for he has grown very fond of *me*, and I return it for your sakes, though he deserves it too, for he is perfectly good-natured and tractable – but he is not beautiful like his *god-dog* as Mr Selwyn called my poor late favourite; especially as I have had him clipped; the shearing has brought to light a nose an ell long; and as he has now *nasum rhinocerotis*, I do not doubt but he will be a better critic in poetry than Dr Johnson, who judged of harmony by the principles of an author, and fancied, or wished to make others believe, that no Jacobite could write bad verses, nor Whig good.

I passed so many evenings of the last fortnight with you, and consequently am the more sensible of the deprivation – and how dismal was *Sunday* evening compared to those of last autumn! For my part I know that my affection has done nothing but increase; though, were there but one of you, I should be ashamed of being so strongly attached at my age. Being in love with both, I glory in my passion, and think it a proof of my sense. Why should not two affirmatives make a negative, as well as the reverse? and then a double love will be wisdom – for what is wisdom in reality but a negative? It exists but by correcting folly; and when it has peevishly prevailed on us to abstain from something we have a mind to, it gives itself airs, and inaction pretends to be a personage, a nonentity sets up for a figure of importance.

Have you shed a tear over the Opera House? or do you agree with me, that there is no occasion to rebuild it? The nation has long been tired of operas, and has now a good opportunity of dropping them. Dancing protracted their existence for some time – but the *room-after* was the real support of both, and was like what has been said of your sex, that they never speak their true meaning but in the postscript of their letters. Would not it be sufficient to build an *after-room* on the whole emplacement, to which people might resort from all the assemblies! It should be a codicil to all the diversions of London; and the greater the concourse, the more excuse there would be for staying all night, from the impossibility of ladies getting their coaches to drive up. To be crowded to death in a waiting room at the end of an entertainment is the whole joy; for who goes to any diversion till the last minute of it? I am persuaded that instead of retrenching St Athanasius' Creed, as the [3rd] Duke of Grafton proposed, in order to draw *good company* to church, it would be more efficacious, if the congregation were to be indulged with an afternoon in the vestry; and instead of *two or three being gathered together*, there would be *all the world*, before prayers would be quite over.

Wednesday

I calculated too rightly; no letter today! – yet [I am not] proud of my computation; I would rather have heard of you today; it would have looked like keeping your promise – it has a bad air, your forgetting me so early! Nay, and after your scoffing me for supposing you would not write till your arrival I don't know where! You see I think of *you* and write every day, though I cannot dispatch my letter, till you have sent me a direction. Much the better I am indeed for your not going to Swisserland! Yorkshire is in the glaciers for me! Miss *Agnes* was coy, and was not so flippant of promising me letters – well, but I do trust *she will* write. I smile against the grain, and am seriously alarmed at Thursday being come and no letter! but I have such perfect faith in the kindness of both of you, as I have in your possessing every virtue, that I cannot believe but some sinister accident must have prevented my hearing from you. I wish Friday was come!

Friday 26

My anxiety increases daily, for I still have no letter. Next to your having met with some ill luck, I should be mortified at being forgotten so suddenly. Of any other vexation I have no fear. So much goodness and good sense as you both possess, would make me perfectly easy, if I were really your husband. I must then suspect some accident, and shall have no tranquillity till a letter puts me out of pain. Jealous I am not, for two young ladies cannot have run away with their father to Gretna Green. Hymen, Hymenaee, bring me good news tomorrow, and a direction too, or you do nothing!

Saturday

Io, paen! Io Tonton! – at last I have got a letter, and you are all well! and I am so pleased, that I forget the four uneasy days I have passed – at present I have neither time or paper to say more, for our post turns on its heel and goes out the instant it is come in. I am in some distress still, for, thoughtless creature, you have sent me no direction. If you do receive this, I beseech you never forget, as you move about, to send me new directions.

Do not be frightened at the enormity of this – I do not mean to

[21]

continue so four-paginous in every letter. Adieu, Adieu! Adieu! all three.

Your dutiful son-in-law and most affectionate husband

H.W.

PS. I beg pardon, I see on the last page of your letter there is a direction.

To be left at Post House, York   Strawberry Hill
[Redirected to Middleton near Pickering]   June 30, 1789

I am more an old Fondlewife than I suspected, when I could put myself into such a fright on not hearing from you exactly on the day I had settled I should – but you had promised to write on the road; and though you did, your letter was not sent to the post at the first stage, as Almighty Love had concluded it might be, and as Almighty Love would have done; and so he imagined some dreadful calamity must have happened to you – but you are safe and I will say no more on what has not happened. Pray, present my duty to Grandmama, and let her know what a promising young grandson she has got.

Were there any such thing as sympathy at the distance of two hundred miles, you would have been in a mightier panic than I was, for on Saturday sennight going to open the glass case in the Tribune, my foot caught in the carpet and I fell with my whole weight against the corner of the marble altar, on my side, and bruised the muscles so badly, that for two days I could not move without screaming. I am convinced I should have broken a rib, but that I fell on the cavity whence two of my ribs were removed, that are gone to Yorkshire. I am much better both of my bruise and my lameness, and shall be ready to dance at my own wedding when my wives return. Philip,* who has been prowling about by my order, has found a clever house, but it is on Ham Common, and that is too far off; and I think Papa Berry does not like that side of the water, and he is in the right. Philip shall hunt again and again, till he puts up better game.

So you was not quite satisfied, though you ought to have been transported with King's College Chapel because it has no aisles, like every common cathedral – I suppose you would object to a bird of paradise, because it has no legs, but shoots to heaven in a *trait*, and does not rest on earth.

*Walpole's Swiss valet.

[22]

I am delighted that my next letter is to come from Wife the Second. I love her as much as you – nay, I am sure you like that I should. I should not love either so much, if your affection for each other were not so mutual. I observe and watch all your ways and doings, and the more I observe you, the more virtues I discover in both – nay, depend upon it, if I discern a fault, you shall hear of it. You came too perfect into my hands, to let you be spoiled by indulgence. All the world admires you, yet you have contracted no vanity, advertise no pretensions; are simple and good as nature made you, in spite of all your improvements – mind, *you* and *yours* are always, from *my* lips and pen, of what grammarians call *the common of two*, and signify *both*; so I shall repeat that memorandum no more.

What a confusion of seasons! The haymakers are turning my soaked hay, which is fitter for a water-souchy, and I sit by the fire every night when I come home – Adieu! I dare not tap a fourth page, for when talking to you, I know not how to stop.

Visitors were allowed to see Strawberry Hill on certain days, conducted by Anne Bransome, the housekeeper, and by procuring tickets in advance. No more than four visitors were allowed at a time and children were forbidden.

Five days after Walpole had written this letter, the Bastille was stormed, the French Revolution had begun. Walpole's account of events is based mostly on hearsay and was not necessarily correct. Necker, the Swiss banker, was Louis XVI's Director-General of Finance and consequently his adviser. The Duc de Châtelet, former Ambassador to England, Colonel of the French Guards, fled to Belgium but returned later to Paris and was guillotined in 1793. Duc de Broglie, Maréchal de France, was obliged to leave France and joined the ever-increasing mass of émigrés. The Duke and Duchess of Devonshire had been in Paris on their way to Spa where the Duke hoped to cure his gout and his wife to ensure a pregnancy, sanguine as to its beneficial waters.

Made of basalt, Walpole's bust of Jupiter Serapis, restored but for the head by Mrs Damer, had been acquired from the Barberini collection by Sir William Hamilton and subsequently sold to the Duchess of Portland, on whose death it was bought by Walpole. At his sale it passed to William Beckford and thence through Beckford's younger daughter, Susan Duchess of Hamilton, to Hamilton Palace.

The Cholmondeley family played no small part in Walpole's life, but here it is Mrs Francis Cholmely of Brandsby Hall, Yorkshire, whom Mary had known since her return from abroad and had probably met on an earlier visit to her grandmother at Middleton, a village not far distant from Brandsby.

To Post House, York [as before]   Strawberry Hill
                                                                July 9, 1789

You are so good and punctual, that I will complain no more of your silence – unless you are silent. You must not relax, especially till you can give me better accounts of your health and spirits. I was peevish before with the weather, but now it prevents your riding, I forget hay and roses and all the comforts that are washed away, and shall only watch the weathercock for an east wind in Yorkshire. What a shame that *I* should recover from the gout and bruises, as I assure you I am entirely, and that *you* should have a complaint left! One would think that it was *I* was grown young again, for just now, as I was reading your letter in my bedchamber, while some of my *customers* are seeing the house, I heard a gentleman in the Armoury ask the housekeeper as he looked at the bows and arrows, 'Pray does Mr Walpole shoot?' – No, nor with pistols neither and since my double marriage have suspended my quiver in the Temple of Hymen. Hygeia shall be my goddess, if she will send you back blooming to this region.

I wish I had preserved my correspondence in France as you are curious about their present history, which I believe very momentous indeed. What little I have accidentally heard, I will relate, and will learn what more I can. On the King's being advised to put out his talons, Necker desired leave to resign, as not having been consulted, and as the measure violated his plan. The people hearing his intention thronged to Versailles, and he was forced to assure them from a balcony that he was not to retire. – I am not accurate in dates, nor warrant my intelligence, and therefore pretend only to send you detached scraps. Force being still in request, the Duc du Châtelet acquainted the King, that he could not answer for the French Guards – Châtelet, who from his hot arrogant temper I should have thought would have been one of the proudest opposers of the people, is suspected to lean to them. In short, Marshal Broglie is appointed Commander-in-Chief, and is said to have sworn on his sword that he will not sheathe it till he has plunged it into the heart of *ce gros banquier genevois* – I cannot reconcile this with Necker's stay at Versailles. That he is playing a deep game is certain – It is reported that Madame Necker tastes previously everything he swallows. The Duke and Duchess of Devonshire, who were at Paris, have thought it prudent to leave it.

Thus, you see, the crisis is advanced far beyond orations, and wears all the aspect of civil war. I fear the present want of temper grasps at so much that they may defeat their own purposes; and where loyalty has for ages been the predominant characteristic of a nation, it cannot be eradicated at once. Pity will soften the tone of the moment, and the nobility and clergy have more interest in wearing a royal than a popular yoke, for great lords and high priests think the rights of mankind a defalcation of their privileges. No man living is more devoted to liberty than I am – yet blood is a terrible price to pay for it! A martyr to liberty is the noblest of characters; but to sacrifice the lives of others though for the benefit of all, is a strain of heroism that I could never ambition.

It was lucky for me that you inquired about France; I had not a halfpenny-worth more of news in my wallet.

Tonton's nose is not I believe grown longer, but only come to light by being clipped: when his beard is recovered, I dare say he will be as comely as my Jupiter Serapis. In his taste he is much improved, for he eats strawberries, and is fond of them – and yet they never were so insipid, from want of sun and constant rain. One may eat roses and smell to cherries and not perceive the difference from scent or flavour. If tulips were in season, I would make a rainbow of them to give other flowers hopes of not being drowned again.

I believe you will make me grow a little of a newsmonger, though you are none; but I know that at a distance in the country letters of news are a regale. I am not wont to listen to the batteries on each side of me at Hampton Court and Richmond; but in your absence I shall turn a less deaf ear to them in the hopes of gleaning something that may amuse you; though I shall leave the manufactures of scandal for their own home-consumption: you happily do not deal in such wares. Adieu! I used to think the month of September the dullest of the whole set, now I shall be impatient for it.

PS. I am glad that you are [to] go to Mrs Cholmondeley [Cholmeley]:

[25]

she is extremely sensible and agreeable – but I think all your particular friends that I have see are so.

Lady Dudley, who makes an entrance in the next letter, had not yet embarked on her third marriage (there was a fourth still to come). Her manor house was within a short step of Teddington. Mrs Pepys, who suffered such a grievous aqueous robbery by sending all her belongings by river to Chelsea Reach, was the daughter of William Dowdswell, Chancellor of the Exchequer, and the wife of William Weller Pepys, Master in Chancery. Richard Owen Cambridge had been at Eton and Oxford with Walpole. He entered at Lincoln's Inn, married soon after and came to live in Twickenham Meadows four years after Walpole at Strawberry Hill. They had never been intimate, the variance in their tastes was too pronounced. Cambridge, or 'Cambridge everything' as Walpole was known to call him in derisory terms, was a sporting man, active on the river as on horseback, as was his wife. A family man, a regular attender at the parish church, an early riser and much interested in the private affairs of his neighbours. Always cheerful and well-informed, he was a congenial friend to many and numbered Johnson, Boswell, Gibbon and Reynolds among them. His younger son, the Revd George Owen Cambridge, later Archdeacon of Middlesex, had excited Fanny Burney's love in the years 1783-85 but no marriage proposal had been volunteered and Fanny Burney had continued to suffer, 'unwilling to abandon hope'.[8]

The whole Court moved with George III and Queen Charlotte and the Princesses to Weymouth where the King was to have 'a few dips in the Sea'.[9] The journey lasted several days with a stop at Mount Edgcumbe, the family seat of Viscount Mount Edgcumbe. Within ten days he was raised to an earldom. Laura Countess Waldegrave, wife of her first cousin, the 4th Earl, was the granddaughter of Walpole's elder brother, Sir Edward Walpole, and consequently Horace Walpole's great-niece.

It was ten years since David Garrick had died and his widow, whom Walpole preferred, was reluctant to welcome anyone but close friends to Garrick's villa on the river at Hampton where she continued to live after his death. The Rt Reverend Beilby Porteus was a noted Bishop of London from 1787 to 1808. Keeper of the Privy Seal of Scotland, James Stuart-Mackenzie, and his wife, Lady Elizabeth, had a villa across the river at Petersham for the summer. Monsieur Dutens, a French protestant clergyman, was a close friend, while Baron de Breteuil succeeded Necker for a short space and as an émigré was appointed a kind of roving Ambassador to the European Courts by the French King. Madame de Calonne was newly married to the ex-Minister of Finance who had joined the émigrés.

Strawberry Hill
July 10, 1789

How angry you will be with me! and how insincere you will think all professions! Why, here is Lady Dudley's house let under my nose, let in my own lane, and for a song! – *Patienza! mie care* – I am as white as snow. It had no bill upon it, though it was advertised, but not in my newspaper, and who knows truth or falsehood but from their own paper? It is true too that had I had any inkling of the matter, I should not have inquired about it, for the rent asked was two hundred a year – The land would pay the rent – but then you must have got your hay in before the rains – and you must have been wiser than I, to have done that, and in hay concerns I don't know that the heads of two wives are better than that of one thousand; and after all, had not you been shrewder than a Master in Chancery, it would have cost you three hundred pounds extraordinary before you could have shown your faces, as I am sure at least *I* should choose to have *my* wives appear – Why there is poor Mrs Pepys with not a rag of linen but the shift on her back.[10] They sent their whole history by water: It was a most tempestuous night; the boatmen dreading a shipwreck cast anchor in Chelsea Reach, intending to put to sea next morning – but before day break pirates had carried off the whole cargo to the value, Mr Cambridge says, of said three hundred pounds. Now, am I as false or negligent as I thought I was? You both and Papa Berry together could not be so mad, as I was myself at first, when I suspected that I had missed Palazzo Dudley for you.

As I keep a letter constantly on the anvil going on for you, I shall, before this gets its complement, tell you that I know more. The House of Edgcumbe set out in perilous haste to prepare the Mount for the reception of their Majesties if they are so inclined, but were stopped at Pool for want of post-horses, all being retained for the service of the

Court. The royal personages arrived, and Lady Mount was in the midst of the reiteration of her curtsies, when the mob gathering and pressing on her, she was seized with a panic, clung to her Lord, and screamed piteously, till a country fellow said to her, 'What dost thee make such a hell of a noise for? Why nobody will touch thee.'

The incessant and heavy rains are alarming; the corn begins to be laid, and fair weather is now wanted as much for use as for pleasure: It costs me a pint of wine a day to make my servants amends for being wet to the skin every time I go abroad. Lord and Lady Waldegrave have been with me for two days, and could not set foot out of doors. I drank tea at Mrs Garrick's with the Bishop of London and Mrs Porteous, and they were in the same predicament.

Wednesday, 15th

My motive for sending this away with abortive notice, is, not to delay giving you an account of the news I heard this morning. Mr Mackinsy and Lady Betty are with me this morning, and he showed me a letter he had just received from Monsieur Dutens: a courier arrived yesterday with prodigious expedition from the [3rd] Duke of Dorset [Ambassador to France] – Necker has been dismissed and was thought set out for Geneva; an offer of his post has gone to Breteuil, who is in this country. Everything at Paris was in the utmost confusion and firing of cannon for four hours there had been heard on the road. All this is confirmed by a courier from the D. and Duchess of Devonshire who were setting out precipitately: that messenger had been stopped three times on his route, being taken for a courier from that court, but was released on pretending to be dispatched by the *Tiers Etat*. Madame de Calonne told Dutens yesterday that the newly encamped troops desert by hundreds – but if the firing of the cannon was from the Bastille, and whence else it should proceed I know not, it looks as if the King were not quite abandoned – Oh! but what a scene! how many lives of quiet innocent persons may have been sacrificed, if the artillery of the Bastille raked that multitudinous city! – I check myself, for what million of reflections present themselves. I shall wish to send you accounts fresh and fresh, but I only catch by accident and by rebound.

We have no enemy but St Swithin; but if he persists in his *quarantaine* he will be a very serious one.

I have scarce left myself any room for conjugal *douceurs* – but as you see how very constantly you are in my thoughts, I am at least not fickle, my affection for both is so compounded into one love, that I can think of neither separately. Frenchmen often call their mistresses *mes amours*, which would be no Irish in me. – Adieu! *mes amours*!

Ex Officinâ Arbutianâ
July 19, 1789

Such unwriting wives I never knew! and a shame it is for an author and what is more, for a printer, to have a couple so unletteral. I can find a time amidst all the hurry of my shop to write small quartos to them continually. In France, where nuptiality is not the virtue the most in request, a wife will write to her consort, though the *doux billet* should contain but two sentences, of which I will give you a precedent; a lady sent the following to her spouse: '*Je vous écris, parce que je n'ai rien à faire; et je finis, parce que je n'ai rien à vous dire.*' I do not wish for quite so laconic a *poulet* – besides, your Ladyships *can* write. Brevity, Mesdames, may be catching – don't pretend not to care, for you are dying for news from France, but not a spoonful shall you have from me today.

Two friends of Walpole are mentioned, Lady Cecilia, who lived at Hampton, married to General Johnston, by no means young yet with traces of beauty and no less vanity than wit. (Their daughter, Mrs Anderson, eloped when very young; she and her husband make appearances in these letters.) Mrs Boscawen, widow of the Hon. Edward Boscawen, Admiral of the Blue, whose grace of manner was recorded by many. Alone among these, Necker's son-in-law, Baron de Staël was familiar to Mary Berry through their association in Paris in the spring of 1785.

To Post House at York   Strawberry Hill
[Redirected: 'Weldrake']   July 29, 1789
I have received two dear letters from you of the 18th and 25th, and though you do not accuse me, but say a thousand kind things to me in the most agreeable manner, I allow my ancientry, and that I am an old fond, jealous and peevish husband, and quarrel with you, if I

do not receive a letter exactly at the moment I please to expect one. You talk of mine, but if you knew how I like yours, you would not wonder that I am impatient, and even unreasonable in my demands. However, though I own my faults, I do not mean to correct them. I have such pleasure in your *letters* (I am sorry I am here forced to speak in the *singular number*, which by the way is an Iricism) that I *will* be cross if you do not write to me perpetually. The quintessence of your last but one was in telling me you are better – how fervently do I wish to receive such accounts every post – but who can mend, but old I, in such detestable weather? – Not one hot day; and if a morning shines the evening closes with a heavy shower.

The first object in my thoughts being a house for you, which I cannot find yet, I will only say that Lady Cecelia tells me that she has acquainted you that at Bushy Gate may be had most reasonably – pho! but when? – at the end of September! I told her she was horribly mistaken, and that it is by the end of August you will want one. She would not have been in such an error, if she had calculated by a certain almanac in my heart.

Of French news I can give you no fresher or more authentic account than you can collect in general from the newspapers; but my present visitants and everybody else confirm the veracity of Paris being in that anarchy that speaks the populace domineering in the most cruel and savage manner, and which a servile multitude broken loose calls liberty, and in which in all probability will end in their being more abject slaves than ever – and chiefly by the crime of their *Etats*, who, had they acted with temper and prudence might have obtained from their poor undesigning King a good and permanent constitution. My intelligence reaches me by so many rebounds, that you must not depend on anything I can tell you. I repeat, because I hear, but draw on you for no credit. Having experienced last winter, in superaddition to a long life of experience, that in Berkeley Square I could not trust to a single report from Kew, can I swallow implicitly at Twickenham the distorted information that comes from Paris through the medium of London!

Friday night 31st

My company prevented me finishing this. Part left me at noon, the residue are to come tomorrow. Today I have dined at Fulham along with Mrs Boscawen, but St Swithin played the devil so, that we could not stir out of doors, and had fires to chase the watery spirits.

Mrs Boscawen saw a letter from Paris this morning, which says Necker's son-in-law was arrived, and had announced his father-in-law's promise of return from Basle. I do not know whether his honour or ambition prompt this compliance – surely not his discretion. I am much acquainted with him, and do not hold him great and profound enough to quell the present anarchy. If he attempts to moderate the King, I shall not be surprised if he falls another victim to tumultuary jealousy and outrage. All accounts agree in their violence of the mob against the inoffensive as well as against the objects of their resentment, and in the provinces, where even women are not safe in their houses.

Though wife Agnes's pen lies fallow, I hope her pencil does not. I will write but to one if but one will write to me, and I will not keep a new name I have just assumed, that of

Horace Fondlewives

The exposure of the young ladies to a mixed company at the York races was not one to appeal to Walpole, particularly since the Prince of Wales, with his notorious reputation for dalliance, was also attending the racecourse. (In a later letter, however, he ascribes his reluctance to something else besides.) The allusion to a third wife was, of course, to Mrs Fitzherbert. The red livery was peculiar to the royal house and was to be avoided. Of this Walpole could speak with knowledge for his widowed niece, Maria Countess Waldegrave, had married HRH the Duke of Gloucester, brother to the King, and an unfortunate union it had turned out to be.

To Post House, York [as before]   Strawberry
Thursday night, Aug. 6, 1789
By your letter of 1st and 3rd which I received this morning, you surprise me by complaining of my silence, when I thought I had talked your *eyes* to death. If I did pause, it was to give you time to answer. If eight letters, and those, no scraps, in less than forty days, are not the deeds of something more than a correspondent, I wish I may never be in love again. If you have not received all these, the devil take the post house at York! By your answers I should not think above one had miscarried.

[31]

I am not going to complain again, but to lament. I now find I shall not see you before the end of September – a month later than I expected would be nothing to an old husband, but it is a century to a husband that is old. Mrs Damer, who passed Saturday and Sunday here with her parents, and I settled it with them that Mr Berry and you two should meet us at Park Place the beginning of September. Now you will make me hate that month more than ever. Long evenings without a fire are tiresome, and without two wives insupportable!

The arrival of Necker, I suppose, has suspended the horrors of Paris for a moment, till the mob find that he does not propose to crown them all in the room of their late King. I shall go to London tomorrow for one night, yet I am not likely to see anybody that knows much authentic.

I am rejoiced that you do not go to the York races. Whatever I do myself, I should not like to have the P of Wales have two or *three* wives. Believe me, who have some cause for knowing, there is nothing so transitory as the happiness of red liveries! The person who will gain most by your delay will be Tonton, whose long nose begins to recover its curled rotundity. It is the best-tempered quiet animal alive, which is candid in me to own, as he, as long as it is light, prefers my footboy, or a bone on the lawn, to my company. In the evening as I allow him to lie on every couch and chair, he thinks me agreeable enough. I must celebrate the sense of Fidelle, Mrs Damer's terrier. Without making the slightest gesture, her mistress only said to her, 'Now Fidelle, you may here jump on any chair you please'; she instantly jumped on the settee; and so she did in every room for the whole two days she stayed. This is another demonstration to me that dogs understand even language as far as it relates to their own affairs.

Now I have cleared my character, and that harmony is quite re-established I will not attempt to eke out my letter, only to say I am sorry there is but one pen in your family – I hinted in my last, that I would compound for a pencil. Of all your visits, that cost me a month, I grudge the least that to your grandmother and aunt, as I can judge how happy you make them – It is a good symptom too for your husband: duty and gratutude to parents are seldom, I believe, ingredients in bad wives. Adieu!

Yours most cordially and constantly,

H.W.

To Agnes Berry   Strawberry Hill
Post House, York   Aug. 13, 1789

I have received at once most kind letters from you both – too kind, for
you both talk of gratitude – Mercy on me! Which is the obliged? and
which is the gainer? Two charming beings, whom everybody likes and
approves; and who yet can be pleased with the company and conversation and old stories of a Methusalem? or I, who at the end of my days
have fallen into a more agreeable society than I ever knew at any
period of my life? I will say nothing of your persons, sense or accomplishments; but where, united with all those, could I find so much
simplicity, void of pretensions and affectations? This from any other
man would sound like compliment and flattery; but in me, who have
appointed myself your guardian, it is a duty to tell you of your merits,
that you may preserve and persevere in them. If ever I descry any
faults, I will tell you freely of them. Be just what you are, and you may
dare my reproofs.

I will restrain even reproaches, though in jest, if it puts my sweet
Agnes to the trouble of writing when she does not care for it. It is the
extreme equality of my affection for both, that makes me jealous if I do
not receive equal tokens of friendship from both – and though nothing
is more just than the observation of two sisters repeating the same
ideas, yet never was that remark so ill applied. Though your minds are
so congenial, I have long observed how originally each of you ex-
presses her thoughts.

I have heard of a house at Teddington likely to be vacant by your
time, and have ordered an indirect inquiry to be made. It is much
nearer to Twickenham than t'other side of Bushy Park. Goodnight.

To Post House, York   Strawberry Hill
                                        Thursday night, Aug. 20, 1789

If the worst comes to the worst, I think, I can secure you a house at
Teddington, a very comfortable one, very reasonably, and a more
agreeable one than the Cecilian destination at Bushy Gate – at least
more agreeable to my Lord Castlecomer, for it is nearer to my half.
That Strawberry proverb I must explain to you for your future use.
There was an old Lady Castlecomer, who had only one son, and he
had a tutor called Roberts, who happened to break his leg. A visitant
lamented the accident to her Ladyship: the old rock replied, 'Yes.

indeed, it is very inconvenient to my Lord Castlecomer!' This saying was adopted forty years ago in the phraseology of Strawberry, and is very expressive of that selfish apathy towards others, which refers everything to its own centre, and never feels any shock that does not vibrate in its own interest.

The house in question is at the entrance of Teddington; you may shake hands with Mr Pepys out of the window. A Mrs Armstrong took it for one year at fourscore pounds, but is tired of making hay and minded to leave it at Michaelmas; but says her landlord [Wickes] has behaved so well towards her, that though she will pay the whole, she will give it up to him at quitting it. I sent to him to inquire what he would ask for October and November – he replied, I should name my price, and I am to have the refusal. I think he cannot accept above £20 at most. All I now dread is Mrs Armstong's loitering into October. Tell me your pleasure on this.

Lady Harriot [Conyers] was here the other morning with her daughters, and I showed them the whole house myself, as they are excellent people and the daughters have taste: the youngest especially struck me by her knowledge of good pictures which she immediately showed she understood. This of my house being shown is a dangerous subject for me to tap, such a grievance is it become – I have actually tickets given out till the middle of the week after next – I write two or three every day, or as many excuses – Pray come, and make my evenings at least pleasant.

Summer is arrived at last, though as much after the due time, as if it was one of the *ton*. It is more bounteous however, and will bless the poor by lowering bread. The whole face of the country is spread with luxurious harvests and gilt by shining suns.

Mr & Mrs Anderson are cooing tête-à-tête at Hampton, as if they were Venus's own turtles left at home in her stable. I have exhausted all my nothings, and if I have no letter from you, shall send this away, meagre as it is, because I want to know your will about Teddington villa.

Friday afternoon

Monsieur de Teddington has been with me and is all-accommodating – if Mrs Armstrong will not stay till after the first week in October. I asked his price – he said, should I think ten guineas a month too much – if I did, he would lower – therefore no doubt you may have it for eighteen for the two months, and you may tell me to offer sixteen. Pray let me have your answer soon, for I will convey to Mrs A. that she will hurt her landlord if she lingers beyond St Michaelmas.

I think, if my account should suit you, the best way will be, as soon as you arrive in town, for Mr Berry and you two to come and lodge with me for a day or two, and then you can go and view your future nest at your leisure, and *that* you may insert, with a little cavil at the price, in your answer to me, which will make your assent conditional.

To Post House, York [Redirected   Strawberry Hill
'Thos. Cayley Esq.,   Thursday evening, Aug. 27, 1789
Middleton near Pickering']
I jumped for joy, that is, my heart did, which is all the remain of me that is in *statu jumpante*, at the receipt of your letter this morning which tells me you approve of the house at Teddington. How kind you was to answer so incontinently! I believe you borrowed the best steed from the races. I have sent to the landlord to come to me tomorrow but I could not resist beginning my letter tonight, as I am at home alone with a little pain in my left wrist; but the right one has no brotherly feeling for it, and would not be put off so.

Mrs Armstrong's secession is doubly fortunate. Your last year's mansion is actually taken by Lord Cathcart, and what is incredible, his wife is to lie in there – It must be in the round summer-house; and though its person may have tempted her as an *étui* at present, I should think, as it is three parts of glass, it could not have allured any pregnant woman, unless she expected to be delivered of a melon.

You must not expect any news from me, French or homebred; I am not in the way of hearing any. About royal progresses paternal or filial, I never inquire, nor do you, I believe, care more than I do. The small wares in which the societies at Richmond and Hampton Court deal, are still less to our taste. I will break off here, and finish my letter when I have seen your new landlord. Goodnight!

Friday

Well! I have seen him, and nobody was ever so accommodating! He is as courteous as a candidate for a county. You may stay in his house till Christmas if you please, and shall pay but twenty pounds: and if more furniture is wanting, it shall be supplied. Mrs

[35]

Armstrong talks of not quitting but the first week in October; but as she is prodigiously timorous about her health, he thinks the first round showers will send her to London. In any case you know you may come and stay here in your conjugal castle, till the house of your separate maintenance is vacant for you. I was curious to learn whence Mr Wickes contracted all this *honnêteté*: I do not believe I have discovered, for all I can trace of his history, is, that he married a dowager mistress of [Lieutenant] General Harvey, whom the General called Monimia, though not the meekest of her calling, and with whom (Wickes) she did not at all agree. I am sure she was the aggressor, as he has captivated Mrs Armstrong and me by his flowing benignity. Besides I have no notion how one can use one's wife ill, even if one has two.

Besides the cohue *at Wentworth House, Earl Fitzwilliam's vast, imposing mansion near Rotherham in the West Riding, displaying a range of nineteen bays, and wings and pavilions besides, Walpole was ill-disposed to the possibility of the sisters being disregarded. Wentworth Castle, near Barnsley, also in Yorkshire, was the seat of the Earl of Strafford. But here was gossip to impart – something he had enjoyed all his life despite his words to the contrary. (Sir William Hamilton knew his man when he remarked that he could rely upon 'the most articulate and intelligent gossip of the day'.)[11] The gossip was that the King's third son, the sailor William Duke of Clarence, had taken a villa at the bottom of Richmond Hill for a few months with 'nothing but a short green apron to the river', facing across to the Cambridges' house, and had installed there a well-known London prostitute, Polly Finch. Bored, however, with her lover she had abandoned him, some said on account of his addiction to perusing aloud the* Lives of the Admirals, *others that 'she was soon sacrificed to the scruples of suburban society'.[12] This may have been true, for Mrs Cambridge and the 'blatant beast' (Walpole's name for that arch-gossip, Lady Greenwich, who lived across the river at Sudbrook House) appear to have been of one mind as to the unseemliness of such an establishment. Lord Glenbervie exclaimed that 'the Duke is an absolute nuisance at Richmond. People do not like to receive him in their house.'[13] It was not long before this young and jovial scion of the royal house pursued a more willing and fascinating enchantress.*

To Post House, York   Strawberry Hill
[Redirected as before]   Sept. 4, 1789

I was charmed that Mr Berry ratifies my negotiation for the house at Teddington; and I do not doubt *now* but Mrs Armstrong will quit it even before Michaelmas; for though Saturday last was so glorious, it was the setting, not rising sun of summer. It rained a torrent all Sunday evening; so it has done almost every day since, and did last night and does at this instant. I grieve for the incomplete harvest; but as it is an ill rain that brings nobody good, I must rejoice if it washes away Dame Armstrong. Mr Wickes I am sure will give me the earliest notice of her departure.

You ask whether I will call you wise or stupid for leaving York races in the middle – neither: had you chosen to stay, you would have done rightly; the more young persons see, where there is nothing blameable, the better as increasing the stock of ideas early will be a resource for age. To resign pleasure to please tender relations is amiable, and superior to wisdom; for wisdom, however laudable, is but a selfish virtue. But I do decide peremptorily that it was very prudent to decline the invitation to Wentworth House, which was obligingly given; but as I was very proud for you, I should have disliked your being included in a mobbish kind of *cohue*. *You two* are not to go where any other two misses would have been equally *priées*; and where people would have been thinking of the princes more than of the Berrys – Besides, princes are so rife now, that besides my *sweet* nephew in the Park [HRH Duke of Gloucester] we have another at Richmond: the Duke of Clarence has taken Mr Henry Hobart's house, point-blank over against Mr Cambridge's, which will make the good woman of that mansion cross herself piteously, and stretch the throats of the *blatant beast* at Sudbrook, and of all the other pious matrons *à la ronde*, for his R.H. to divert lonesomeness, has brought with him a Miss Polly Finch, who being still more averse to solitude, declares that any tempter would make even paradise more agreeable than a constant tête-à-tête.

I have talked scandal from Richmond like its gossips, and now by your queries after Lady L[uxborough] you are drawing me into more, which I do not love; but she is dead and forgotten, but on the shelves of an old library or on those of my old memory which you will be routing into. The lady you wot of then was the first wife of Lord Catherlogh, before he was an earl, and who was the son of Knight the

South Sea cashier, and whose second wife lives here at Twickenham. Lady Luxborough, a high-coloured lusty black woman, was parted from her husband upon a gallantry she had with Dalton the reviver of *Comus*, and a divine. She retired into the country, corresponded, as you see by her letters, with the small poets of that time, but having no Theseus amongst them, consoled herself, as it is said, like Ariadne, with Bacchus. This might be a fable like that of her Cretan Highness – no matter; the fry of little anecdotes are so numerous now, that throwing one more into the shoal is of no consequence if it entertains you for a moment, nor need you believe what I don't warrant. Gramercy for your intention of seeing Wentworth Castle; it is my favourite of all great seats; such a variety of ground, of wood and water; and almost all executed and disposed with so much taste by the present Earl! The new front is in my opinion one of the lightest and most beautiful buildings on earth – and pray like the little Gothic edifice and its position in the menagerie; your husband recommended it and had it drawn by Mr Bentley from Chichester Cross. Don't bring me a pair of scissors from Sheffield; I am determined nothing shall cut our loves, though I should live out the rest of Methusalem's term as you kindly wish, and as I can believe, though you are my wives, for I am persuaded my Agnes wishes so too, don't you?

Adieu! – for three weeks I shall say, *Sancte Michael*, or *ora pro nobis*. – You seem to have relinquished your plan of sea-coasting – I shall be sorry for that: it would do you good.

To Post House, York
Strawberry Hill
Sept. 18, 1789

I don't wonder that your grandmother is unwilling to part with you, when you sacrifice the amendment of your health to her, and give up bathing for her satisfaction – but between ourselves I do not admire her for accepting the sacrifice. You bid me be very kind to make up for your parting with her and your friends – I am like poor Cordelia,

> – I am sure my love's
> More pond'rous than my tongue –

She reserved half her affection from her father for her husband – I will keep none of mine from my wives for my grandmother – but I promise nothing; come and try.

I will see Mr Wickes, and know more particularly about Mrs

Armstrong's motions: I shall be a little fearful of haggling with him, lest I should sour his complaisance which hitherto has been all sugar. Still I will not be grandmaternal, and prefer myself to your interests.

I have been a prisoner in my own house for some days in consequence of a violent fall I had last week, in which it is wonderful that I lost nor life, nor limb, nor even a bone. I went to sit with my second cousins the three Philippses on Hampton Court Green; it was dusk, there was a very low step at the door, I did not see it, it tripped me up, I fell headlong on the stones, and against the frame of a table at the door, and battered myself so much, that my whole hip is as black as my shoe for about half a yard long, and a quarter wide, besides bruising one hand, both knees, and my left elbow, into which brought the gout next day. Now pray admire my lightness; if I had weighed a straw, what mischief might not have happened to me? Nay, I have had very little pain; and the gout, not to be out of the fashion, is gone too, and I should have been abroad this morning, if I had not preferred writing to you.

Mrs Cambridge's prayers have been heard: the Duke of Clarence has already taken another villa at Rohampton; and besides being so soon tired, I suppose he will now new-furnish that in a week more. I shall go to Park Place on Monday for two or three days, and then come back to be ready to receive you – but you have not been very gracious, nor said a word of accepting my invitation till the house at Teddington is ready for you. Pray let me know when I may expect you, that I may not enter into any engagement even for an evening.

As the hour of my seeing you again approaches, and as I have nothing of the least importance to tell, I shall try not to lengthen this to its usual complement. Essays, that act the part of letters are mightily insipid things, and when one has nothing occasional to say, it is better to say nothing.

The weather has been so cold since Monday, that for these two days I have had a carpenter stopping chinks in window frames and listing the door of the blue room which I destine to wife Agnes: winds will get into these old castles. Sultana Maria is to sleep in the red room, where the Sultan himself resides when he has got the gout, and which his Haughtiness always keeps very comfortable. Adieu!

To Somerset Street   Strawberry Hill
                                        Wednesday night, Sept. 30, 1789

When an ancient gentleman marries it is his best excuse, that he wants a nurse; which I suppose was the motive of Solomon, who was the wisest of mortals, and a most puissant and opulent monarch, for marrying a thousand wives in his old age, when I conclude he was very gouty. I in humble imitation of that sapient king, and no mines of Ophir flowing into my exchequer, espoused a couple of helpmates.

I do not want you – on the contrary, I am delighted that you did not accept my invitation. I should have been mortified to the death to have had you in my house, when I am lying helpless on my couch, or going to bed early from pain. In short, I came from Park Place last Thursday with an imflammation in my foot from a chalkstone, which I was obliged to have lanced the next morning, and it is not well yet. Nay, it has brought the gout into the knee of the same side, and I suffered a good deal yesterday evening, and blessed myself you were not here – did you think it would ever come to that? In the meantime here is the state of your affairs: Mr Wickes goes into Norfolk tomorrow for three weeks to shoot. I told him you was much displeased at his asking new terms, and that till you should come to town, I could say nothing positive to him, and he must not depend on anything till then. He was all penitence and complaisance. I told him I must have a lease signed: he said there was no necessity for it. O yes, I said but there is. He answered, if I would send one down to him signed by Mr Berry he would sign it too – but what I shall do, when I know your determination, is to send to Mr Wickes a copy of the few lines which Mr Pepys, whom I have consulted twice, had from Lady Dudley, and which shall specify that you are to pay but £20 in full of all demands from the time you shall take possession of the house to December 25th, and when Wickes returns that agreement signed, Mr Berry will sign it too. Thus you see I have acted with the utmost caution, nor have been to the house, nor sent anybody to see it that Wickes might not say we have taken possession.   Now hold a council incontinently, and let me know its decree or why should not Mr Berry come to me immediately, if I cannot come, as I fear. You know here is a dinner and a bed always at his service, which will save a great deal of time.

I am not quite for having your house in town new painted at this time of year when it cannot dry fast. There is nothing so very unwholesome as the smell of new paint. Cannot you make shift as it is for another year? I never perceived its wanting it – you do not propose to give assemblies or concerts.

Thus I think I have foreseen and said all that can be necessary – and perhaps more like a nurse than a person that wants one.

Be sure that I find you both looking remarkably well – not that I have any reason for desiring it, but as I am not able to nurse you – Adieu!

The matter was concluded and the Berrys moved into the house at Teddington. Might one perhaps detect a disinclination on the Berrys' side to be all but forced into following Walpole's wishes? We do not know why they returned direct to town – without, it appears, sending word that that was their intention– rather than the blue, the red rooms at Strawberry Hill. And was the object of painting the London house to delay the arrival at Teddington, embracing unremitting evening visits to Strawberry Hill? Also, the semi-jocular conjugal references must have worn a bit thin.

However, to have them so close at hand was a delight to Walpole, who, in consequence, remained longer at Strawberry Hill than was his usual practice. When they returned to London in the middle of December, so did he. But Mary had been ill and Walpole composed for her the following verses. To these, despite ill-health, Mary collected herself sufficiently to reply.

TO MISS MARY BERRY

The beauty, learning, eloquence,
With every grace of social sense,
And all with unaffected ease,
Without pretensions sure to please;
With every virtue that endears,
Why raise my wishes less than fears?
'Tis nought that heaven denied thee wealth;
Ah, why withold its dearer blessing – health?

[Inscribed by Mary Berry]: 'December 1789 wrote when I was very ill in answer to some complimentary lines from the Honourable H. Walpole.'

Though pain with unrelenting Sway
My languid frame subdues
Can I with common thanks repay
The wishes of thy Muse?

Ah no! my *heart* no languor knows,
In every feeling strong
Dwells with delight on all it owes
Thy friendship, converse, song.

The voice of praise still charms my Ear
Yet not deceived, I see
Thy verse but tells in language clear
What I should strive to be –

To Mary Berry, December 1789
An apology for Miss Berry's Paleness
In imitation of Waller. By H.W.

True on her cheek the Damask rose
Too seldom or too faintly blows;
Less does the venal mimic art
To that fair cheek its dyes impart,
E'en Hebe's bloom would ill replace
The sensibility and grace
That sweetly beams from Mary's face:
As the white lily would but lose
If tinged by Flora's brightest hues.

Dec. 1789

*Although in the summer of 1790, when the correspondence is resumed,
the French émigrés were in abundance at Richmond and even included
the Duke of Orléans (Philippe Egalité) calling himself a Capet, the
earliest branch of French kingship (as the Bourbons were to be the
last), Walpole felt he had little news with which to entertain the Berrys
at Lymington, Hampshire, where they had gone for invigorating sea
air. On their way they had stayed with Lady Ailesbury and General*

Conway at Park Place, a house magnificently situated on the wooded hills at Henley, high above the river. Their visit to his dearest friends had done nothing to reconcile Walpole to the fearsome plan they had embarked upon which would remove them from his vicinity both at Twickenham and in London in the early autumn for very many months. The Berrys were to go abroad, with Italy as their objective, more especially to obtain health in a temperate climate. Possibly also as living was cheaper abroad. They had now been in England five years and Mary, inclined to restlessness, wished to revisit the marvels of their earlier sojourn; Agnes one supposes was of a like mind. Might it also be possible that the kindly attentions of their new great friend were in some measure restrictive to the conduct of their own lives? Did Mr Berry find the regular evenings at Strawberry awkward and protracted?

To Post Office, Lymington   Strawberry Hill
                                                                   July 2, 1790

My neighbourhood, though Richmond is brimful of French and English, furnishes no more entertainment than usual, for which I am much more sorry on your account than on my own, for my letters will not be amusing. My personal history is short and dull. I have made my chief visits; my offices advance, and I have got in most of my hay, and such a quantity, that I believe, I believe it will pay for half a yard of my building. All news has centered in elections; I care about none; nor have listened to any. They, and the press-gangs have swept the roads of foot-pads and highwaymen, who hide themselves, or are gone to vote. Whether they who used to come to see my house are of either complexion I don't know, but I have less demand for tickets than usual – what else can I tell you?

France seems more likely to ripen to confusion; they go on levelling so madly, that I shall wonder if everybody does not think himself loosened from all restraints and bound to conform to none – a pretty experiment to throw society with all its improved vices and desires into a state of nature, which in its outset had many of them to discover, and no worse instrument than the jawbone of an ass to execute mischief with. That serene prince the Duke of Orleans has bowed to the abolition of titles, and calls himself *Monsieur Capet*, from whom he may be descended, if he is not from the Bourbons; but as he has failed in being such another usurper, I wonder he did not avoid the allusion.

You are sure I must want matter, not inclination when I do not send you what pedants call a *just volume*. Pray return from Lymington with blooming countenances, you must sit for your pictures before your long journey. I have not mentioned that article lately, because you have both looked so pale – nor indeed has the subject been so agreeable, as when I first proposed it – portraits are but melancholy pleasures in long absences! With what a different emphasis does one say adieu! for a month, and for a year! – I scarce guess how one can say the latter – alas! I must learn!

In Walpole's letters until the Berrys' departure there was a fair amount of self-pity; also fear for their safety on their route to Italy. The Berrys had engaged to spend some weeks near Strawberry Hill on returning from Lymington, to which scheme Walpole showed some costiveness though no doubt he was pleased enough when they lodged in Montpelier Row, Twickenham for several weeks in August. Meanwhile there was Netley Abbey to speak of, the thirteenth-century Cistercian monastery founded by Henry III who was also its patron; Lyndhurst, the capital town of the New Forest also on the way to Lymington, the King's House being that of the Lord Warden of the New Forest, the Duke of Gloucester (whom Walpole cordially disliked); Lady Herries, wife of the banker in whose house in St James's Square he had first seen the Berrys; and a sneer at Lord Lansdowne who showed sympathy with the Jacobins.

Walpole's friend, Lady Diana Beauclerk, a good amateur artist, lived with her husband at Little Marble Hill. Her brother, the 4th Duke of Marlborough, had come over from Syon House with his wife. The later evening visit was not greatly successful, both because of the twilight and because Walpole had Lady North to attend upon at Bushy House.

George Cholmondeley, Walpole's great-nephew (not to be confused with George James Cholmondeley, 4th Earl of Cholmondeley) would marry Marcia Pitt in August. He was the eldest son of of the Hon, and Revd Robert Cholmondeley, the second son of the 3rd Earl, who had married Polly[14] (Mary), who like her elder sister Peg Woffington, the celebrated actress, had risen from a Dublin gutter. Their father had been a bricklayer; their mother sold watercress on the Dublin streets to pay off debts. Peg's intelligence and acting ability had brought her to the London stage opposite Garrick, with whom she had lived for a number of years. Polly tried her luck in the theatre but without success and in 1746 married the Revd Robert Cholmondeley.

Post Office, Lymington   Strawberry Hill
                                        Saturday night, July 3, 1790

How kind to write the very moment you arrived! but pray do not think that, welcome as your letters are, I would purchase them at the price of any fatigue to you – a proviso I put in already against moments when you may be more weary than a journey to Lymington. You make me happy by the good accounts of Miss Agnes; and I should be completely so, if the air of the sea could be so beneficial to you both, as to make your farther journey unnecessary to your healths at least for some time; for – and I protest solemnly that not a personal thought enters into the consideration, I shall be excessively alarmed at your going to the Continent, when such a frenzy has seized it. You see by the papers that the flame has burst out at Florence – can Pisa be secure? Flanders can be no safe road – and is any part of France so? I told you of the horrors at Avignon. The demon of Gaul is busy everywhere – nay, its imps are here! Horne Tooke declared on the hustings t'other day that he would exterminate those *locusts* the nobility. Lord Lansdown whose family name I suspect to have been Petit (a French one) not Petty, like Monsieur Capet would waive his marquisate to compass a revolution.

The *Etats* are as foolish as atrocious, have printed lists of the surnames which the latest noblesse are to assume or resume, as if people did not know their own names. I like a speech I have heard of the Queen. She went with the King to see the manufacture of glass, and as they passed the Halles, the *poissardes* huzzaed them; 'Upon my word,' said the Queen, 'those folks are civiller when you visit them, than when they visit you.' – This marked both spirit and good humour – For my part, I am so shocked at French barbarity that I begin to think that our hatred of them is not national prejudice, but natural instinct; as tame animals are born with an antipathy to beasts of prey.

[45]

I feel all the kindness of your determination of coming to Twicken-ham in August, and shall certainly say no more against it, though I am certain that I shall count every day that passes, and when *they are passed*, they will leave a melancholy impression on Strawberry, that I had rather affixed to London. The two last summers were infinitely the pleasantest I ever passed here, for I never before had an agreeable neighbourhood. Still I loved the place, and had no comparisons to draw. Now, the neighbourhood will remain, and will appear ten times worse, with the aggravation of remembering *two months* that may have some transient roses, but I am sure, lasting thorns.

You tell me I do not write with my usual spirits – at least I will suppress, as much as I can, the want of them – though I am a bad dissembler. Miss Cambridge told me you had charged her to search for a house for you – I did bid Philip, but I believe not with the eagerness of last year, and I am persuaded that she will execute your commission punctually.

You do not mention the cathedral at Winchester, which I have twice seen and admired. Nor do you say anything of Netley, charm-ing Netley. At Lyndhurst you passed the palatial hovel of my royal nephew who I have reason to wish had never been so, and did all I could to prevent his being.

The home chapter will be as dull as usual. On Tuesday is to come Lady Herries and her clan. The week before last I met the Marlboroughs at Lady Di's. The Duchess desired to come and see Strawberry again, as it had rained the whole time she was here last. I proposed the next morning: no, she could not, she expected company to dinner, she believed their brother Lord Robert would dine with them – I thought that a little odd, as they have just turned him out for Oxfordshire; and I thought a dinner no cause at the distance of four miles. In her Grace's dawdling way she could fix no time; and so on Friday at half an hour after seven, as I was going to Lady North's, they arrived; and the sun being setting and the moon not risen, you may judge how much they could see through all the painted glass by twilight.

It has rained all day and I have not been out of my house: in the morning I had three or four visitors, particularly my nephew George Cholmondeley with an account of his marriage settlements and the toothache. Tonight I am writing to you comfortably by the fireside, for we are forced to raise an English June in a hot-house like grapes.

Pray tell me as much of your personal history and what company you have. I care much more about Lymington, than all the elections in the kingdom – and I seem to think that you interest yourself as much about *les amusements des eaux de Strawberri*. Good night.

From Strawberry Hill Walpole was keeping the sisters well-informed of the barbarities committed in France, but there were still the diversions of the river to impart. Ragman's Castle, which took its name from a public house once on the site, now lived in by Mr George Hardinge, was close to Orleans House and a little over a mile downstream from Strawberry. Lady Dudley's house was barely a half mile from Walpole's in the reverse direction.

The liaison between the 4th Earl of Cholmondeley and the extremely pretty Mme de St Alban, a French courtesan, was well known. His mistress from 1785, she remained so until his marriage in 1791, having borne him two or three children.

To Post House, Lymington   Strawberry Hill
                        Friday [Saturday] night, July 10, 1790
I begin my letter tonight, but shall not send it away till I hear again from you, that our letters may not jostle without answering one another – but how can I pass my solitary evenings so well as by talking to you? I laid on my couch for three days, but as never was so tractable a gout as mine, I have walked all over the house today without assistance.

I did long to peep at my building, but as it has been a cold *dog-day*, I would not risk a relapse, and about dinner we had a smart shower – well, you cry, and was it worth while to write only to tell me it is cold? We know that at Weymouth [Lymington] – Oh! yes, it was to tell you otherguess news than of heat or cold overhead. In short, as whatever may directly or indirectly affect you and your sister, is my principal occupation at present.

Till some of the ferment in Europe subsides, it would be very unadvised to change this country for another. Mrs Boscawen, who came to visit my gout this morning, told me that Mr Prescot, coming from Avignon was thrown into prison in France and detained there all night before suffered to prosecute his journey through France. The

Duchess of Gloucester who called on me afterwards, says the like troubles are broken out in Swisserland – Surely this is not a season for expeditions to the Continent!

General Conway in his last letter asked me if it was not a theme to moralize on, this earthquake that has swallowed up all Montmorencis, Guises, Birons, and great names? I reply, it makes me *immortalize*; I am outrageous at the destruction of all the visions that make history delectable – without some romance it is but a register of crimes and calamities, and the French seem preparing to make their country one universal St Bartelemi; they are instructing the populace to lay everything waste! What is to restrain them? Will they obey these masters who tell them, preach to them, that all are equal – but who, good men! pay themselves twelve livres a day propagating that doctrine – Oh! go not into that conflagration, nor whither its sparks extend! Come to the banks of the gentle Thames – nor strow its shores with alarm and anxiety by leaving them. How I wished for you today – yes, don't you believe me, and particularly at three o'clock. Mrs Boscawen was sitting with me here in the blue bow-window: in a moment the river was covered with little yachts and boats, the road and the opposite meadow with coaches, chaises, horsemen, women and children. Mr George Hardinge had given three guineas to be rowed for by four two-oared boats from his Ragman's Castle to Lady Dudley's and back, so we saw the confluence go and return. I had not heard of it, but all Richmond had, and was descended from its heights.

12th

It is but Monday evening and I expect no letter until tomorrow, but I must go on; I have new horrors and dangers to relate. Monsieur Cordon, who was Sardinian minister here, and now at Paris, fell under the displeasure of the new despots of the mob: they met a man who they took for Cordon; and *sans dire gare!* hanged him. Madame de St Alban, who you know is a pinchbeck-niece of mine, was returning to Lord Cholmondeley from Paris, but was arrested at the gate, and had all her papers seized and examined. While I was writing this paragraph, Mrs Grenville called to see me; and had just seen a Mrs Hamlyn lately returned from Italy with her husband; between Boulogne and Calais they were stopped *seven times* by vagabonds liberty drunk; and obliged to drink with them.

I am still confined, and like others who are well, sitting by the fire

– in short, one must have fire-summer if sun-summer is not to be
had. Mrs Anderson and Mr Wheeler called on me this morning from
Hampton; she looks lean and ill, and goes to Ramsgate: her parents
next week to Tunbridge for a month. One would think all England
were ducks, they are forever waddling to the water – but I must stop;
I shall not have a inch of paper for tomorrow.

*Almost a year after the publication of a book by Pennant, the
naturalist and traveller, a volume of* Additions and Corrections *was
published to which Walpole added his own.*

*Penelope Lady Rivers was the wife of the first Baron Rivers; to
Walpole she was 'all loveliness within and without'. The Comtesse
d'Artois, Marie-Thérèse de Savoie, had left Paris the previous year
and predeceased her husband who, in 1824, succeeded Louis XVIII as
Charles X, King of France.*

To Post House, Lymington   Strawberry Hill
                                             July 17, Saturday, 1790
I have received yours of the 14th and since you seem so determined
on your journey, I shall say little more on the subject, though if my
arguments have no weight, yours, I assure you, are as far from con-
vincing me; when there is so much danger, does it become a jot wiser
to run the contrary risk. That our papers are very untrue, is certain;
but nothing upon earth is less true than that they have exaggerated
the barbarities in France.

My week of confined evenings have been employed in writing
notes to Mr Pennant's *London*. Ever since the appearance of *Les
Rues de Paris** I had been collecting notices for such a work, though
probably now should not have executed it. When Mr Pennant had
something of such an idea the winter before last, I told him such
hints as I recollected – but as he is more impetuous than digestive, I
had not looked out my memorandum, and he has made such a
bungling use of those I gave him that I am glad I furnished him with
no more.

What can I say more? Nothing tonight, but that Philip and I have

*More precisely *Essaies historiques sur Paris, 1754-7*, in five volumes, by Poullain de
Saint-Foix.

looked and inquired and can find nothing here that even calls itself a ready-furnished house.

Monday 19th

I came to town yesterday, and at the door my maid told me that two persons had called to inquire, who had heard that I was dangerously ill, and even supposed dead – to be sure at my age that would be no miracle; but as upon my honour I have seen myself every day, and know nothing of any illness I have had but a fillip of gout, I cannot believe there is any truth in those reports.

Had you been at Lyons lately you might have been obliged to receive most condescending civilities from two of the greatest personages in France. Lady Rivers has written to my sister that she was at Lyons when two Amazons arrived there, deputed by their legislative body *Mesdames les Poissardes* to invite the *late* Comtesse d'Artois to return to Paris; and those two ambassadresses lodged in the same hotel. Lady R was told that she ought to wait on them – not she indeed – Oh! yes, you had much better – and so she found she had. They received her very graciously, and said 'Nous nous reverrons.' – How could I imagine that it is not charming travelling through France! I go into Kent tomorrow; how you will envy me if I meet a detachment of *poissardes* on the road to Chevening to create Earl Stanhope no peer! Good night!

Lee Priory, near Canterbury, long since demolished, had been enlarged and gothicized for Mr Thomas Barrett mainly through the influence of Walpole, who admired it excessively when he visited it in 1788. When Mary Berry was there in 1794 she could not show the same enthusiasm. But it is worth remembering that there is no indication of the Berrys' opinion of the astonishing Gothic creation on the bank of the Thames; whether or not they admired it or simply accepted it as the fantasy of their benefactor, there is no divining.

Sophia Walpole had been born to Lady Mary Churchill, Sir Robert Walpole's daughter by his mistress whom he later married. Lady Mary was Walpole's favourite of his sisters and brothers. She in turn married Charles Churchill, a natural son of Marlborough's General Churchill and Mrs Oldfield, the notable actress. Sophia, their daughter, married a kinsman, a Walpole of Wolterton.

Squibs of Savile Row, a well-known auctioneers, had been owned by a man of that name who went bankrupt in 1784. At a later date the place was adapted to a puppet theatre and under the ownership of Lord Barrymore, who had bought it in 1790, it had acquired the distinction of a theatre. Farquhar's The Beaux Stratagem *was given with much success and the Prince of Wales attended; this was followed by a 'select supper party at* two *in the morning'.*

To Post House, Lymington   Strawberry Hill
                                            Friday night, July 23, 1790

I arrived at Lee on the day and hour I had promised Mr Barrett. I found his house complete and the most perfect thing ever formed! Such taste, every inch so well finished and the drawing room and eating room so magnificent! I think if Strawberry were not its parent, it would be jealous. My journey too delighted me: such a face of plenty and beauty; the corn, the hay harvest, the cherry orchards, the hop grounds, all in their different ages so promising or so fulfilling! All the farms and hedges so tight and neat, and such rows of houses tacking themselves on to every town – and on t'other side what an answer is coming from France!

I went to carry my niece Sophia Walpole home last night from her mother's, and found Little Burlington Street blocked up by coaches. Lord Barrymore, his sister Lady Caroline, and Mrs Goodall the actress, were performing *The Beaux Stratagem* in Squib's auction room which his Lordship has converted into a theatre. I do not know the rest of the company, nor are you probably curious. Having now emptied my pouch of news, I will come to your letter of the 20th which I have received.

I thank you for saying at least that you will take time to consider before you finally determine on your journey. I do not promise myself much from that consideration, for if you *can* still hesitate, it must be by the *coup de baguette* of some guardian angel that the face of Europe can be tranquillized in two months. The position of France indeed may be much worse; but the talisman which I conclude you possess, and that is to convey you invulnerable or invisible through that nation of barbarians, must have as much virtue as it had a fortnight ago – and as I have no amulet that can lull asleep my fears for you, I am not at all comforted nor quieted by the composing draught you have sent me. Those alarms have sent *me* on considering too, and unless you have reasons unknown to me, those you did give me, appear by no means adequate to so strange a fancy as that of leaving your country again, when it is and appears to everyone else, the only country in Europe at present that one would wish to be in. I fear my dread of letting my self-love preponderate over my attachment to dear you and dear Agnes made me too rashly forbear to contend against your scheme. It appears to me a wild uncomfortable plan, and therefore I ascribe it to a volatile roving humour, or to some motive of which I am ignorant, and into which I have no right to inquire.

Mrs Udney of the following letter would eventually be appointed under-governess to Princess Charlotte by whom she was much loved. Her husband, Robert Udney, an Aberdonian of genial liberality was well-informed and owned a good collection of pictures. The Revd Daniel Lysons, topographer and sometime assistant curate of Putney was engaged in writing a history of the villages and churches within ten miles of London (The Environs of London, 1792-6). *When, on the death of the 3rd Lord Orford, Horace Walpole succeeded to the earldom he appointed Lysons his chaplain.*

In July 1784 and within three years of her husband's death, Hester Thrale had married Gabriel Piozzi, an Italian musician and singer from Brescia. This had shocked her friends and after many years of close friendship, Dr Johnson, voicing his grave displeasure, had broken with her. A large party was to celebrate the Piozzis' sixth wedding anniversary; it was also a kind of housewarming as Streatham Park, the Thrales' large house in Surrey, had been let for a number of years and had now been reclaimed by its owner. Set in its own park with a moat dividing the south and north lawns, there was much to be done to put order to the shrubberies, the walled garden and the 'graperies'.

To Post House, Lymington   Strawberry Hill
                                                      Thursday, July 29, 1790
If you give yourself an air and pretend to write dull letters, which I defy you to do when they are to pass through the medium of my eyes, I will lay you a wager that this shall beat you hollow. One comfort is,

that if I have nothing to say, I trust it will be the last that you will receive till I see you, and therefore if it is as dull as the last scene in any comedy, no matter.

I have most seriously been house-hunting for you. I saw bills on two doors in Montpelier Row – but neither are furnished – and yesterday to a larger at Teddington, but it was not only stark naked, but tumbling down. You shall come to me, and then we will see what can be done.

You are in the right to look better, and I would advise Agnes to do so too as fast as possible, for to tell you the truth I feel myself growing inconstant – I have seen Mrs Udney – Oh! she is charming, looks so sensible and – unluckily, so modest – but then as Mr Udney looks as old and decrepit as I do, there may be some hopes.

At night

Mr Lysons the divine and I have been this evening to see the late Duke of Montagu's at Richmond, where I had not been for many years. Formerly I was much there, but *her* Grace broke with me on what I had said in my *Noble Authors* [1758] of her grandfather Marlborough, as if I had been the first to propagate avarice! The new garden that clambers up the hill is delightful and disposed with admirable taste and variety. It is perfectly screened from human eyes, though in the bosom of so populace a village; and you climb till at last, treading the houses under foot, you recover the Thames and all the world at a little distance. I am amazed that it is not more talked of – and I am glad Mrs Udney did not see me in my ascent or descent – I was no very graceful figure as Mr Lysons was dragging me up and down. I will take care to make love on plain ground – and things do go on well, for at my return I found a note from Mrs Udney to invite me to a concert on Sunday, so I must have made some impression, for I never saw her till yesterday morning.

Adieu! how glad I am to have no more of these empty letters to write!
PS. Mr Lysons was last Monday at Mrs Piozzi's fête at Streatham. Five and forty persons sat down to dinner. In the evening was a concert, and a little hopping, and a supper.

Walpole mentioned the 'Abbé', a name he gave to the Revd Norton Nicholls, a friend of the poet Thomas Gray. Nicholls, though taking

Holy Orders, had more of a literary cast of mind and an aptitude for society such as to remind Walpole of the worldly priests of the Courts of Versailles and Paris.

Since Lord Cholmondeley, though the father of illegitimate children, had never yet married, his uncle, the Revd Richard Cholmondeley, was heir presumptive, with his son, George Cholmondeley (of an earlier letter), in succession after his father.

To Somerset Street   Strawberry Hill
                                                    Monday night, Aug. 2, 1790
It has rained all day. I had ordered my coach to go to Richmond in the evening, but bade it set up again, and preferred having the fires lighted. Miss Cheap is certainly your true friend, for she told me that Mrs Udney, whom I took for two and twenty, is eight and thirty. There I found the Abbé singing glees. He came to Mr Barrett's a day later than he had promised: I had insisted that he had been warbling at the Worcester and Gloucester music meeting.

My nephew George Cholmondeley is to be married on Saturday. *Madame St Alban* is breeding, I told him I hoped his cousin the Earl will not disinherit him for a ready-made heir. I would allow her to be a Duchess [of St Albans] but then it would be without changing *her name*. Goodnight, I am glad I shall say so in person on Thursday.

Writing to the sisters on the day of their departure, Walpole set down in terms of affection all that he felt for them and his fears that age might prevent his seeing them again. Thomas Kirgate, who had come to Walpole in the late 1760s as his printer, acted in these late years when Walpole suffered from gout in the hands, as his amanuensis.

Agnes's Death of Cardinal Wolsey *was a watercolour copy of William Lock's oil portrait of the same subject and was to find an honourable place among Walpole's prints and drawings. He already owned two of her works,* Arcadia, *and another unidentified. The Duchess of Gloucester's reaction to this new addition, to which Walpole refers in a subsequent letter, was probably one of distaste for its creator. There is no question that his niece, who was fond of*

Walpole, was also jealous of his attachment to Mary and one day, unable to suppress her feeling, exclaimed: 'Do you mean to marry Miss Berry, or do you not?' 'That is as Miss Berry herself pleases,' came the equable rejoinder.[15]

The Duchess was not alone in her foreboding; Lady Mary Churchill was of the same mind and of this both Mary and Agnes were well aware.

Meanwhile, on 10 October the Berrys' journey from 26 North Audley Street, their newly acquired house, ended nine hours later at the Old Ship, Brighton, where they spent the night. Carriage and baggage were placed on a hired forty-ton sloop the next day and in the evening sailed for Dieppe. Mary went to bed immediately and never stirred till their arrival twenty-four hours later. She mentions no sea-sickness in her Journal, though she does to Walpole, which perhaps accounts for the twenty-four hours in bed. Passing through Rouen there was of course something to be compared with England: 'The Quay to the Seine, which here is as broad as the Thames at Kew Bridge'; and away they hurried to Paris.

The Berrys had not been there since 1785 and a vast change was noticed in the populace and in the places of 'public resort', the streets ('hardly a gentleman's carriage to be seen'), the Palais Royale, the Tuileries 'filled with people of the lowest class, with a very small proportion of those one can suppose above it'.

To Poste restante à Lyon, France   [Strawberry Hill]
               Sunday, Oct. 10, 1790
             The day of your departure
Is it possible to write to my beloved friends and refrain from speaking of my grief for losing you, though it is but the continuation of what I have felt ever since I was stunned by your intention of going abroad this autumn. In happy days I smiled and called you *my dear wives* – now I can only think of you as *darling children* of whom I am bereaved! As such I have loved and do love you; and charming as you both are, I have had no occasion to remind myself that I am past seventy-three. Your hearts, your understandings, your virtues, and the cruel injustice of your fate, have interested me in everything that concerns you; and so far from having occasion to blush for any unbecoming weakness, I am proud of my affection for you, and very

proud of your condescending to pass so many hours with a very old man, when everybody admires you, and the most insensible allow that your good sense and information (I speak of both) have formed you to converse with the most intelligent of our sex as well as your own; and neither can tax you with airs of pretension or affectation. Your simplicity, and natural ease set off all your other merits – all these graces are lost to me, alas! when I have no time to lose!

I have found the frame of Wolsey, and tomorrow morning Kirgate will place him in it, and then I shall begin pulling the Little Parlour to pieces that it may be hung anew to receive him. I have also obeyed Miss Agnes, though with regret for on trying it I found that her Arcadia would fit the place of the picture she condemns, which shall therefore be hung in its room, though the latter should give way to nothing else, nor shall be laid aside, but shall hang where I shall see it almost as often. I long to hear that its dear paintress is well. You will tell me the truth though she in her own case and in that alone, allows herself mental reservation.

I have not spoken to a single person but my own servants since we parted last night. My future letters shall talk of other things, whenever I know anything worth repeating – or perhaps any trifle, and the frequency of my letters will prove there is no forgetfulness – if I live to see you again, you will then judge whether I am changed – but a friendship so rational and so pure as mine is, and so equal of both, is not likely to have any fickleness of youth, when it has none of the other ingredients. It was a sweet consolation to the short time I may have left, to fall into such a society – no wonder then that I am unhappy at that consolation being abridged. I pique myself on no philosophy, but what a long use and knowledge of the world has given me, the philosophy of indifference to most persons and events. I do pique myself on not being ridiculous at this very late period of my life; but when there is not a grain of passion in my affection for you two, and when you both have the good sense not to be displeased at my telling you so (though I hope you would have despised me for the contrary) I am not ashamed to say that your loss is heavy to me, and that I am only reconciled to it by hoping that a winter in Italy and the journeys and the sea air will be very beneficial to two constitutions so delicate as yours. Adieu! my dearest friends – it would be tautology to subscribe a name to a letter, every line of which would suit no other man in the world but the writer.

[56]

Walpole had now a sustained interest in making over to the Berrys the small house not 500 yards to the south of his own. This had given him a new purpose. It had been empty for a few years since the death of his friend Kitty Clive, the leading comic actress of her day, in no way inferior to Sarah Siddons, though of a very different genre. Popular, witty, ugly, vulgar, good-humoured and generous in most respects, Drury Lane had made her fortune. She had retired from the stage in 1769 and had been Walpole's tenant, pensioner and neighbour until 1785. They met regularly and often; in the evenings they would walk together in the meadows. He had called the house Cliveden, a proper analogy to its usage. Now Walpole would make some additions to the house and assign it to the Berrys; Little Strawberry Hill would be their home and they his very close neighbours.

Good Miss Barbara Cecilia Seton, a cousin of the girls on their mother's side, had stopped at the Cambridges' house on her walk from Richmond, aware that there she might pick up information to quieten Walpole's anxieties regarding the travellers.

To Posta restante, Torino   [Strawberry Hill]
                                        Tuesday, Oct. 12, 1790
Yesterday was so serene and the wind so favourable, that I hoped the packet was ready and that you sailed. I wish for a brisk wind to carry you swiftly; yet if I could hold the bag, I should open it so timorously, that Boreas would not be able to squeeze his puffed cheeks through the vent, though I might hear of you sooner. Oh! how you have made me long to dig deep into the almanac, and even into that of next year, though it is most prodigal in me to be willing to hurry away a day, who may have so few in the bank.

Yesterday morning I had just framed Wolsey and hung him over the chimney of the Little Parlour, when the Duchess of Gloucester came, and could scarce be persuaded it was the work of Agnes – but who else *could* have painted it? – This was my employment yesterday – but not the only one – for I had my lawyer with me to prepare for securing Cliveden, if I should not have another almanac; and he is to bring me a proper *clause* on Monday next.

                                                At night
This will be only a journal of scraps, till you are settled somewhere,

and I can write regularly. Moreover, it is the only way of filling random letters – unless I were to indulge myself on the theme that for your sakes I will avoid. I am little likely here to learn or do anything worth repeating; yet if you will be content with trifles, my wanting better subjects shall not be an excuse for not writing. It is a common plea with the unwilling; and persons abroad, I know, are often told by their correspondents, who have not the grace of friendship before their eyes, that they did not send them news, concluding that they had better information. I ask no punctuality of replies, nay beg you to restrain them. I have certainly nothing to do that I like half so well as writing to you two. Do but tell me in short notes your stations, your motions and intentions, and particularly how you both do, and I shall be content: I do give you my word I shall. Never, I beseech you, let the person who studies your well-being the most, be accessory to causing you the least trouble, disquiet or disorder. That is a positive injunction. Good night.

Wednesday night, 13th

I received your kind letter from Brighth[elmstone] this morning, and give you a million thanks for it. It gives me some hopes that you might be landed on Tuesday morning before the wind changed and rose – but it revived a thousand more anxieties. I do not like a vessel smaller than the packet; and the tempestuous wind of yesterday shocks me, lest it should have overtaken you at sea. That good soul Miss Seton walked over from Richmond to communicate her letter to me – how I love her for it! And she had previously called at the Cambridges' to consult him, where his son George, who has often crossed to Dieppe, assured her the vessel would put back to England, or put into Boulogne on change of the wind – It may be so, but I cannot get out of my head the storm of yesterday, every blast of which made me quake and I tremble more now lest you should have been in its power! Oh! when shall I hear you are safe! When you are settled anywhere I shall be more composed, and will think of the more insignificant things of the world.

Friday, 15th

Words cannot tell what I have felt and do now feel! The storm on Tuesday terrified me beyond measure and so I have remained till this minute that Mrs D[amer] has most humanely sent me an express to tell me you are landed. I am not composed enough to say anything else –

[58]

*Mr Ogilvie's mishap which Walpole recounts would have inter-
ested Mary, for even if she did not know him she would have
known of his connection with Lady Ailesbury and Mrs Damer.
The year after the death of the 1st Duke of Leinster, Mr William
Ogilvie had married his widow, the Dowager Duchess; there were
two daughters of the marriage. Mr Ogilvie had been the Scottish
tutor of the Leinsters' younger sons. The Dowager Duchess was the
sister of the Duke of Richmond whose wife was Lady Ailesbury's
daughter by her first marriage, and consequently Mr Damer's half-
sister.*

*Major-General Charles O'Hara, Commandant at Gibraltar, the
Berrys' acquaintance in Rome in 1784 must have been mortified,
not so much by the appointment of Major-General Sir Robert
Boyd to the Governorship of Gibraltar, as by the assignment of
Major-General Sir Henry Calder as Lieutenant-Governor, a posi-
tion O'Hara coveted and to which rumour had given currency.*

*Walpole's unalterable dislike of Dr Johnson was based on the
Doctor's contempt for Thomas Gray's poetry; also for Matthew
Prior's work which he placed in the same category.*

To Poste restante, Torino   Saturday night, Oct. 16, 1790
Not having been out of my house these three days, nor scarce seen a
soul in it, I am not yet come to my worldly talk, but hope to be able
to entertain you a little soon – arrive but at Turin. I know nothing
but two events, not likely to please you. Poor Mr Ogilvie has been
near killed at Goodwood by an astonishing indiscretion of his own.
He went, yes, and with one of his daughters, and without even a
stick, into an enclosure where the [3rd] Duke keeps an elk. The
animal attacked him, threw him down, gored him, bruised him – in
short, he is not yet out of danger.

Boyd is made Governor of Gibraltar, and somebody I know not
whom, is appointed lieutenant-governor in the place of your friend
O'Hara – I know not how or why, but shall be sorry if he is mortified, and you consequently.

                                Sunday noon
Here is your letter from Dieppe as I expected, and strange it is, that
as much as I abhor sea-sickness myself, I am very hard-hearted
about yours – to have only been less sick than usual, when I would

have compounded for your both rivalling the cascades of St Cloud.

I think it is probable that good Miss Seton may take a walk hither after church, as October is dressed out in all its diamonds; I have my coach ready to convey her back if she does – if not, I will call on her this evening; we must drink the health of your sea-sickness.

Sunday night

If I could continue to predict as well as I have done today, I would turn prophet, and I know what I would fortell. Miss S. did come to me, and we had an hour and a half of comfortable conversation, and nobody interrupted us, nor would any mortal have been welcome – you may guess the topics. She saw Wolsey over his chimney in a comely frame of black and gold, and tomorrow the paper-man comes to new-hang the room in sober brown suiting the occasion. As she was going she desired me to read to her Prior's *Turtle and Sparrow*, and his *Apollo and Daphne*, with which you were so delighted, and which though scarce known, are two of the wittiest and genteelest poems. There should be new way-posts on our common roads to some of our best poets, since Dr Johnson from want of taste and ear and from mean party-malice defaced the old indexes as the mob do milestones.

To Posta restante, Torino   Strawberry Hill
                                          Monday 25 [October 1790]
The Little Parlour is new hung, and Wolsey has been installed this morning, with shouts of *Viva Santa Agnese*! – with these festivities I must conclude for this post – disposed as I am to be always writing to you two, be sure matter, *outward* matter only is wanting. I send you trifles, lest I should omit anything you might like to know, especially as I know not when you will see an English newspaper. You are not to answer any of those trumpery articles – let me write, it amuses me.

PS. I have just permitted four foreigners to see my house, though past the season, because all their names end in *i's* and I must propitiate Italians, when you are, as I hope, on Hesperian ground.

In Paris, at the Hotel d'Orléans, rue des Petits Augustins, and driving around the Boulevards, the Berrys saw a great deal to approve, though Mary admitted that 'the first city in the world is at present in déshabile'. The late buildings had an air of grandeur that London had never been able to attain. 'Witness that enormous mass of littlenesses at Somerset House,' she wrote. A friend, the Duc de Levis, Deputé de la Noblesse de Dijon, conducted them to the National Assembly in the Tuileries in what had formerly been the Manège and here Mary was astonished to find seldom less than three or four people vociferously addressing the President at the same time while he, vainly ringing a great bell, sought to silence them. At the Champs de Mars, the large covered pavilion circled by trees with an altar in the middle made only of canvas and boards, deeply impressed the family who were reminded of ideal landscapes of Greece by Poussin. The remains of the Bastille were also inspected.

Passing rapidly through Fontainebleau they reached Pougues on 19 October and from there wrote to Walpole. This was the time of the vendanges and their drunken postilions all but broke up the carriage in their endeavour to reach their destination swiftly. But this was not the first of their vehicular misfortunes. Shortly before Fontainebleau the bed of the carriage had broken and between Pouges and Nevers there was nearly an hour's delay to get the drag mended.

To Poste restante à Florence   Strawberry
                                                          Sunday, Oct. 31, 1790
Perhaps I am unreasonably impatient, and expect letters before they can come. I have got one today – but alas! from Pougues only, 11½ posts short of Lyons! We have had summer till Wednesday last, when it blew a hurricane – I said to it, 'Blow, blow, thou winter wind, I don't mind you now.' But I have not forgotten Tuesday 12th.

I am glad you had the amusement of seeing the National Assembly: did Mr B. find it quite so august as he intended it should be? Your description, and of the Champs de Mars were both admirable; but the altar on boards and canvas seems a type of their perishable constitution, as their air balloons were before. French visions are generally full of vapour, and terminate accordingly.

You license me to direct this to Bologna, but I prefer Florence, for you will not lose more time by its waiting for you, than by its being sent after you; and I always think that the less complicated the manoeuvres of the post, the safer.

You say nothing of your healths – how are Miss Agnes's teeth? Don't omit such essential articles. I promise not to omit a tittle that I can think you would like to know; and in that light nothing will seem too insignificant to tell you. Even articles that would scarce do for home consumption, acquire a value, I know by coming from home. Those wretched tattlers, that one so justly despises on their own dunghill, are welcome abroad in hopes of finding a barley-corn or two that are eatable.

Before leaving England Mary and Agnes had subjected themselves, at Walpole's request, to sitting to Miss Anna Foldsone (Mrs Mee) for their portraits in miniature.

In France bullocks were put to the carriage to help the horses over hilly country and when at Lyons the Hôtel de Provence was reached, there was little to detain them there other than a few purchases made and arguments with the voituriers *over their charges; then on to Chambéry with a night at Bourgoin. It was on leaving there that they experienced some reverse over their passports and had their trunks searched for papers and on Mary inquiring whether everything having now been turned* dessus des-sous, *they were content, a corporal, 'a saucy lad', replied in the most impertinent manner:* 'Non, je ne suis pas content, et ne parlez pas tant vous, cela ne vous fera aucun bien.'

To Poste Restante à Florence   Park Place
                                                                Nov. 8, 1790
I am out of humour with Miss Foldsone; though paid for, she has not sent me your pictures; and has twice broken her promise of finishing them.

I have taken a great liberty which I hope Mr B. will forgive, though a breach of trust. Having only a coach myself, and Saturday being very wet, and being afraid of a bad hired chaise, I did allow myself to use his hither – I will do so no more.

                                              Strawberry, 9th, at night
This morning before I left Park Place I had the relief and joy of

receiving your letter of Oct 24 from Lyons – as you have met with no impediments so far I hope you got out of France as well as through it. I am not surprised at your finding *voiturins* or anybody or anything dearer: where all credit and all control are swept away, every man will be a tyrant in proportion to his necessities and his strength. Societies were invented to temperate force – but it seems, force was liberty – and much good may it do the French with being delivered from everything but violence! – which I believe they will soon taste pro and con.

You make me smile by desiring me to continue my affection – have I so much time left for inconstancy? For three score years and ten I have not been very fickle in my friendships – in all those years I have never found such a pair as you and your sister; should I meet with a superior pair – but then they must not be deficient in any one of the qualities which I found in you two – why perhaps I may change – but with that double mortgage on my affections, I do not think you are in much danger of losing them. You shall have timely notice if a second couple drops out of the clouds and falls in my way.

Nov 11th

As the Parl[iament] will meet in a fortnight and the town be plumper, my letters may grow more amusing, though, unless the weather grows worse, I shall not contribute my leanness to its *embonpoint*. Adieu!

To Miss Seton Strawberry Hill
Nov. 13, 1790

Dear Madam,

I received a letter last night from Chamberry, where our dear friends were safely arrived. They were a little troubled in the last village in France and had their trunks ransacked with some insolence; but that was all. Thank God! they are out of that distracted country! You probably have heard from them too; but I would not risk your not knowing it as soon as I could inform you of it – and now we have nothing to apprehend. I am with great regard, Madam,

Your most obedient servant,
Hor. Walpole

Moving on from Chambéry, Mary had with great trouble and ex-
pense secured a voiturier *to take them to Turin with four horses for*
the carriage and a bidet for one of the servants, but two days out of
Chambéry a further mishap occurred. Shortly before Lanslebourg,
the road and the jolting were so bad that on reaching the village of
St André where the streets were narrow, the projecting roof of a
house was hit by one of the imperials and a falling stone broke the
fastening staples, removing the top of the lantern and breaking the
check-brace. The carriage had to be taken to pieces at Lanslebourg,
but surprisingly undiscouraged they drove on to Turin the next
day, 1 November. Here the disappointment of finding no letters
from England was severe. (The omission of not marking them 'par
Paris' *had led to their going round by Germany.) Discovering some*
friends, the Berrys were urged to stay a day or two and attend the
hunt at Stuminigi, which Mary described as 'driving about till we
heard the stag was killed', *and then delighting in watching the King*
of Sardinia ('a very gentlemanlike old man, easy and dignified in his
manner' – *in fact incompetent and extravagant), the Prince of Pied-*
mont, 'the oddest, ugliest looking being I ever beheld', 'il abuse du
privilège non seulement qu'ont les hommes, mais les princes, d'être
laids', *and the Comte d'Artois, he mercifully better-looking than*
when she had last seen him. The dress, ugly in itself, was gay and
pretty in the field; the men all wore the red faced with blue and
broad silver lace uniforme de chasse. *Continuing on their road they*
reached Parma from Piacenza and there found at the printing office
an impression of 300 copies that had just been completed of Wal-
pole's Castle of Otranto, *destined for Edwards, the London book-*
seller; also five copies on vellum.

To Poste restante à Florence   Strawberry Hill
                                                      Nov. 13, 1790
Oh! yes, yes, Chamberry is more welcome than Turin, though I
thought nothing could make me so happy as a letter from the latter
– but Chamberry is nearer, and has made me easy sooner. What a
melancholy forlorn object did I think that antique capital of a dismal duchy formerly!

  With what anxiety did I read your letter when you were in the
hands of the savages of Bourgoin! I figured them with scalping

[64]

knives and setting up a war-whoop! but you are all safe – and I shall not have another panic until you are returning. Pray burn all my letters; I trembled when they were ransacking your trunks, lest they should meet with any of them: for though I was very cautious while you were in France, I was afraid that my eagerness to learn your arrival at Turin, might be misinterpreted, though meaning nothing but impatience to know you are out of France, into which I hope you will never set your foot more, but return home through Swisserland and Flanders, which I conclude will be resettled shortly. At any rate, I insist on your burning this, that you may not forget it and have it in your trunk. I was the more alarmed, as I have lately heard that Lord Bruce and Mr Lock, whom Miss Agnes has rivalled, riding out in Languedoc, escorted by two national guards, and the former spitting, the wind carried the spittle on one of those heroes, on which they seized our countrymen and imprisoned them all night in a sentry-box, for imprisonment is the characteristic of liberty, and when all men are equal, accidents are punished, as only crimes used to be.

By the way, you affront my dear city, by calling it a *dirty place* – so far from that, it is smug, beautiful, *sublimibus alta columnis*, and deserves to be the metropolis of Europe. Chamberry has made amends for a great deal – and I will pass a few – oh! I fear more than a *few* months contentedly – but then there is to come a journey back – the sea to cross, which I shall not leave out of my reckoning, a second time! All may be forgotten, if I see you next autumn at Cliveden, at *your own* Cliveden, alias, little Chamberry.

I know nothing, nothing at all; but I go to town tomorrow for two days and may pick up something.

Berkeley Square – Tuesday 15th
I might as well be in a country village; you will not be a tittle the wiser for my being in London, which is still a solitude. If I learn nothing more before tomorrow morning, when I shall return to Strawberry, I shall let this amble to Florence without a word more. Adieu!

In the next letter Walpole refers to Audley Street, for the Berrys had

[65]

given up their house in Somerset Street and had taken 26 North Audley Street before their departure, with a view to letting it now but to having a London home to return to. Mr Cambridge would shortly effect a lease. The street was a short one leading into Grosvenor Square which perhaps gave it a mild gentility though inhabited mostly by tradesmen, stay-makers, victuallers, decorators, peruke-makers. To Walpole its advantage lay in its being closer to Berkeley Square.

To Poste restante à Florence [Strawberry Hill]
[Forwarded 'á Pisa'] Thursday, Nov. 18, 1790
Miss Foldson has not yet sent me your pictures: I was in town on Monday and sent to reproach her with having twice broken her promise: her mother told my servant that Miss was at Windsor drawing the Queen and Princesses – That is not the work of a moment – I am glad *all* the Princes are not on the spot.

I think of continuing here till the weather grows very bad, it has not been at all yet, though not equal to what I am rejoiced you have found. I have no Somerset or Audley Street to receive me; Mrs Damer is gone too; the Conways remain at Park Place till after Christmas: it is entirely out of fashion for women to grow old and stay at home in an evening – They invite you indeed now and then, but do not expect to see you till midnight, which is rather too late to begin the day, unless one was born twenty years ago. I do not condemn any fashions, which the young ought to set, for the old certainly ought not; but an oak that has been going on it old way for an hundred years, cannot shoot into Maypole in three years because it is the mode to plant Lombardy poplars.

Walpole had a pleasant circle of friends on whom he could count for entertainment in the evening. The Boufflers with their daughter-in-law with her harp were among the émigrés but in the midst of recounting the dissipations of Richmond society a letter arrived – from Agnes it seems – telling of a frightening adventure, perhaps adjusted so as not to alarm its recipient. In her Journal Mary wrote of an intrepid undertaking in filthy weather needing determination to get as far as Reggio from Parma; Modena, their objective, could not be reached in a day owing to ceaseless pouring rain and a 'rushing torrent' where a brick bridge had to be crossed with the fields under water.

Leaving Reggio two days later and crossing the swollen River Secchia in a boat, they reached Modena, providing a night's halt on the road to Bologna and from there to Florence, arriving on 14 November.

The Duke of Queensberry, who was about to entertain the Prince of Wales with the Duke of Clarence and Mrs Fitzherbert at his palatial house on the river at Richmond, was the lecherous 'old Q', in youth 'the most brilliant, the most fashionable, most dissipated young man in London, the leading character at Newmarket, the support of the gaming table, the person most universally admired by the ladies'.[16] Now sixty-five years old, debauched, and in his dotage, ogling and leering at any pretty girl, he survived Walpole by several years.

Queensberry House, to which his guests were invited, had formerly belonged to George 3rd Earl of Cholmondeley. Built in 1708 on part of the ten acres which had once embraced Henry VIII's Richmond Palace and close to the river beside what is now known at Cholmondeley Walk, it had been a place much liked by Charles I. Afterwards sold, and passing through various hands, the Duke bought it in 1780 and filled it with the fine collection of paintings originally from Lord Clarendon's home at Cornbury; these had subsequently passed to the Duchess of Queensberry.

It was from this house overlooking a broad sweep of the river that the Duke, wearied by the praise of the view and the compliments of his friends, pronounced with the utmost indifference: 'What is there to make so much of in the Thames? I am quite weary of it; there it goes, flow, flow, flow, always the same.'

To Mary and Agnes Berry   Strawberry Hill
Poste restante à Florence   Friday night, Nov 27[26], 1790
[Forwarded 'Pisa']

I am waiting for a letter from Florence, not with perfect patience, though I could barely have one, even if you did arrive as you intended on the 12th – but twenty temptations might have occurred to detain you in that land of eye-and-ear-sight.

I am still here; the weather though very rainy is quite warm, and I have much more agreeable society at Richmond with small companies and better hours than in town, and shall have till after

Christmas, unless great cold drives me thither. Lady Di, Selwyn, the Penns, the Onslows, Douglases, Mackinseys, Keenes, Lady Mt Edgcumbe all stay, and some of them meet every evening. The Boulfflerses too are constantly invited, and the Comtesse Emilie sometimes carries her harp, on which they say she plays better than Orpheus; but as I never heard him on earth, nor *chez* Proserpine, I do not pretend to decide.

Mr C[ambridge] sent me notice yesterday that he and his daughter have let your house very favourably for *five* months – will you forgive me when I own I was glad it was for no longer?

Sunday 28. Particularly to Miss *Agnes*
Though I write to both at once, and reckon your letters to come equally from both, yet I delight in seeing your hand with a pen as well as with a pencil and you express yourself as well with the one as with the other. Your part in that which I have been so happy as to receive this moment, has singularly obliged me by your having saved me the terror of knowing you had a torrent to cross after heavy rain. No cat is so afraid of water for herself, as I am grown to be for you. That panic which will last for many months adds to my fervent desire of your returning early in the autumn. Precious as our insular situation is, I am ready to wish with the Frenchman that you could somehow or other get to it by land, 'Oui, c'est une île toujours, je le sais bien: mais par exemple en allant d'alentour, n'y aurait-il pas moyen d'y arriver par terre?'

Richmond, my metropolis, flourishes exceedingly. The D. of Clarence arrived at his palace there last night between eleven and twelve as I came from Lady Douglas. His eldest brother and Mrs Fitzherbert dine there today with the D. of Queensberry and his Grace who called here this morning, told me, on the very spot where lived Charles I and where are the portraits of his principal courtiers from Cornbury. Q has taken to that palace at last, and has frequently company and music there in an evening. I intend to go.

I suppose none of my Florentine acquaintances are still upon earth. I lived then with Sir Horace Mann in Casa Mannetti in Via de' Santi Apostoli* by the Ponte di Trinità. Pray worship the works of Masaccio, if any remain, though I think the best have been burnt in a church. Fra Bartolomeo too is one of my standards for great ideas; and Benvenuto Cellini's Perseus a rival of the antique.

*A slip for Via S. Spirito.

Circumstances over which Walpole had no control sent him into a fever of acute distress, for on 9 December when returning in the evening from Richmond he found on his table a letter from Mary voicing her disappointment that the family had had no letters from England awaiting them at Turin, except for one from Mrs Damer. How they had miscarried, and why, was a matter of the utmost disturbance to Walpole. He replied hastily saying he would seek safe means of reaching her and meanwhile was able to share his agitation with Miss Seton.

To Miss Seton
Strawberry Hill
Dec. 11, 1790

Instead of your making apologies to me, dear Madam, for the length of your letter, it is I who owe a thousand thanks to you for it. I can never be weary of hearing from you, or about our dear friends, though so unhappy at their present vexatious disappointment. I had a letter from Mary and what adds to my surprise at their want of all letters from England is, that I have assuredly received every one of theirs. I will wait till the next foreign post comes in, and if then I find that they are still in the same letterless situation, I will inquire at the office of the Secretary of State or of Lady Bristol, mother of Lord Hervey Minister at Florence, or of some foreign minister, whether I cannot get leave to send one letter at least in one of their packets.

I cannot wish them during winter to think of returning rather than live in perfect ignorance of all their friends; but since this misfortune has happened, I do trust it will open their eyes on the dangers and inconvenience of living out of their own country. Mr Berry is a healthy man and not an old one, but how frequently has it occurred to me how dreadful would be the situation of two handsome unmarried women if they found themselves in a foreign country without a protector, and curtailed in their circumstances! I dare mention this to you, dear Madam, as I am sure it will not pass your own lips, unless you could artfully a little while hence, when they do receive letters, suggest a hint. I saw with grief before they went, and now perceive by the melancholy reflections in Agnes's letter to you, how much chagrin and disappointment had driven them to take this imprudent journey, and therefore I do but feel the more for them, and attribute all to the true causes, their vile great-uncle, and almost an unjust uncle.

Your most obliged and obedient servant

Hor. Walpole

At Florence the Berrys put up at Maget's and occupied the same rooms as they had had six years previously. But there were still no letters from home, a melancholy circumstance to them all.

Although still somewhat harassed by the uncertainty of his letters reaching their destination, Walpole had so far overcome his despondency as to be able to send local news to Italy. Sarah Siddons, after nearly two years' absence from Drury Lane, returned there in the role of Isabella in Thomas Southern's tragedy, Isabella, or The Fatal Marriage. *It was in this part that Mrs Siddons had conquered London at Drury Lane in 1782, where her success had been outstanding. By 1786 she was on visiting terms with Walpole and later became an intimate friend of Mrs Damer. The Hon. Mrs Bouverie was a notable beauty with great charm of manner and of superior taste.*

Lulled into some kind of tranquillity for his friends, Walpole was rudely shaken afresh by a letter towards the end of the year from Mr Berry himself, with the most dire hint that their sojourn abroad might be extended. While Walpole's note to Miss Seton is on the sour side, his reply to Mr Berry is most unsporting.

To Mary and Agnes Berry   Strawberry
At Florence or Pisa   Friday night, Dec. 17, [1790]
Last week I received your first from Florence with an account of your shocking disappointment at finding no letters from England there or at Turin, though all yours have come regularly to me and Miss Seton so you may be satisfied that your grandmother has been under no alarm about you. A French packet from Calais to Dover sunk in the great storm on Tuesday with all the crew, thirty persons, and I suppose the mails too. Permission has been brought me to send *this* in Lord Hervey's packet, which sets me to writing with confidence.

In the uncertainty of any of my letters reaching you, I must, till I know they do, use many repetitions. The most material are, that your house in Audley Street is let for six months at seven guineas a week; and Mr G. Cambridge has sold Mr Berry's horse. Cliveden was secured for you both in form yesterday morning.

Mrs Siddons is playing again to crowded houses. For my own history I am still resident here. We have had several beautiful days, a vast deal of rain and high winds, but scarce any cold. Richmond is still full, and will be so till after Christmas. The Duke of Clarence is there and every night at Mrs Bouverie's, Lady Di's at home or at the Duke of Queensberry's, with suppers that finish at twelve. I have been at three – but I do not think seventy-three just suited to twenty-five, and therefore have excused myself from as many – and believe I shall settle in town before New Year's Day, though the hours in London even of old folk, are not half so reasonable as those of this young prince, who never drinks or games, and is extremely good humoured and well bred.

To Miss Seton   Strawberry Hill
                                                        Dec. 21, 1790
Dear Madam, I have received your letter and conclude that at the same time you received one from me, and from our friends too.

I am not quite delighted at their seeming to be so much pleased with Florence a second time, though it is sure that I wish them happy anywhere and everywhere; but I had rather they could find felicity in England.

You will excuse my saying no more now, for though I write this myself, I have a little gout in my left wrist – but I beg you will not mention it to them, for it is going off.

Adieu! my dear Madam
                                          Yours most sincerely,
                                              Hor. Walpole

To Mr Robert Berry   Strawberry Hill
à la poste restante à Florence   Dec. [22], 1790
[Forwarded 'Pisa']
Dear Sir, If your letter did not give me so much pleasure from many particulars, I should be vexed at your thinking it necessary to thank me for an affection, by which I am certainly the greater gainer. At my great age, and decrepit as I am, what could happen so fortunate to me

in the dregs of life, as to meet with you and your daughters, and them very pretty young women universally admired, and still more from their virtues, sweet tempers, knowledge and such funds of good sense, as makes them company for the most sensible of both sexes as you constantly have seen – was not this an acquisition to value as I do, when you allowed me to enjoy myself so much of your society? – Indeed I sometimes reproach myself and say 'Did I not engross too much of their time, and may not my blind self-love have contributed to deprive me of that blessing?' Yes, I know I was unreasonable – and may never be so happy again! Can I at past 73 depend on a great life? – I am not so vainly sanguine. Nay, can I be so unjust as to wish to shorten their stay in a country to which they are so partial? Yet human nature, though worn out, cannot, with all its reason, philosophy, and what is much stronger in me, friendship, put itself so entirely out of the question, as to eradicate every hope that they may have a wish to return home; though you alarm me, sir, when you speak hypothetically of being in England by the annual period of your setting out – should there be any *if* in the case, I doubt there will be no *if* for me – Forgive my returning your favour by this melancholy strain; I am too weak to command myself, and the best advice I can give to your daughters, is to gratify their own, and so reasonable inclinations and ascribe my grief to what I should myself and would allow to be dotage, if there were one spark of ridiculous love in my affection for your daughters, and which is equal for both.

On reading what I have been writing, I perceive I have omitted half my words. In fact your letter arrived at nine tonight, and affected me so much, that I began to answer it the instant I had read it, and have written in great precipitation -

Thursday, 23rd

My head was so confused last night, and I have made so many inter-lineations, that I can scarce read it myself – if you cannot, you will have no loss. When I went to bed, the wind was very high, yet I got to sleep. At half an hour after four I was waked by such volleys of thunder, lightning, hail, and then a torrent of rain, as I believe was never known in this temperate clime two days before Christmas. I thought my little castle would be crushed under the bombardment. The lightning darted down the chimney, through the crevices of the shutters and the linen curtains of my bed: Some of my servants and others of the village got [out] of their beds – yet I find no mischief done here, nor yet, anywhere else.

I propose settling in town the beginning of next week, and after the holidays shall probably be less sterile.

Adieu! dear Sir.

Yours most cordially,

H.W.

Having reached Florence, the object of their journey, the Berrys remained there a bare four weeks, removing to Pisa on 11 December. The cold of a Florentine winter was the reason Mary gave Walpole but the account she herself wrote down at a much later date concerning their first visit to Florence in May 1784 bears testimony, together with Mr Berry's letter to a friend of the present date, that it was fear of lack of principle, of possible indelicacy and dissipation amongst the English society in which they found themselves that persuaded her it was not the place for two young women with a father of irresolute character.

'At Florence was our first stop', she had written about that former visit, 'and here for the first time I began to feel my situation, and how entirely dependent I was on my own resources for my conduct, respectability, and success. My father, with the odd inherent easiness of his character had abandoned the world, entirely forgetting that on him now depended the success and happiness of his two motherless daughters. I soon found that I had to lead those who ought to have lead me instead of finding in [my father] a tutor and protector. Strongly impressed as I was that honour, truth and virtue were the only roads to happiness, and the society in which I was about to live, depended entirely on my own conduct and exertions, the whole powers of my mind were devoted to doing always what I thought right and knew would be safe, *without a consideration for what I knew would be* agreeable.*'*

Most probably the same argument was advanced on this occasion, for when writing to his friend Bertie Greatheed, Mr Berry made reference to: 'My daughters not choosing to form any liaison *with some of our countrywomen who happen to be here at present, nor to give offence by shunning their company, made us resolve to spend the three winter months [at Pisa], and to return to Florence in March.'[17]*

Meanwhile they were consorting with the noble family of Corsini and going to their ballet champêtre, *attending balls and other forms of entertainment. Already profiting from the "change of air' since leaving England, Agnes had 'recovered her complexion'.*

But this was a vexatious time for Walpole, suffering from a severe attack of gout and rheumatism and irked by Mr Berry's letter to him regarding his Continental plans. Mrs Siddons, whom he had known now for some time, was unwell and various causes were given for her illness which at the time was referred to as 'a very serious state of ailment'. A couple of years elapsed before it was found that 'Her complaint turns out to be the P[ox] given by her husband'.[18] *But the greater sadness was the death of his old friend George Selwyn, whom he had known since he was eight years old. A wit, misogynist, lacking in ambition, drawn to watching executions of criminals, this enigmatic character was nevertheless devoted to dogs and children, this last sentiment blossoming in his care for the little Mie-Mie (illegitimate child of his friend Lord March) who later married the disreputable 3rd Marquess of Hertford.*

Poste restante à Florence   Strawberry Hill
[Forwarded 'Pisa']   Jan. 2, 1791
I have just been delighting myself in settling Cliveden – then came Mr Berry's letter which after relating your plan, and mentioning your intention of being at home by the period of your setting out, talked of a visit to Swisserland, which I dreaded would detain you, and then said, '*all subject to correction and alteration*' – Those words went to my heart, as if threatening prolongation of your term, though perhaps meaning only the intervening time – in short, I quite despaired!

I have had the gout in my hand for above a fortnight now; it mends very slowly indeed – but I have been much worse since with the rheumatism, which joined it, and still possesses that whole arm and shoulder. I have been quite immovable, but by two servants; I have written all this in my lap without stopping; so you may be sure I am not very bad.

Monday 3rd
Lady Mt Edgcumbe [has] been here from Richmond this morning, and says Mrs Siddons has suffered so much by her late exertions that she has relapsed, and they think must quit the stage.

Berkeley Square
Sat. Jan. 22, 1791

[Entire letter in Kirgate's hand]

I have been most unwillingly forced to send you such bad accounts of myself, but as I could not conceal all, it was best to tell you the whole truth. Though I do not know there was any real danger, I could not be so blind to my own age and weakness, as not to think that with so much gout and fever the conclusion might very probably be fatal, and therefore it was better you should be prepared for what might happen. The danger appears to be entirely over; I have no fever, have a very good appetite, and sleep well. Emaciated, and altered, I am incredibly, as you would find were you ever to see me again – But this illness has dispelled all visions! And as I have so little prospect of passing another happy autumn, I must wean myself from whatever would embitter my remaining time by disappointments.

Tuesday the 25th

I have had another good night, and clearly do mend. I even hope that in a fortnight I shall be able to write a few lines with my own hand, which makes me less solicitous to lengthen my letter now.

I am on the point of losing, or have lost, my oldest acquaintance and friend, George Selwyn, who was yesterday at the extremity. These misfortunes, though they can be so but for a short time, are very sensible to the old; but him I really loved, not only for his infinite wit, but for a thousand good qualities.

Walpole's comments on Semiramis, his name for Catherine II of Russia, refer to her second war with Turkey and her invasion of Poland. Meanwhile the so-called Sultan of Mysore, Tippoo Sahib, had concluded peace with Britain after the Mysore war, but by his assault on territory belonging to the Raja of Travancore the British invaded Mysore and after Cornwallis's victory at Seringapatam in 1792 he was obliged to relinquish much of his country.

Henry Dundas, 1st Viscount Melville, was at this time Member of Parliament for Edinburgh and soon to be Home Secretary. A genial, bustling, red-faced Scot, given to the bottle, he was a popular figure in the House of Commons. The vignette of the scheming Jane Duchess of Gordon (she would marry three daughters to dukes) commanding the rising Home Secretary in peremptory tones to call

[75]

*her servant since he was used to speaking, is a masterpiece of comedy
which Walpole would not miss. No mention is ever made of Mary
Berry's sense of humour. One hopes she too caught the piquancy of
the situation.*

[Berkeley Square]
Saturday, Jan. 29, 1791

[Part of letter in Kirgate's hand]
Voici ma propre écriture! the best proof that I am recovering. I now
rather think it was hussar gout attacking in flying squadrons the
outposts – no matter which. My countenance was so totally altered,
that I could not trace myself. Its outlines have returned to their posts,
though with deep gaps. This is a true picture and too long an one of
self – and too hideous for a bracelet – apropos your sweet Miss
Foldsone I believe is painting portraits of *all* our princesses, to be sent
to all the princes upon earth, for though I have sent her several
written duns, she had not deigned even to answer one in writing -

Pray delight in the following story; Caroline Vernon, *fille d'hon-
neur* [to Queen Charlotte], lost t'other night £200 at faro, and bade
Martindale* mark it up; he said he would rather have a draft on
her banker – oh! willingly; and she gave him one. Next morning he
hurried to Drummond's, lest all her money should be drawn out.
'Sir', said the clerk, 'would you receive the contents immediately?' –
assuredly – 'Why, sir, have you read the note?' Martindale took it, it
was, 'Pay to the bearer 200 blows well applied.' The nymph tells the
story herself – yet I think the clerk had the more humour of the two.

Sunday evening

I wish that complaining of people for abandoning me were an infallible recipe for bringing them *back*! – but, I doubt it will not do in
acute cases. Today I had a crowd of visits; but they all come past two
o'clock, and sweep one another away before any can take root; my
evenings are solitary enough, for I ask nobody to come; nor indeed
does anybody's evening begin, till I am going to bed. I have outlived daylight, as well as my contemporaries – What have I not survived? the Jesuits, and the monarchy of France – and both without a
struggle! Semiramis seems to intend to add Constantinople to the
mass of revolutions – but is not her permanence almost as wonderful

*In charge of a public gaming table.

as the contrary explosions! I wish – I wish we may not be actually flippancying ourselves into an embroil with that Ursa Major of the North Pole. What a vixen little island are we, if we fight with the Aurora Borealis and Tippoo Sahib at the end of Asia at the same time! – You, damsels, will be like the end of the conundrum.

You've seen the man, who saw these wondrous sights.

The Duchess of Gordon, t'other night, coming out of an assembly said to Mr Dundas, 'Mr Dundas, you are used to speak in public, will you call my servant?'

Berkeley Square
Friday, Feb. 4, 1791

I see and thank you for all the kindness of your intention, but as it has the contrary effect from what you expect, I am forced for my own peace to beseech you not to continue a manoeuvre that only tantalizes and wounds me. In your last you put together many friendly words to give me hopes of your return – but can I be so blind as not to see that they are vague words – did you mean to return in autumn, would you not say so? would the most artful arrangement of words be so kind as those few simple ones? In fact, I have for some time seen how little you mean it, and for your sakes I cease to desire it. The pleasure you expressed at seeing Florence again, which, forgive me for saying, is the joy of sight merely, for can a little Italian town and wretched Italian company, and travelling English lads and governors, be comparable to the choice of the best company of so vast a capital as London, unless you have taken an aversion to England? and your renewed transports at a less and still more insipid town Pisa – these plainly told me your thoughts, which vague words cannot efface – you then dropped, that you could let your London house till next Christmas, and then talked of a visit to Swisserland – and since all this, Mrs Damer has warned me not to expect you till *next spring* – I shall not, nor do I expect *that next* spring – I have little expected this next! My dearest Madam, I allow all my folly and unreasonableness and give them up and abandon them totally. I have most impertinently and absurdly tried *for my own sake merely*, to exact from two young ladies above forty years younger than myself a promise of sacrificing their rooted inclinations to my whims and satisfaction –

[77]

but my eyes are opened, my reason is returned, I condemn myself – and I now make you but one request, which is, that though I am convinced it would be with the most friendly and good-natured meaning possible, I do implore you not to try to help me to delude myself any more. You never knew half the shock it gave me when I learned what you had concealed from me, your *fixed* resolution of going abroad last October – and though I did in vain deprecate it, your coming to Twickenham in September, which I knew and from my inmost soul believe was from mere compassion and kindness to me – yet it did aggravate my parting with you – I would not repeat all this – but to prevail with you, while I do live, and while you do condescend to have any friendship for me, never to let me deceive myself. I have no right to inquire into your plans, views or designs, and never will question you more about them. I shall deserve to be deluded if I do – but what you do please to say to me, I beg may be frank – I am in every light too weak to stand disappointment – now – I cannot be disappointed. You have a *firmness* that nothing shakes – and therefore it would be unjust to betray your good nature into any degree of insincerity. You do nothing that is not reasonable and right, and I am conscious that you bore a thousand times more from my self-love and vanity than any other two persons but yourselves would have supported with patience so long. Be assured that what I say, I think, feel and mean. I now wish you to take no one step, but what is comfortable to your views, interests and satisfaction. It would hurt me now to interfere with them. I reproach myself for having so un-generously tried to lay you under any difficulties, and I approve your resolution in adhering steadily to your point. Two posts ago I hinted that I was weaning myself from the anxiety of an attachment to two persons that must have been so uneasy to them, and has ended so sorrowfully to myself – but that anxiety I restrict solely to the desire of your return: my friendship, had I years to live, could not alter or be shaken; and there is no kind of proof or instance of it, that I will not give you both while I have breath.

I have vented what I had at my heart and feel relieved. Do not take ill a word I have said. Be assured I can love you as much as ever I did and do, though I am no longer so unjust as to prefer my own satisfaction to yours. Here I drop the subject -

Monday 7th

Though the Parliament is met, and the town, they say, full, I have not heard a tittle of news of any sort, and yet my prison is a coffee-house in a morning, though I have been far from well this whole week. If you are curious to know the chief topic of conversation, it is the rival opera houses, neither of which are opened yet, both saying the other is falling down.

To Walpole, who had generously offered the Berrys the invaluable advantage of drawing on his account at his Charing Cross banker if in need of funds, it must have been like the turning of a knife in the wound occasioned by their departure, when he read that owing to this kindness they felt able to lengthen the duration of their stay abroad.

Berkeley Square
Feb. 12, 1791

I have received your *two* letters of 17 Jan. and 24th with an account of your objects and plans, and the latter are very much what I expected, as before you receive this, you will have seen my last. Indeed you most kindly offer to break so far into your plan, as to return at the beginning of the next winter; but as that would, as you say, not only be a sacrifice, but risk your healths, can anything upon earth be more impossible than for me to accept or consent to such a sacrifice? Were I even in love with one of you, could I agree to it? Should I be a friend at all, if I wished you, for my sake, to travel in winter over mountains, or risk the storms at sea, that I have not forgotten when you went away? Can I desire you to derange a reasonable plan of economy, that would put you quite at your ease at your return? Have I any pretensions for expecting still less for asking such or any sacrifices? Have I interested myself in your af-fairs only to embarrass them? – The only point on which I can make a shadow of complaint, is your talking of what I did to assist your going, as a reason for your wishing to stay longer abroad – that would be *hard* indeed on *me* and would be punishing me severely for doing you a trifling service! – but when you have other and substantial reasons for not returning before spring twelvemonth, it is useless to talk to the other. I shall not forget how very un-reasonable I have been myself, nor shall I try to forget it, lest I should be so silly again; but I earnestly desire to be totally silent on a subject that I have totally abandoned, and which it is not at all improbable I may never have occasion to renew.

Your other letter talks as kindly as possible on my illness. One comfort however I have, which is conviction that all my pains have been and are gout not rheumatic, which I dread much more as less likely to leave me. A lover, especially one of seventy-three, would not give you these details – but though I have been unreasonable, and I suspect, vain; I am not ridiculous – let us pass to better, that is, to any other subjects.

Miss Foldsone is a prodigy of dishonest impertinence – I sent her word a week ago by Kirgate that I was glad she had so much employment, but wished she would recollect that your pictures had been paid for these four months. She was such a fool as to take the compliment seriously and to thank me for it, but verbally, and I have heard no more – so I suppose she thinks me as drunk with *her* honours as she is – I shall undeceive her, by sending for the pictures again and telling her I can get twenty persons to finish them as well as she can – and so they could the likenesses, and I doubt, better.

I believe I am rather worse than I know (and yet you need not be alarmed) for some of my relations, who never troubled themselves much about me grow very attentive and send me game and sweetmeats, which rather do me good, for they make me smile – and though this fit may be going, they are sure I cannot grow younger.

It is not known whether the Berrys had seen General O'Hara since their meeting in Italy seven years ago, but they would have agreed with Walpole, and consequently with General Conway, that he had been treated disgracefully in having been overlooked for the post of Lieutenant-Governor of Gibraltar.

The King's Theatre in the Haymarket (the Opera House) had been rebuilt after its destruction by fire though had not yet reopened. The company had migrated to the Pantheon in Oxford Street, which though built for concerts and balls had also been intended 'for a kind of winter Ranelagh' but was now fitted up as an opera house. There the King and Queen attended a performance soon after its opening in February.

The history of myself will be short, but sweet: my pains are all gone, and if there is dry weather, I think I shall get out next week; but I am so afraid of a relapse, that I will run no risks – I am content to be at ease: what calls have I abroad?

Our papers say General Ohara is arrived, but as General Conway has not seen him, he concludes him performing quarantine.

The Pantheon has opened, and is small, they say, but pretty and simple; all the rest ill-conducted, and from the singers to the scene-shifters imperfect; the dances long and bad, and the whole performance so dilatory and tedious, that it lasted from eight to half an hour past twelve.

The rival theatre is said to be magnificent and lofty, but doubtful whether it will be suffered to come to life – in short, the contrast will grow politics; *Dieu et mon Droit* supporting the Pantheon, and *Ich Dien* countenancing the Haymarket – it is unlucky that the amplest receptacle is to hold the minority!

20th

Ohara is come to town – you will love him better than ever; he persuaded the captain of the ship, whom you will love for being persuaded, to stop at Lisbon that he might see Mrs Damer. Ohara has been shockingly treated!

Is it not strange that London in February and Parliament sitting, should furnish no more paragraphs! yet confined at home, and in everybody's way, and consequently my room being a coffee-house from two to four, I probably hear all events worth relating as soon as they are born, and I send you them before they are a week old. When I go out again, I am likely to know less; I go but to few and those the privatest places I can find, which are not the common growth of London – nor but to amuse you, should I inquire after news. What is a juvenile world to me, or its pleasures, interests and squabbles? I scarce know the performers by sight.

The Comtesse du Barry, once the maîtresse en titre *of Louis XV, was now nearing fifty and as Lord Glenbervie expressed it: 'very fat and clumsy'.*[19] *She had come to London to identify the large number of fine jewels stolen from her house at Louveciennes in January. The*

thieves, who had brought their spoil to England for sale, had been
apprehended. The Lord Mayor of London at that time was John
Boydell, the well-known engraver. At Chantilly, home of Louis-
Joseph Prince de Condé, the park had been overrun and partly
destroyed while the daughters of Louis XV, Mesdames Adelaïde and
Victoire, aunts to the present King, had been stopped from leaving
Paris.

The Berrys would have received Walpole's earlier letter chronicling
his dismay at the likelihood of their prolonging their time abroad. It
was probably Mary who thought it best, albeit a sacrifice, to relieve
his distress and return by the late autumn.

Poste restante à Florence   Berkeley Square
[Forwarded 'Pisa']   Feb. 26, 1791

I have no letter from you to answer, nor anything new that is in the
least interesting to tell you. There has been a fragment of a rehearsal
in the Haymarket; but still the Pantheon remains master of the field
of battle: the vanquished are preparing manifestoes; but *they* seldom
recover the day.

Madame du Barry is come over to recover her jewels, of which she
has been robbed – not by the National Assembly, but by four Jews
who have been seized here and committed to Newgate. Though the
late Barrymore acknowledged her husband to be of his noble blood,
will she own the present Earl for a relation, when she finds him
turned strolling player? If you want bigger events you may piddle
with the havoc made at Chantilly, which has been half demolished by
the rights of men; as the poor old Mesdames have been stopped by
the rights of the *poissardes*; for, as it is true that extremes meet,
the moment despotism was hurled from the throne, it devolved to
the mob, whose majesties not being able to write their names, do
not issue *lettres de cachet*, but execute their wills with their own
hands; for hanging which degrades an executioner *ne déroge pas* in
sovereigns – witness the Czar Peter the Great, Muley Ishmael [Sultan
of Morocco], and many religious and gracious African monarchs.

After eleven weeks of close confinement, I went out yesterday to
take the air, but was soon driven back by rain and sleet, which soon
ripened to a tempest of wind and snow, and continued all night; it
does not freeze, but blows so hard, that I shall sally out no more, till

[82]

the weather has recovered its temper – I do not mean that I expect Pisan skies.

Monday evening

The east winds are making no amends; one of them has brought me twins. I am sorry to find that even Pisa's sky is not quite sovereign, but that you have both been out of order, though thank God! quite recovered both! If a Florentine March is at all like an English one, I hope you will not remove thither till April. Some of its months, I am sure, were sharper than those of our common wear are; we have scarce had one day without every variety of bad weather, with a momentary leaf-gold of sun.

I wish you had not again named October or November. I have quite given up those months, and am vexed I ever pressed for them, as they would break into your reasonable plans, for which I abandon any foolish ones of my own – but I am a poor philosopher, or rather am like all philosophers, have no presence of mind, and must study my part before I can act it. A long journey in November would be the worst part you could take, and I beseech you not to think of it – for me you see I take a great deal of killing – nor is it so easy to die as is imagined.

Madame du Barry was to go and swear to her jewels before the Lord Mayor – Boydell, who made excuses for being obliged to administer the oath *chez lui*, but begged she would name her hour; and when she did, he fetched her himself in the state coach, and had a mayoroyal banquet ready for her. She has got most of her jewels again.

Poste restante à Florence   Berkeley Square
[Forwarded 'Pisa']   March 5, 1791

One may live in a vast capital and know no more of three parts of it than of Carthage. When I was at Florence, I have surprised some Florentines by telling them that London was built like their city (where you often cross the bridges several times in a day,) on each side of the river, and yet that I had never been but on one side, for then I had never been at Southwark. When I was very young and in the height of the opposition to my father, my mother wanted a large parcel of bugles, for what use I forget. As they were out of fashion she could get none. At last she was told of a quantity in a little shop in an obscure alley in the City: we drove thither, found a great stock, she bought it and bade the proprietor send it home – he said, 'Whither?' – to Sir Robert Walpole's. He asked coolly 'Who is Sir Robert Walpole?'

T'other morning a gentleman made me a visit and asked if I had heard of the great misfortune that had happened? The Albion mills are burnt down. I asked, where were they? – supposing they were powder mills in the country that had blown up. I had literally never seen or heard of the spacious lofty building at the end of Blackfriars Bridge. At first it was supposed maliciously burnt – and it is certain the mob stood and enjoyed the conflagration of a monopoly – but it had been on fire, and it was thought extinguished. The building had cost an hundred thousand pounds, and the loss in corn and flour is calculated at £140,000 – I do not answer for the truth of the sums, but it is certain that Palace Yard and part of St James's Park were covered with half-burnt grain.

This accident and my introduction have helped me to a good part of my letter; for you must have observed that even in this overgrown town, the winter has not been productive of events. Scandal I hate, and would not send you what I thought so; but it is not doubted now but two of our finest ladies, sisters, have descended into the *basse cour* of the Alley with Jews and brokers, and waddled out with a large loss of feathers though not so considerable as was said – yet 23 thousand makes a great gap in pin-money. You will find the initials of both, without going so far as the fifth letter of the alphabet.*

Goodnight! I have two days to wait for a letter that I may answer – stay, I should tell you that I have been at Sir Joseph Banks's† literary saturnalia, where was a Parisian watchmaker, who produced the smallest automaton that I suppose was ever created. It was a rich snuffbox, not too large for a woman. On opening the lid, an enamelled bird started up, sat on the rim, turned round, fluttered its wings, and piped in a delightful tone the notes of different birds, particularly the jug, jug, of the nightingale. It is the prettiest plaything you ever saw – the price tempting – only five hundred pounds. The economist the P[rince] of W[ales] could not resist it and has bought one of those dickeybirds. If the maker finds such customers, he will not end like one of his profession here, who made the serpent in *Orpheus and Euridice*, and who fell so deeply in love with his own

*The Duchess of Devonshire and her sister, Viscountess Duncannon.
†President of the Royal Society.

works, that he did nothing afterwards but make serpents of all sorts and sizes till he was ruined and broke.

The Mesdames are said to be safely out of France, after being stopped three times. The Lord Mayor did not fetch Madame du Barry in the city-royal coach, but kept her to dinner. She is gone but returns in April.

Tuesday morning

I find your letter on my table, but as it only talks of your life at Pisa, and of the community of apartments, which appears as bad as Buxton or Harrowgate, I have nothing to add but to wonder how anyone can seek such an uncomfortable life a second time. Adieu!

Poste restante à Florence   Berkeley Square
[Forwarded 'Pisa']   March 11, 1791

The Haymarket Theatre opened last night with an opera gratis. It is computed that four thousand persons accepted the favour, and the theatre is allowed to be the most splendid and convenient, let Naples say what it will; the singers very indifferent, the dancers (Vestris and Hilsberg) and the dances, charming. – Still it is probable there will be no more representations, for people cannot get much by giving operas for nothing.

I have a solution of Miss Foldsone: she has a mother and eight brothers and sisters, who make her work incessantly to maintain them, and who reckon it loss of time to them, if she finished any pictures that are paid for beforehand – That however is so very uncommon that I should not think the family would be much the richer. I do know that Lord Carlisle paid for the portraits of his children last July and cannot get them from her – at that rate I may see you before your pictures!

Monday 14th

You letter which I received this morning at breakfast, whets no reply, being merely carnivalesque – but you are going to more royal festivities at Florence with their Neapolitan and Tuscan majesties and dukedoms. Shall not you call at Charing Cross on that account – let me know in time.

The *Great Turk* [Catherine of Russia] has sent us rather a *de haut en bas* answer to our proposal of mediating to hinder her removing to Constantinople; we have frowned at the rate of eighteen men of war

– still, keeping up our dignity costs us so dear, that I hope we shall let her go to the Black Sea and be d---d!

Poste restante à Florence   Strawberry Hill
[Forwarded 'Pisa']   Saturday, March 19, 1791
I did not begin my letter on customary Friday, because I had nothing new to tell or to say. The town lies fallow – not an incident worth repeating as far as I know. Parliament manufactures only bills, no politics: I never understood anything useful; and now that my time and connections have shrunk to so narrow a compass what business have I with business? I have ventured hither for change of air – and to give orders about some repairs at Cliveden.
                    B[erkeley] Sq[uare], Monday evening
I am returned, and find the only letter I dreaded, and the only one I trust that I shall ever not be impatient to receive from you. Though ten thousand times kinder than I deserve, it wounds my heart, as I find I have hurt two of the persons I love the best upon earth, and whom I am most constantly studying to please and serve. That I soon repented of my murmurs you have seen by my subsequent letters. The truth, as you may have perceived, though no excuse, was, that I had thought myself dying and should never see you more; that I was extremely weak and low, when Mrs D's letter arrived and mentioned her supposing I should not see you till spring twelvemonth. I am perfectly well again; and just as likely to live one year as half an one. Indulge your pleasure in being abroad while you are there. I am now reasonable enough to enjoy your happiness, as my own. Convince me you are in earnest by giving me notice that you will write to Charing Cross – I will look on that as clearer proof of your forgiving my criminal letter, than your return before you like it. Forgive then, my dearest friends, what could proceed from nothing but too impatient affection; most truly you did not deserve my complaints. I do not think I shall be faulty to you again.

Poste restante à Florence   Berkeley Square
[Forwarded 'Pisa']   Sunday, March 27 1791
Mr Pitt has notified that he is to deliver a message from the King tomorrow to the House of Commons on the situation of Europe; and should there be a long debate, I may not gather the particulars till

Tuesday morning, and if my levee lasts late, shall not have time to write to you – Oh! now are you all impatience to hear *that* message – I am sorry to say that I fear it is to be a warlike one. The Autocratrix swears, d---n her eyes, she *will* hack her way to Constantinople through the blood of 100,000 more Turks, and that we are very impertinent for sending her a card with a sprig of olive. On the other hand Prussia bounces and huffs and claims our promise of helping him to make peace by helping him to make war; and so in the most charitable and pacific way in the world, we are, they say, to send twenty ships to the Baltic, and half as many to the Black Sea – this, little Britain, commonly called Great Britain, is to dictate to Petersburgh and Bengal, and cover Constantinople under those wings that reach from the North Pole to the farthest East! – I am mighty sorry for it, and hope we shall not prove a jackdaw that pretends to dress itself in the plumes of imperial eagles!

If we bounce abroad, we are more forgiving at home; a gentleman who lives at the east end of St James's Park has been sent for by a lady, who has a large house at the west end,* and they have kissed and are friends, which he notified by toasting her health in a bumper at a club the other day. I know no circumstances, but am glad of it – I love peace public or private – not so the chieftains of the contending theatres of harmony. Taylor in wondrous respectful terms and full of affliction, has printed in the newspapers an advertisement declaring that the Marquis's [of Salisbury] honour the Lord Chamberlain did in one season, and that an unprofitable one, send *orders* (you know, that is, tickets of admission without paying) into the Opera House, to the loss of the managers of £400 – servants, it is supposed, and Hertfordshire voters – eke and moreover, that it has been sworn in Chancery that his Lordship, not as Lord Ch[amberlain], has stipulated with Gallini and O'Reilly that he, his heirs and assigns should preserve the power of giving those detrimental *orders* in perpetuity. The immunity is a little new: former Chamberlains, it seems, even *durante officio*, have not exercised the privilege – if they had it.

Sunday night

I have proved in the right in determining to let this depart on Tuesday, for the martial message is only to be delivered tomorrow, and to be taken into consideration the next day; thence I could not send you the result till Friday, when I may possibly write again.

* The Prince of Wales at Carlton House, the Queen at Buckingham House.

Poste restante à Florence   Berkeley Square
                                                      Thursday, March 31, 1791

I postpone my farther answer to your last, till I have satisfied *Mr*
Berry's curiosity about the war with Semiramis. The King's martial
message was adopted on Tuesday by both Houses – but the measure
is exceedingly unpopular, and even some impression was made on the
Court-troops. The Ministerialists affect to give out that matters will
not ripen to war; as if our blustering would terrify a woman, in
whom fear of no sort seems to predominate. More this deponent
knows not.

We have no other positive news since my Tuesday's letter. There is
no peace between the opera theatres: the Haymarket rather triumphs.
They have opened twice, taking money, in an evasive manner,
pretending themselves concerts; the singers are in their own clothes,
the dancers dressed, and no recitative – a sort of opera dishabille.
Threats of arrest have been thrown out, but *no coup de main*. Some
think the return of the judges from the circuit is awaited – but
perhaps the court is sensible of having begun by doing wrong.

I feel every week the disagreeableness of the distance between us:
each letter is generally three weeks on its passage, and we receive
answers to what one must often forget one has said: and cannot
under six weeks learn what one is anxious to know. Balloons, had
they succeeded, would have prodigiously abridged delays – but
French discoveries are not, I believe, endowed with duration; when
they have broken necks and cut throats, they find the world forced to
content itself with old inventions. French levity never takes disappointment into its calculations.

This must be a short letter, for even London, you see, cannot
furnish a whole sheet once a week: however, I had rather leave half
my paper blank, than have any campaign-work to fill it with. Europe
at present is in a strange ferment, distracted between the demons of
republicanism and universal monarchy – at least Prussia and we say
that Semiramis aims at the latter – if she does, we at least might wish
her removed to Constantinople – she would be farther off. Nay, I
am so ignorant, as to imagine, that, if there, she would cultivate
and restore Greece, etc. and be a better customer than the Turks.
Nor am I disposed to think Prussia a substantial ally; it is a fic-
titious power that would have shrunk to little again with its creator,*

*Frederick the Great - his successor was Frederick William II.

had the successor been an inactive prince. Attention, treasures and a most formidable army he has; but if war dissipates his hoards, and diminishes his force, which the squandor of his wealth will weaken too, *adieu! panier, vendanges sont faites* – these are my speculations – I don't know whether they have come into the head of anybody else, nor care whether they deserve it.

I write to amuse you and myself, and only reason, because I have nothing better to send you. I am far from fond of dissertationary letters, which present themselves humbly, but hope to rank as essays – I must be in sad want of nonsense, when I talk seriously on general topics.

I have gossiped to anybody's heart's wish; and the deuce is in it, if any letters are worth receiving, that have the fear of wisdom before their eyes. Adieu to *Arno's vale* till next Friday.

To Horace Walpole the rumblings of the Russian-Turkish War were as nothing compared to the news – shattering as it was to him – that Mary had tumbled down a bank in the neighbourhood of Pisa and had cut her nose. This dire piece of information was repeated to all friends and was reported to Mrs Damer on her return from a journey to Portugal and was still being commented on in mid May. In writing to Mary Berry Mrs Damer not only referred to Mary's 'milk diet', promising not to speak of it to Walpole, but also described his very apparent irritation at her also receiving letters from Mary.

Mrs Siddons, in spite of her 'lowered vitality', was 'as expressive as she had ever been known to be' and resembled her brother, John Philip Kemble, a fine actor, in 'their general style of solemn and alarming grandeur', though this resemblance was an 'outer rather than an inner nature'. Kemble's art was a studied art; hers was natural, she was an artist born.[20] Elizabeth Farren's gifts were of a different nature. She had started her theatrical career as a child in a strolling company where they announced their arrival by a beat on the drum which she carried, thus making a saving in handbill expenditure. She had come a long way since those early days and had for some years been acclaimed as the finest comedy actress of the English stage, giving her place to Dorothy Jordan on her retirement. Her special line was to represent the highly-bred fashionable woman in a comedy of manners ('though with too great an apparent *consideration of what she thinks genteel*'),[21] *a role she perfected when marrying the 12th Earl of Derby to whom she had been attached for eighteen years as all the world knew and accepted. 'Will Miss Farren's coronet never be put on?'*[22] *sighed Mrs Piozzi to the Revd Daniel Lysons. It was not until 1797 that Miss Farren 'exchanged the buskin for a coronet'.*[23]

Poste restante à Florence   Strawberry Hill
                                                      Sunday night, April 3, 1791
Oh! what a shocking accident! how I detest your going abroad more than I have done yet in my crossest mood! You passed unhurt through the cannibals of France and their republic of *larrons* and *poissardes*, who terrified me sufficiently – but I never expected that you would dash yourself to pieces at Pisa! You say I love truth and that you have told me the exact truth – but how can fear believe? You say you slept *part* of the night after your fall – oh! but the other part! was not you feverish? A little comfort I have had even since I received the horrid account – I have met Mrs Lockhart and she has assured me that there is a very good surgeon at Pisa – if he is, he must have blooded you directly. I wish you had had some arquebusade water. How you must have suffered by washing the wound with vinegar, though rightly! When I am satisfied that you have not hurt yourself more than you own, I will indulge my concern about the outside of your nose, about which I shall not have your indifference. I am not in love with you, yet fully in love enough not to bear any damage done to that perfect nose or to any of all your beautiful features – then too I shall scold at your thoughtlessness – how I hate a party of pleasure! It never turns out well; fools fall out, and sensible people fall down! – Still I thank you a million times for writing yourself – if Miss Agnes had written for you, I confess I should have been ten times more alarmed than I am – and yet I am alarmed enough! My sweet Agnes, I feel for you too, though you have not the misery of being a thousand miles from your wounded sister, nor are waiting for a second account.

Not to torment you more with my fears when I hope you are almost recovered, I will answer the rest of your letter. General Ohara I have unluckily not met yet: he is so dispersed and I am so confined in my resorts and so seldom dine from home, that I have not seen him even at General Conway's. When I do, can you imagine that we shall not talk of you two – yes, and your accident I am sure will be the chief topic. As our *fleets* are to dethrone Catherine Petruchia, Ohara will probably not be sent to Siberia. Apropos to Catherine and Petruchio, I supped with their representatives, Kemble and Mrs Siddons, t'other night at Miss Farren's. Mrs Siddons is leaner, but looks well: she has played Jane Shore and Desdemona, and is to play in *The Gamester*; all the parts she will act this year. Kemble, they say, shone in *Othello*.

This morning has been as warm, as if the day had been born at Pisa; and Cliveden, where I have been giving some orders, did not look ugly.

Walpole's great-nephew, George James, 4th Earl (and in 1815 1st Marquess) of Cholmondeley, married Lady Georgiana Charlotte Bertie, daughter of the late 4th Duke of Ancaster, who with her sister was joint hereditary Lord Great Chamberlain of England. Mr George Cholmondeley had been married the previous August and his wife was pregnant (the child was still-born) and until now he had been in line for his cousin's title. His mother, Polly Cholmondeley, would have been at Mrs Buller's party, a close friend of Walpole, but he had felt himself unable to attend. Since Walpole went out of his way on an earlier occasion (3 July 1790) to comment at George Cholmondeley being racked with the toothache and on 15 April of this year 'he is speechless with the headache', he gives the impression that he finds this great-nephew something of a valetudinarian.

Lady Elizabeth Waldegrave, Walpole's great-niece and daughter by marriage of the 3rd Earl Waldegrave, was the second wife of the aged 5th Earl of Cardigan,[24] Constable of Windsor Castle. He died without issue and the succession descended to his nephew, Robert Brudenell, whose mother was Woman of the Bedchamber to Queen Charlotte.

Poste restante à Florence   Berkeley Square
                                                             10 April, 1791
I have little news for you though I begin writing today. If anybody asks me for news, I answer 'Yes, and very bad, Miss Berry has had a terrible fall, and cut her beautiful nose!'.

What novelties there are I will dispatch – at present my gazette would lie in a nutshell; and were it not for the oddity of what happened to myself for two days together, my intelligence would be like the common articles of a newspaper – On Wednesday my nephew Lord Cholmondeley came and acquainted me that he is going to be married to Lady Charlotte Bertie, who accepted of him – 'But,' says he, 'you will be so good as not to mention it yet, for I am now going to the Duchess of Ancaster to ask her consent' – which her grace did not refuse.

The next day Captain Waldegrave came, and almost in the same words, the parties excepted, notified a match between his sister Lady Elizabeth, and Lord Cardigan, 'But you must not mention it yet, for the Earl is only now gone to the King to ask his leave.' – I did not know I was so proper a Cato to be trusted with love-tales – I doubt George Cholmondeley and his new wife, and the mothers of both are not delighted with the former match; and Brudenel and his mother will be terribly disappointed with the latter, after the old Earl had lain fallow for so long. I remember when he married his former wife, they both looked so antique, that I said, they may have grandchildren, but they certainly will have no children – now it seems his Lordship means to have a great-grandson. I was to have met the mother Mrs Cholmondeley last Friday at Mrs Buller's, but the latter turned a very small party into a ball, and I desired to be excused, for though I have married two wives at once, when many years older than Lord Cardigan, I did not choose to jig with Master Buller's friends the officers of the Guards.

I can tell Mr Berry nothing more of our Russian war, but that it is most exceedingly unpopular, and it is supposed Mr Pitt will avoid it if he possibly can. You know I do not love Catherine Petruchia Slayczar, yet I have no opinion of our fleet dethroning her.

Monday

The Abbé [Nicholls] has come in, and distracted me with news for which I do not give a straw, nor would have listened to but that you like my telling you all I hear. Your acquaintance Mrs Horace Churchill, one of my seventy and I don't know how many nephews and nieces, has just presented me with one more of the first gender: Madame de St Alban gave me two of the other – but perhaps might as justly have bestowed them on somebody not so rich in nepotism.

Poste restante à Florence   Berkeley Square
                                                   Friday night, April 15, 1791
My preface will be short, for I have nothing to tell. I go to Strawberry
tomorrow in this jubilee spring that comes but once in fifty years, and
shall return on Monday trusting to be met by a letter from Pisa with a
prosperous account of all I wot of.

I have seen Ohara, with his face as ruddy and black, and his teeth
as white as ever, and as fond of you too, and as grieved for your fall
as anybody – but I. He has got a better regiment.

                                        Strawberry, Sunday night past eleven
You choose your time ill for going abroad this year; England never
saw such a spring since it was fifteen years old. The warmth, blossoms and verdure are unparalleled.

                                            Berkeley Square, Monday 18th
Oh! what a dear letter I have found! and from both at once! I should
not be pleased with the idleness of the pencil, were it not owing to the
chapter of health, which I prefer to everything, high as I hold 'The
Death of Wolsey'. The moment I enter Strawberry, I hasten into the
Little Parlour, which I have new-hung for his reception.

My ambition is to pass a summer with you two established at
Cliveden – I shall not reject more if they come – but one must not be
presumptuous at seventy-three; and though my eyes, ears, teeth and
motion have still lasted to make life comfortable, I do not know that I
should be enchanted if surviving any of them; and having no desire to
become a philosopher, I had rather be unaturally cheerful than affec-
tedly so; for patience I take to be only a resolution of holding one's
tongue and not complaining of what one feels – for does one feel or
think the less for not owning it?

Though London increases every day, I believe you will think the
town cannot hold all its inhabitants, so prodigiously the population is
augmented. I have twice been going to stop my coach in Piccadilly
(and the same has happened to Lady Ailesbury) thinking there was
a mob, and it was only nymphs and swains sauntering or trudging.
T'other morning i.e. at two o'clock, I went to see Mrs Garrick and
Miss H[annah] More at the Adelphi, and was stopped five times before
I reached Northumberland House, for the tides of coaches, chariots,
curricles, phaetons, etc., are endless. Indeed the town is so extended,
that the breed of chairs is almost lost, for Hercules and Atlas could not
carry anybody from one end of this enormous capital to the other.

[93]

How magnified would be the error of the young woman at St Helena who some years ago said to a captain of the Indiaman,'I suppose London is very empty, when the India ships come out.' Don't make excuses then for short letters, nor trouble yourself a moment to lengthen them.

Eleven at night

Oh! mercy! I am just come from Mrs Buller's, having left a very pleasant set at Lady Herries's, and for such a collection! eight or ten women and girls, not one of whom I knew by sight, a German count, as stiff and upright as the inflexible Dowager of Beaufort, a fat dean and his wife, he speaking Cornish, and of having dined today at Lambeth, four young officers, friends of the boy Buller who played with one of them at tric-trac, while the others made with the Misses a still more noisy commerce, and not a creature but Mrs Cholmondeley who went away immediately, and her son who was speechless with the headache, that I was the least acquainted with; and to add to my sufferings, the Count would talk to me of *les beaux arts*, of which he knows no more than an oyster –

I have this moment received a card from the Duchess Dowager of Ancaster to summon me for tomorrow at three o'clock – I suppose to sign Lord Cholmondeley's marriage articles with her daughter. The wedding is to be this day sevennight – save me, my old stars! from wedding-dinners! but I trust they are not of this age. I should sooner expect Hymen to jump out of a curricle and walk into the Duchess's dressing-room in boots and dirty shirt.

Following the Duke of Leeds's resignation as Secretary of State for Foreign Affairs owing to ill-health and the objection to his conduct of affairs with Russia, Lord Grenville was appointed in his place.

Charles James Fox, Whig statesman, joined with the Prime Minister in advocating the abolition of the slave trade but this measure was not effected until 1807. Walpole's 'sable moiety' represents the body of French colonial mulattos who the previous year had requested that they too should benefit from the Declaration of the Rights of Man.

Poste restante à Florence Strawberry Hill
April 23, 1791

Today, when the town is staring at the sudden resignation of the

Duke of Leeds, asking the reason, and gaping to who will succeed him, I am come hither with an indifference that might pass for philosophy as the true cause is not known, which it seldom is. Don't tell Europe, but I really am come to look at the repairs of Cliveden, and how they go on; not without an eye to the lilacs and the appleblossoms; for even *self* can find a corner to wriggle into, though friendship may fit out the vessel. Mr Berry may perhaps wish I had more political curiosity; but as I must return to town on Monday for Lord Cholmondeley's wedding, I may hear before the departure of the post, if the seals are given: for the Duke's reasons, should they be assigned, shall one be certain? His intention was not even whispered till Wednesday evening.

The abolition of the slave trade has been rejected by the House of Commons, though Mr Pitt and Mr Fox united earnestly to carry it. Our wedding is over, very properly, most of the women in white, and no diamonds but on the Duke's wife; and nothing of ancient fashion, but two brides-maids: the endowing purse I believe has been left off, ever since broad pieces were called in and melted down. We were but eighteen persons in all, chiefly near relations of each side, and of each side a friend or two; Sir Peter Burrel* gave away the bride: the poor Duchess-mother wept excessively; she is now left quite alone, her two daughters married, and her other children dead – she herself I fear in a very dangerous way. She goes directly to Spa, where the new-marrieds are to meet her. We all separated in an hour and a half. The Elliot girl was there, and is pretty – she rolls in the numerous list of my nephews and nieces. Mrs Horace Churchill has just given me one of the former, and Mrs George Cholmondeley is bringing another of one sort or other, and could not be at the wedding tonight, no more than his father and mother, who to my surprise were not invited.

I have exhausted my gazette – and this being both Easter and Newmarket week, I may possibly have nothing to tell you by tomorrow sennight's post, and may wait till Friday sennight, of which I give you notice, lest you should think I have had a fall and hurt my nose, Good night!

The visit of the Countess of Albany to England created something of a stir. This rather dim German princess, Louise de Stolberg, with

*Sir Peter Burrell, Bt, was married to the bride's sister.

the sparkling blue eyes, fair skin and lively manner, had married on Good Friday, 1772, at the age of nineteen the Young Pretender, Charles Edward Stuart, Bonnie Prince Charlie, and more recently self-styled Earl of Albany. The bridegroom was over fifty. Four years later she was carrying on a clandestine affair with Count Vittorio Alfieri, dramatic poet from Piedmont. A legal separation was effected in 1784 and thereafter she lived with Alfieri in Paris in the rue de Bourgogne, but following the Pretender's death in Rome in 1788 they lived together mostly in Florence on the Lungarno. When Alfieri died (1803) she lived with the French painter François Xavier Fabre, and remained with him until her own death in 1824. On her maternal side she was descended from the 3rd Earl of Ailesbury and thus claimed relationship with Caroline Lady Ailesbury and her daughter by her first marriage, the Duchess of Richmond.

Mrs Swinburne of Hamsterley Hall, Co, Durham, later the home of Robert S. Surtees, creator of 'Jorrocks', had been acquainted with the Countess of Albany and Alfieri in Paris; she had also known the Empress Maria Theresa and her two daughters.

Poste restante à Florence   Berkeley Square
                                                             May 4, 1791
Nothing more is known of the Russian war, or the new Secretary of State, nor why the last resigned. The Duke of York is gone to Berlin, and the press continues alert – That looks all martial – but the stocks are philosophic and keep their temper. The Prince of Wales is much out of order, spits blood, and fainted away after his levee on Monday.

General Conway has had a great escape; he was reviewing his Blues on Friday, previous to their being reviewed yesterday by the King. The ground was so slippery, for we have had much rain, that his horse fell down and rolled over him, and he had only his arm and leg much bruised; yet so much bruised that yesterday he was forced to write to the King to excuse his appearance, and last night he was lamer than I am.

Here is arrived the pinchbeck Queen Dowager of England, alias the Countess of Albany. I have not much royal curiosity left, yet I have to see her, and will be satisfied, for as she is great-niece to Lady Ailesbury, and cousin of the Duchess of Richmond, they must visit

[96]

her, and they will make some assembly or private party for her. At present they say she is going to see Mrs Swinburne in Yorkshire, who it seems is the friend of all sorts of queens.

Charles James Fox had always supported what might now be called the rights of man and was outspoken in his favour of the French Revolution. On 6 May a dramatic incident took place in the House of Commons during a debate when Burke renounced Fox's friendship.

Mrs Damer's return from six months in Portugal was welcomed with rapture by Walpole.

Poste restante à Florence   Berkeley Square
                                                    May 12, 1791

If you were really my wives, I could not be more generally applied to for accounts of you; of which I am proud – I should be ashamed, if at my age it were a ridiculous attachment. I have one general wish that you may be amused while you stay by the natives of any nation: and I thank you a thousand times for confirming your intention of returning by the beginning of November, which I should not desire *coolly*, but from the earnest wish of putting you in possession of Cliveden while I live, which everybody would approve, at least not wonder at (Mr Batt, to whom I communicated my intention, does extremely) and the rest would follow of course, as I had done the same for Mrs Clive.

The Prince is recovered; that is all the domestic news, except a most memorable debate last Friday in the House of Commons. Mr Fox had most imprudently thrown out a panegyric on the French Revolution. His most considerable friends were much hurt, and protested to him against such sentiments. Burke went farther, and vowed to attack those opinions. Great pains were taken to prevent such altercation, and the P of W is said to have written a dissuasive letter to Burke – but he was immovable – and on Friday he broke out, and sounded a trumpet against the plot, which he denounced as carrying on here. Prodigious clamour and interruption arose from Mr Fox's friends; but he, though still applauding the French, burst into tears, and lamentations on the loss of Burke's friendship, and endeavoured to make atonement; but in vain, though Burke wept too – in short, it was the most affecting scene possible, and undoubtedly *an unique* one, for both the commanders were in earnest and *sincere*. Yesterday a second act was expected – but mutual friends prevailed that the contest should not be renewed – nay, on the same bill Mr Fox made a profession of his faith, and declared he would venture his life in support of the *present* constitution by King, Lords and Commons – in short, I never knew a *wiser* dissertation, if the newspapers deliver it justly, and I think all the writers in England cannot give more profound sense to Mr Fox than he possesses. I know no more particulars, having seen nobody this morning yet.

You know my infinity of nephews and nieces – I am always at a wedding or christening. Two nights ago I was godfather with Lord Chatham and Princess Sophia of Gloucester (represented by Miss Dee) to Horace Churchill's newborn son: It is christened *Chatham Horace*, but is to be called by the latter – it could not, while young, be called *Chat, Chat!*

Friday morning 13th

Last night we were at Lady Fred. Campbell's, the usual cribbage party: Conways, Mount Edgcumbes, Johnstones – at past ten Mrs Damer was announced! Her parents ran down into the hall and I scrambled down some of the stairs – She looks vastly well, was in great spirits, had been twelve hours at sea from Calais, and had rested but four days at Paris from Madrid – We supped and stayed till one o'clock, and I shall go to her as soon as I am dressed. Madrid and the Escurial she owns have gained her a proselyte to painting which her statuarism had totally engrossed – in her, no wonder. Of Titian she had no idea (nor have I a just one, though great faith) as at Venice all his works are now coal-black – but Rubens she says amazed her, and that in Spain he has even grace.

Prince Henry Stuart, Cardinal Duke of York and brother of the Young Pretender, had lived all his life in Rome. Walpole already possessed commemorative medals of his father, James, the Old Pretender, the 'King over the Water', and of his mother, Princess Clementina Sobieska. Thomas Coutts, banker to the house of Hanover, had been received by the Cardinal at Frascati where 'a large medal struck in honour of his accession to his unsubstantial throne had been delivered into Mr Coutts's hand for acceptance by George III'.[25]

Poste restante à Florence   Berkeley Square
                                        Thursday, May 19, 1791

Your letter of the 29th for which you are so good as to make excuses
on not sending it to the post in time, did arrive but two days later
than usual – but make no more excuses – I reproach myself with
occasioning so much waste of your time, that you might employ
every hour, for it is impossible to see all that the Medicis had collected or encouraged in the loveliest little city and in such beautiful
environs – nor had I forgotten the Cascines, the only spot containing
English verdure.

You are learning perspective to take views; I am glad; can one have
too many resources in one's self? Internal armour is more necessary
in your sex than weapons to ours. You have neither professions nor
politics, nor ways of getting money like men. in any which, whether
successful or not, they are employed. Scandal and cards you will both
always hate and despise as much as you do now; and though I shall
not flatter Mary so much as to suppose she will ever equal the extraordinary talent of Agnes in painting, yet as Mary like the scriptural Martha is occupied in many things, she is quite in the right to
add the pencil to her other amusements.

The Countess of Albany is not only in England, in London, at this
very moment I believe in the palace of St James – not restored by as
rapid a revolution as the French, but as was observed last night at
supper at Lady Mt Edgcumbe's by that topsy-turvy-hood that charac-
terizes our present age – Within these two months the Pope [in effigy]
has been burnt in Paris, Madame du Barry, mistress of Louis Quinze,
has dined with the lord Mayor of London, and the Pretender's widow
is presented to the Queen of Great Britain! She is to be introduced to
her great-grandfather's niece, the young Countess of Ailesbury. That
curiosity should bring her hither, I do not quite wonder – less, that
she abhorred her husband; but methinks that it is not very well bred
to his family, nor very sensible. Apropos, I hear there is a medal
struck at Rome of her brother-in-law as Henry IX, which as one of
their papal majesties were so abominably mean as to deny the royal
title to their brother, though for Rome he had lost a crown, I did not
know they allow his brother to assume. I should be much obliged to
you if you could get me one of those medals in copper, ay, and one of
his brother, if there was one with the royal title; I have the father's
and mother's and all the Popes in copper but my Pope Benedict XIV

[99]

is the last, and therefore I should be glad of *one* of each of his successors, if you can procure and bring them with little trouble. I should not be sorry to have *one* of the present Gr[eat] Duke [of Tuscany] and his father; but they should be in copper, not only for my suite, but they are sharper than in silver.

Thursday night.

Well! I have an exact account of the interview of the two Queens from one who stood close to them. The Dowager was announced as Princess Stolberg; she was well dressed, and not at all embarrassed. The King talked to her a good deal, but about her passage, the sea and general topics: the Queen in the same way, but less. Then she stood between the Dukes of Gloucester and Clarence, and had a good deal of conversation with the former, who perhaps may have met her in Italy. Not a word between her and the Princesses, nor did I hear of the Prince, but he was there and probably spoke to her. The Queen looked at her earnestly. To add to the singularity of the day, it is the Queen's birthday – another odd accident at the opera at the Pantheon: Madame D'Albany was carried into the King's box and sat there. It is not of a piece with her going to court, that she seals with the royal arms.

I have been told tonight that you will not be able to get me a medal of the Royal Cardinal, as very few were struck, and only for presents – so pray give yourself but little trouble about it.

Boswell has at last published his long-promised life of Dr Johnson in two volumes in quarto. I will give you an account of it when I have gone through it.

The Hon. Mrs George Hobart, the socially ambitious wife of a man soon to become the 3rd Earl of Buckinghamshire, was of voluminous size, known for her indefatigable activities as well as for her faro table in St James's Square. On leave from Naples, Sir William Hamilton, for many years England's envoy, was accompanied by his mistress of five years, the lovely Emma Hart, soon to be his wife. She was frequently painted by Romney who sometimes represented her posed in a classical 'attitude' for which she was famous. Mrs Montagu was the well-known author and bluestocking who held assemblies in her Portman Square house where intellectuals and literary persons foregathered. Burke's first pamphlet, Reflections on the

French Revolution, *was succeeded by a* Letter from Mr Burke to a Member of the National Assembly.

Poste restante à Florence   Berkeley Square
                                                             May 26, 1791
I am rich in letters from you: You tell me mine entertain you; *tant mieux*; it is my wish, but my wonder, for I live so little in the world, that I do not know the present generation by sight, for though I pass them in the streets, the hats with valances, the folds about the chin of the ladies, and the dirty shirts and shaggy hair of the young men, who have *levelled nobility* almost as much as the *mobility* in France have, have confounded all individuality. Besides, if I did go to public places and assemblies, which my going to roost earlier prevents, the bats and the owls do not begin to fly abroad till far in the night, when they begin to see and be seen. However, one of the empresses of fashion, the Duchess of Gordon, uses fifteen or sixteen hours of her four and twenty. I heard her journal of last Monday – She first went to Handel's music in the Abbey; she then clambered over the benches and went to Hasting's trial in the Hall – after dinner to the play, then to Lady Lucan's assembly; after that to Ranelagh, and returned to Mrs Hobart's faro table; gave a ball herself in the evening of that morning into which she must have got a good way, and set out for Scotland the next day. Hercules could not have achieved a quarter of her labours in the same space of time.

Sir William Hamilton is arrived – his nymph of the attitudes was too prudish to visit the rambling peeress.

George Cholmondeley's wife after a dreadful labour is delivered of a dead child. The rest of my letter must be literary, for we have no news. Boswell's book* is gossiping, but having numbers of proper names, would be more readable, at least by me, were it reduced from two volumes to one – but there are woeful *longuers*, both about his hero, and himself, the *fidue Achates*, about whom one has not the smallest curiosity; but I wrong the original *Achates*; one is satisfied with his fidelity in keeping his master's secrets and weaknesses, which modern led-captains betray for their patron's glory, and to hurt their own enemies, which Boswell has done shamefully, particularly against Mrs Piozzi and Mrs Montagu, and Bishop Percy [of Dromore]. Dr

Life of Samuel Johnson.

Blagdon* says justly, that it is a new kind of libel, by which you may abuse anybody, by saying, some dead person said so and so of somebody alive – Often indeed Johnson made the most brutal speeches to living persons, for though he was good-natured at bottom, he was very ill-natured at top. He loved to dispute to show his superiority. If his opponents were weak, he told them they were fools; if they vanquished him, he was scurrilous – to nobody more than to Boswell himself who was contemptible for flattering him so grossly, and for enduring the coarse things he was continually vomiting on Boswell's own country, Scotland. I expected amongst the excommunicated to find myself, but am very gently treated. I never would be in the least acquainted with Johnson, or as Boswell calls it, had not a just value for him, which the biographer imputes to my resentment for the Doctor's putting bad arguments (purposely out of Jacobitism) into the speeches which he wrote fifty years ago for my father in the *Gentleman's Magazine*, which I did not read then, or even knew Johnson wrote till Johnson died, nor have looked at since. Johnson's blind Toryism and known brutality kept me aloof, nor did I ever exchange a syllable with him; nay, I do not think I ever was in a room with him six times in my days. The first time I think was at the Royal Academy. Sir Joshua [Reynolds] said, 'Let me present Dr Goldsmith to you'; he did. 'Now I will present Dr Johnson to you.' 'No,' said I, 'Sir Joshua, for Dr Goldsmith, pass – but you shall not present Dr Johnson to me.'

Some time after, Boswell came to see me, said Dr J was writing the lives of the poets, and wished I could give him anecdotes of Mr Gray. I said very coldly, I had given what I knew to Mr Mason. B hummed and hawed and then dropped, 'I suppose you know Dr J does not admire Mr Gray' – Putting as much contempt as I could into my look and tone, I said, 'Dr Johnson don't! – humph!' – and with that monosyllable ended our interview – After the Doctor's death, Burke, Sir Joshua Reynolds and Boswell sent an ambling circular letter to me begging subscriptions for a monument for him – the two last, I think impertinently, as they could not but know my opinion, and could not suppose I would contribute to a monument for one who has endeavoured, poor soul! to degrade my friend's superlative poetry – I would not deign to write an answer, but sent down word by my footman, as I would have done to parish officers with a brief, that I would not subscribe. In the two volumes, Johnson says – and very probably

*An army medical officer.

did, or is made to say, that Gray's poetry is *dull*, and that he was a *dull* man! The same oracle dislikes Prior, Swift and Fielding. If an elephant could write a book, perhaps one that had read a good deal would say that an Arabian horse is a very clumsy ungraceful animal – pass to a better chapter –

Burke has published another pamphlet against the French Revolution, in which he attacks it still more grievously. The beginning is very good, but it is not equal, nor quite so injudicious as parts of its predecessor; is far less brilliant, as well as much shorter; but were it ever so long, his mind overflows with such a torrent of images, that he cannot be tedious. His invective against Rousseau is admirable, just and new. Voltaire he passes almost contemptuously. I wish he had dissected Mirabeau too; and I grieve that he has omitted the violation of the consciences of the clergy; nor stigmatized those universal plunderers, the National Assembly, who gorge themselves with eighteen *livres* a day, which to many of them three years ago have been astonishing opulence.

When you return, I shall lend you three volumes in quarto of another work with which you will be delighted. They are state letters in the reigns of Henry VIII, Mary, Elizabeth and James, being the correspondence of the Talbot and Howard families, given by a [6th] Duke of Norfolk to the Herald's Office, where they have lain for a century neglected, buried under dust and unknown, until discovered by a Mr Lodge, a genealogist, who to gratify his passion procured to be made a Persuivant. Oh! how curious they are! Henry seizes an alderman who refused to contribute to a benevolence, sends him to the army on the borders, orders him to be exposed in the front line, and if that does not do, to be treated with the utmost rigour of military discipline. His daughter Bess is not less a Tudor. The mean unworthy treatment of the Queen of Scots is striking; and you will find how Elizabeth's jealousy of her crown and her avarice were at war, and how the more ignoble passion predominated.

Poste restante à Florence   Berkeley Square
                                                    June 2, 1791
Well! I have seen Madam D'Albany, who has not a ray of royalty about her. She has good eyes and teeth; but I think can have had no more beauty than remains, except youth. She is civil and easy, but

German and ordinary. Lady Ailesbury made a small assemblage for her on Monday, and my curiosity is satisfied.

These two days may boldly assume the name of June without the courtesy of England. Such weather makes me wish myself at Strawberry, whither I shall betake myself on Saturday for three days; but shall not be able to settle yet.

Poste restante à Florence   Berkeley Square
                                                                June 8, 1791

Be it known to you, ladies, that from the first of the month June is not more June at Florence. My hay is crumbling away, and I have ordered it to be cut, as sure way of bringing rain.

I have a selfish reason for remonstrating against long letters; I feel the season advancing, when mine will be piteous short, for what can I tell you from Twickenham in the next three or four months? Scandal from Richmond and Hampton Court, or robberies at my own door? The latter are indeed blown already. I went to Strawberry on Saturday, to avoid the [King's] birthday crowd and squibs and crackers; at six I drove to Lord Strafford's, where his goods are to be sold by auction. I returned a quarter before seven, and in the interim between my Gothic gate and Ashe's nursery a gentleman and gentlewoman in a one-horse chair and in the broad face of the sun had been robbed by a single highwayman *sans* mask. Ashe's mother and sister stood and saw it, but having no notion of a robbery at such an hour, in the high road, and before their men had left work, concluded it was an acquaintance of the robbees.

The [5th] Duke of Bedford eclipsed the whole birthday by his clothes, equipage and servants; six of the latter walked on the sides of the coach to keep off the crowd – or to tempt it, for their liveries were worth an argosy. The Prince was gorgeous too. The latter is to give Madame d'Albany a dinner – she has been introduced to Mrs Fitzherbert.

I am glad you repose till your journey commences, and go not into sultry lodgings at the Ascension. I was at Venice in summer, and thought airing on stinking ditches pestilential. after enjoying the delicious nights on the Ponte di Trinità at Florence in a linen nightgown and a straw hat with *improvisatori*, and music and the coffee houses open with ices – at least such were the customs fifty years ago!

The Duke of St Albans has cut down all the brave old trees at Hanworth, and consequently reduced his park to what it issued from, Hounslow Heath – nay, he has hired a meadow next to mine for the benefit of embarkation, and there lie all the good old corpses of oaks, ashes and chestnuts, directly before *your* windows, and blocking up one of my views of the river! – but so impetuous is the rage for building, that his Grace's timber will, I trust, not annoy us long. There will soon be one street from London to Brentford, ay and from London to every village ten miles round. Lord Camden has just let ground at Kentish Town for building fourteen hundred houses – nor do I wonder – London is I am certain much fuller than ever I saw it. I have twice this spring been going to stop my coach in Piccadilly to inquire what was the matter, thinking there was a mob – not at all; it was only passengers. Nor is there any complaint of depopulation from the country: Bath shoots out into new crescents, circuses, squares every year. Birmingham, Manchester, Hull and Liverpool would serve any King in Europe for a capital, and would make the Empress of Russia's mouth water. Of the war with Catherine Slayczar I hear not a breath, and thence conjecture it is dozing in peace.

Mr Dundas has kissed hands for [Home] Secretary of State; and Bishop Barrington of Salisbury is transferred to Durham, which he affected not to desire, having large estates by his wife in the south – but from the Triple Mitre downwards it is almost always true what I said some years ago, that *'nolo episcopari'* is Latin for *'I lie'*. Tell it not in Gath that I say so, for I am to dine tomorrow with the Bishop of London in Fulham.

This morning I went with Lysons the Reverend to see Dulwich College founded in 1619 by Alleyn a player, which I had never seen in my many days. We were received by a smart divine *tres bien poudré* and with black satin breeches – but they are giving new wings and red satin breeches to the good old hostel too, and destroying a gallery with a very rich ceiling, and nothing will remain of ancient but the front, and an hundred mouldy portraits, among apostles, sibyls, and kings of England. On Sunday I shall settle at Strawberry; and then woe betide you on post days! I cannot make news without straw.

With the Berrys' plans fixed for a return in October, Walpole's letter reveals him in good spirits. Mrs Damer wrote to Mary Berry in May *assuring her that 'the certainty he feels of your return with the flattering prospect of enjoying your society makes it not easy to put him out of spirits'. Meanwhile, in Florence Mary was reading Cicero's Letters*, though it is not known which are referred to, only that to Mrs Damer's delight Mary's praise corresponded with her own.*

The weather had promised fair and Mrs Hobart in her Petersham villa Sans Souci had had the felicity of engaging the presence of the Duke of Clarence, who was living at Petersham Lodge, with the actress Dorothy Jordan at her garden fête. Unfortunately the day turned out to be showery and she was 'not a little piqued to get a note from Dorothy which read: "Mrs Jordan presents her compliments to Mrs Hobart and at the request of his Royal Highness the Duke of Clarence begs leave to offer his excuses for not being able to wait on her today, having a previous engagement which he forgot till this morning. Should Mrs Hobart's fête be put off on account of the badness of the weather till Monday or any other day, his Royal Highness will be extremely happy to wait on her." '[26]

Mrs Montagu had given 'an elegant breakfast' to a large and distinguished assembly to view the new and most handsome rooms designed by Bonomi in her Portman Square house. The feather-room whose walls were festooned with feathers sewn together and chiefly worked by Mrs Montagu herself and a few helpers, must have created a singular effect. Of the Queen's visit, accompanied by the Princesses, Mrs Montagu waxed eloquent: 'no pen can describe, no paper contain' the honour Her Majesty's visit had conferred on her.

Poste Restante à Florence

Strawberry Hill
June 14, 1791

I pity you! what a dozen or fifteen unentertaining letters are you going to receive! for here I am, unlikely to have anything to tell you worth reading: You had better come back incontinently – but pray do not prophesy any more; you have been the death of our summer, and we are in a close mourning for it in coals and ashes. It froze hard last night: I went out for a moment to look at my haymakers and was starved – the contents of an English June are, hay and ice, orange-flowers and rheumatisms! I am now cowering over the fire.

*Possibly the English translation of *Letters to Several of his Friends*, 4th edition, 1789, 3 volumes, for R. Dodsey, Pall Mall, London.

Mrs Hobart had announced a rural breakfast at Sans Souci last Saturday; nothing being so pastoral as a fat grandmother in a row of houses in Ham Common. It rained early in the morning; she dispatched postboys for want of cupids and zephyrs, to stop the nymphs and shepherds who attend their flocks in Pall Mall and St James's Street, but half of them missed the couriers and arrived. Mrs Montagu was more splendid yesterday morning and breakfasted seven hundred persons on opening her great room, and the room with the hangings of feathers. The King and Queen had been with her last week – I should like to have heard the orations she had prepared on the occasion. I was neither city mouse nor country mouse. I did dine at Fulham on Saturday with the Bishop of London, Mrs Boscawen, Mrs Garrick and Hannah More were there. Oh! ye ladies of the Common, and ye uncommon ladies in London, have pity on a poor gazetteer, and supply me with eclogues or royal panegyrics! Moreover – or rather moreunder, I have had no letter from you these ten days, I say not this in reproach as you are so kindly punctual, but as it stints me from having a single paragraph to answer. I do not admire specific responses to every article – but they are great resources on a dearth.

Thursday 16, Berkeley Square

Three persons have called on me since I came, but have not contributed a tittle of news to my journal. Two companies had been to see my house last week, and one of the parties, as vulgar people always see with the ends of their fingers, had broken off the end of my invaluable eagle's bill, and to conceal their mischief, had pocketed the pieces. It is true it had been restored at Rome; and my comfort is, that Mrs Damer can repair the damage – but did the fools know that? It almost provokes me to shut up my house, when obliging begets injury!

Ever since the Wars of the Roses the white rose of York had been the emblem of the Stuart kings and Walpole's reference here to the date is a reminder that the birthday (Old Style) of the Old Pretender, the Countess of Albany's father-in-law, fell on the day that as 'King of Great Britain France and Ireland, and Defender of the Faith', George III prorogued Parliament.

The Countess of Huntington Connection was a Methodist sect founded by herself which caught on and flourished to some extent in churches she built in parts of England. When Wesley withdrew from the sect on grounds of diversion of doctrine she supported Whitefield, one of her chaplains, against him. Eventually a reconciliation was effected but without the foremost protagonists and by degrees the sect decreased in numbers and finally expired.

Poste restante à Florence   Strawberry Hill
                                                              June 23, 1791

Woe is me! I have not an atom of news to send you, but that the second edition of *Mother Hubbard's Tale* [Mrs Hobart's] was again spoiled on Saturday last by the rain, yet she had an ample assemblage of company from London and the neighbourhood. The late Queen of France, Madame du Barry was there; and the late Queen of England Madame d'Albany was not. The former, they say, is as much altered as her kingdom and does not retain a trace of her former powers. I saw her on her throne in the chapel of Versailles, and though then pleasing in face and person I thought her *un peu passée*.

It is an anxious moment for the poor French here: a strong notion is spread that the Prince de Condé will soon make some attempt, and the National Assembly by their pompous blustering seem to dread it. Perhaps the moment is yet too early, till anarchy is got to a greater head – but as to the duration of the present revolution, I no more expect it, than I do the millennium before Christmas.

In my last in the description of June for *orange-flowers* pray read *roses*: the east winds have starved all the former; but the latter, having been settled here before the wars of York and Lancaster, are naturalized to the climate, and reck not whether June arrives in summer or winter: they blow by their own old-style almanacs: Madame d'Albany might have found plenty of white ones on her tenth of June – but on that very day she chose to go and see the king in the House of Lords with the crown on his head proroguing Parliament! What an odd rencontre! Was it philosophy or insensibility?

The patriarchess of the Methodists, Lady Huntington, is dead. Now she and Whitfield and Wesley are gone, the sect will probably decline: a second crop of apostles seldom acquire the influence of the founders.

Madame de Genlis, Marquise de Sillery, 'that scribbling trollope, Mme de Sillery', as Walpole described her, was the mistress of the Duc D'Orléans and governess to his children. He supposedly fathered her daughter, Pamela Fitzgerald. The Comte de Provence (Monsieur) was the younger brother of Louis XVI. He and his wife escaped to Belgium at the time of the King's ill-fated flight. With the death of the Dauphin he became heir to the French throne, styling himself Louis XVIII.

Poste restante à Florence   Strawberry Hill
                                                              June 28, 1791

You was right in concluding I should disapprove of your visiting hospitals. One ought to surmount disgust, where it is one's duty, or one can do any good, or perform an act of friendship; but it is a rule with me to avoid any disagreeable object or idea, where I have not the smallest power of redress or remedy. I would not read any of the accounts of the earthquakes in Sicily and Calabria and when I catch a glimpse of a report of condemned malefactors to the Council, I clap my finger on the paragraph, that I may not know when they are to suffer, and have it run in my head. It is worse to go into hospitals – there is contagion into the bargain. I have heard of a French princess, who had a taste for such sights, and once said, 'ill faut avouer, que j'ai vu aujourd'hui une agonie magnifique'. Your tender nature is not made for such spectacles; and why attrist it, without doing any service? One needs not recur to the index of the book of creation to hunt for miserable sufferers. What would I give not to have heard the calamities fallen on the heads of the King and Queen of France? I know no more yet than of their being betrayed and stopped at Clermont six miles from Varennes, and ordered back to Paris, *with their children*! To expect insult, ignominy, and prison, perhaps separation, or death, without a ray of comfortable hope of their infants! That their imprisonment and danger should have been grievous, I do not wonder – but to await dissension amongst the tyrants, and anarchy, was the best chance the King and Queen had in store – but though both will still happen in time I still believe, what advantage either or both will produce to those victims, may be very doubtful. That their flight was ill-advised is plain, from that woefully false step of leaving his recantation behind him, before he was safely out of the country. It

[109]

was strange that his intention being divulged, he should not have learnt the preparations made to prevent it, and desisted! It is equally strange that he should have escaped, though so watched and guarded!

Wednesday 29th

Your Italian paper is thin, but perfectly good. Cliveden will look beautiful with your narcissuses – I wish you were all there today, for we are again soused into Florentine weather, and have scarce had a teacup of rain, which makes us not look so green as the Cascines, though generally we have fifty thousand acres or such verdure – thus I have answered your chief articles.

Late at night

Madame D'Albany at her own desire is to have breakfast here on Saturday; and at her desire, Alfieri too. Whatever her feelings are *here*, she must rejoice at having been only titular Queen of France!

Nine months are gone and over – I trust there are but four to come e'er we meet. Monsieur and Madame have done right in retiring; none of the family should stay in Paris, but a paltry Duke of Orleans, with his affected trull Mad. de Sillery – and I should not be sorry if they were pelted out of it with contempt.

Poste restante à Florence   Strawberry Hill

Monday, July 4, 1791

Mrs Damer has already repaired the eagle's beak with wax, so that he can again receive company; but as that has not force enough to execute commands of Jove, nor to crush the fingers of those who presume to touch his sacred person, he will soon have another of marble. Madame d'Albany and her cicisbeo breakfasted with us on Saturday, and seemed really delighted – consequently, '*c'est la plus grande reine du monde.*' I really found she had more sense than I had thought the first time I saw her – but she had like to have undone all, for when I showed her 'The Death of Wolsey', with which Mrs D is anew enchanted, and told her it was painted by her acquaintance Miss Agnes Berry, she recollected neither of you – but at last it came out that she had called you Miss Barrys – I cannot say, that whitewashed her much in my eyes: how anything approaching to the sound would strike me at any distance of time – which I trust will never, while I exist, exceed four months. Apropos, t'other night I visited at the foot of Richmond Bridge, and found a whole circle of old and young gossips. Miss [Cambridge] assured me you are to be back in October, which I do not repeat as if violating my promise of contenting myself with the very commencement of November; but to give an opportunity of saying that Cliveden will be quite ready to receive you in October; and as I conclude the lease of your house in town will not be out then, your best way will be not to stop a moment in London, but to drive directly hither, and stay all three, etc., with me till you can settle yourselves in Cliveden. This will not only be the most convenient to yourselves, but you are sure the most agreeable to me; and thus you will have time to unpack and arrange yourselves, without being broken in upon for some days by visits, nor expected to make them: with all my warmth for those I love, I have a rebuffing coldness, that does not glue people to a chair in my house.

I will not talk on France, for one is overwhelmed with reports contradicting one another, according to the propensities of the senders and receivers. Of one thing I am certain, of pitying the Queen, which was so generally felt here as soon as the reverse of her escape was known, that I was told that if money could serve her, an hundred thousand pounds would have been subscribed in a quarter of an hour at Loyd's Coffee-House. There is a wretch, a quondam Prince du Sang [Duc d'Orléans], who has snapped at this moment for making himself more ridiculously contemptible than ever, by protesting he does not wish for the regency – which I suppose would as soon be offered to me. I remember an old French refugee here, a Marquise de Montandre who on the strength of her pinchbeck marquisate, pretended to precede our sterling countesses – but being sure of its not being allowed, she thus entered her claim: when at a visit tea was brought in; before the groom of the chambers could offer it to anybody, she called out, 'I would not have any tea'; and then when she had thus saved her dignity, she said to him after the others had been served, 'I have bethought myself; I think I will have one cup.'

Poste restante à Florence   Strawberry Hill
                Tuesday night, July 12, 1791
I must say a syllable about myself – it is the rheumatism. It was almost gone till last Sunday, when the Bishop of London preaching a charity sermon in our church, whither I very, very seldom venture to

hobble, I would go to hear him, both out of civility, and as I am very intimate with him. The church was crammed, and though it rained, every window was open. However, at night I went to bed and to sleep very well; but at two I waked with such exquisite pain in my rheumatic right shoulder, that I think I scarce ever felt greater torture from the gout. Though the gout could never subdue my courage, nor make me take any precaution against catching cold, the rheumatism and Cliveden have made a coward of me. I now draw up my coach glasses, button my breast, and put a hat on the back of my head, for I cannot yet bear it to touch my forehead, when I go into the garden.

The Hon. Mrs Frederick Keppel, Laura, the eldest of Sir Edward Walpole's three illegitimate daughters, had obtained the villa on the river bank a few miles downstream from her uncle's Strawberry Hill, from her late father.

Richard Brinsley Sheridan, notorious for his extravagances – financial and of the heart – had but lately had his reputation tarnished further by his love affair with Lady Duncannon. His wife, the beautiful Elizabeth Linley, a professional singer before her marriage in 1773, still languished as his wife but died of consumption in 1792.

Poste restante à Florence   Strawberry Hill
                                                                July 26, 1791
Ten months are gone of the longest year that ever was born – a baker's year, for it has thirteen months to the dozen! As our letters are so long interchanging, it is not beginning too early to desire you will think of settling the stages to which I must direct to you in your route – nay, I don't know whether it is not already too late; I am sure it will be if I am to stay for an answer to this – but I hope you will have thought on it before you receive this.

Mrs Keppel has let her house at Isleworth to Sheridan for £400 a year – an immense rate – and yet far from a wise bargain; he has just been forced out of his house in Bruton Street by his landlord, who could get no rent from him – almost the night he came to Isleworth, he gave a ball there which will not precipitate Mrs K's receipts.

Thank you for remembering the Cardinal of York's medal; how welcome it will be, for from what hand am I to receive it! There is another dear hand from which I wish I sometimes saw a line! I can and do write to both at once, and think to and of both at once. I shall not think I am as equally dear to both, as they are to me, if I never hear but from one. Mary is constant, but I shall fear Martha is busy about many other things! Mr Berry is so good as to write to me – I say no more.

Poste restante à Florence   Monday night, Aug 8, 1791
My poor letters that you say are not so barren as I foretold they would be in the summer, will now I doubt have the additional *désagrément* of being teasing and full of repetitions. Can one attend to or inquire after news, when one's mind is occupied about one family, and anxious about every step they take? Can one relate with interest what does not interest one?

There is to be a ball at Windsor on Friday for the Prince's birthday, which has not lately been noticed there. Lord Lorn and several other young men of fashion were invited to it. It seems they now crop their hair short and wear no powder, which not being the etiquette yet, the youths, instead of representing that they are not fit to appear so docked, sent excuses, that they were going out of town, or were unavoidably engaged – a message certainly unparalleled in all the books in the Lord Chamberlain's office.

Had Walpole survived until July 1797 he would have learned that 'a Lady Webster' had been married that month to the 3rd Lord Holland following her divorce by an act of Parliament from Sir Godfrey Webster, Bt. In August 1791 she and her husband were in Lausanne where Gibbon was living and where Lord and Lady Sheffield joined them, Lady Sheffield being a close friend of hers.

The Duke of York, second son of George III, had gone to Berlin in search of a bride, whom he found and married there in September 1791. Consent to the marriage was declared in council 'at the Court at Weymouth', where the King was passing part of the summer. Princess Frederica of Prussia, Princess Royal, was niece to Frederick the Great and great-granddaughter of George I.

What had been known as Petersham Lodge had now, during the Duke of Clarence's tenancy, changed its name to Clarence Lodge.

[113]

Poste restante à Florence   Strawberry Hill
                                                                      Aug 10, 1791

Your last gives me a new alarm: I had flattered myself with your
coming directly to Cliveden – I now see a hitch even in that! – I must
be obstinate and foolish indeed, if I nurse any more visions, and
attempt to harmonize ages so dissonant as yours and mine, and attempt to make their purposes coincide – yet I declare, – though my
own happiness has a great share in my plan, its ultimate object is to
make you two a little more comfortable when I shall be out of the
question. If you have any speculations more rational, I relinquish
mine with pleasure. One point I can by no means abandon; set not
your feet on French ground; I hear daily of insults and violence offered to English travelling to or through that frantic country: a Lady
Webster was lately ill-used on the frontiers of Swisserland, and her
pockets would have been ransacked, had not her husband interposed
roughly. You cannot have a lower opinion of that whole nation than I
have; the residents are barbarians, the exiles have wanted spirit, and
neither have any sense.

The Duke of York's marriage is certain; the Duke of Clarence
told me so himself yesterday. He graciously came hither yesterday,
though I had not been to pay my court – indeed I concluded he had
forgot me, as at his age was very natural – Not having cropped
my hair, I went today to thank him – He could not see me, but
sent to desire I would call on him tomorrow – I asked the page at
what hour would be proper; he answered, between ten and eleven –
mercy on me! to be dressed and at Petersham before eleven! I am not
got down to modern hours – but neither am I reverted to those of
Queen Elizabeth, nor to those of Louis Douze, who is said to have
hastened his death by condescending in complaisance to his young
Queen Mary Tudor to dine at so late an hour as eleven in the morning – I at least, before I am so rakish, will wait till the arrival of my
own Queen *Mary*.

Poste restante à Florence   Strawberry Hill
                                                                      Aug. 17, 1791

I have heard today that Lord and Lady Sheffield, who went to visit
Mr Gibbon at Lausanne, met with great trouble and impertinence at
almost every post in France. In Swisserland there is a furious spirit of

democracy or demonocracy; they made great rejoicings on the recapture of the King of France – Oh! why did you leave England in such a turbulent era? When will you sit down on the quiet banks of the Thames!

Wednesday night

I know nothing new, public or private, that is worth telling. The stocks are transported with the pacification with Russia, and do not care for what it has cost to bully the Empress to no purpose, and say we can afford it. The poor French here are in hourly expectation of as rapid a revolution, as what happened two years ago.

[The Revd] Mr [William] Gilpin was here on Saturday, and desired me to say a thousand civil things from him. Lord Derby and the Farrens were to dine here tomorrow, but the Earl has got the gout and the party is put off. Our weather this week has been worthy of Florence, with large showers, very reputable lightning, and a decent proportion of thunder, and yet the warmth has stood the shock bravely. I wish it may keep up its courage till next Monday, when Lord Robert Spencer is to give a cup for a sailing match at Richmond in honour of the Duke of Clarence's birthday.

I shall fill my vacuum with some lines that General Conway has sent me, written by I know not whom, on Mrs Hart, Sir W. Hamilton's pantomime mistress – or wife, who acts all the antique statues in an Indian shawl. I have not seen her yet, so am no judge, but people are mad about her wonderful expression, which I do not conceive, so few antique statues have any expression at all – nor being designed to have it. The [Belvedere] Apollo has the symptoms of dignified anger – the Laocoön and his sons, and Niobe and her family, are all expression and a few more; but what do the Venuses, Floras, Hercules, and a thousand others tell, but the magic art of the sculptor, and their own graces and proportions? – well! no matter – here are the verses –

ATTITUDES – A SKETCH
To charm the sense, the taste to guide
Sculpture and painting long had tried:
Both call'd ideal beauty forth;
Both claim'd a disputable worth:
When nature looking down on art,
Made a new claim, and show'd us Hart;

All of Corregio's faultless line;
Of Guido's air and look divine;
All that arose to mental view
When Raphael his best angels drew:
The artist's spell, the poet's thought
By her to beauteous life is brought.
The gazer sees each feature move,
Each grace awake and breathing love;
From parts distinct a matchless whole:
She finds the form, and gives the soul.

Altogether it is a pretty little poem enough, though not very poetically expressed.

The Duke of Clarence's tweny-sixth birthday on 21 August was the occasion for celebrations on the river. Little wonder that the 'gloomth' of Strawberry Hill seemed oppressive. The Castle Inn at Richmond faced down the river and was much used in summer months when City companies arrived in their barges with bands and music.

Poste restante à Florence   Berkeley Square
                                                    Tuesday, Aug 23, 1791
I am come to town to meet Mr Conway and Lady Ailesbury, and as I
have no letter from you yet to answer, I will tell you how agreeably I
have passed the last three days, though they might have been improved had you shared them, as I wished, and as I *sometimes* do
wish. On Saturday evening I was at the Duke of Queensberry's (at
Richmond, *s'entend*) with a small company, and there was Sir W
Hamilton and Mrs Hart who on the 3rd of next month previous to
their departure is to be Madame l'Envoyée à Naples, the Neapolitan
Queen [Marie Caroline] having promised to receive her in that
quality – here she cannot be presented, where only such over-virtuous
wives as the Duchess of Kingston and Mrs Hastings, who could go
with a husband in each hand, are admitted. Why the Margravine of
Ansbach with the same pretensions, was not, I do not understand –
perhaps she did not attempt it – but I forget to retract and make

amende honorable to Mrs Hart. I had only heard of her attitudes –
and those, in dumb show, I have not yet seen – Oh, but she sings
admirably, has a very fine strong voice, is an excellent *buffa*, and an
astonishing tragedian. She sung Nina in the highest perfection, and
there her attitudes were a whole theatre of grace and various expressions.

On Monday was the boat race. I was in the great room at the
Castle [Inn] with the Duke of Clarence, Lady Di [Beauclerk], Lord
Robert and the House of Bouverie to see the boats start from the
bridge at Thistleworth [Isleworth], and back to a tent erected in Lord
Dysart's meadow, just before Lady Di's windows, whither we went
to see them arrive, and where we had breakfast. For the second heat I
sat in my coach on the bridge – and did not stay for the third. The
day had been coined on purpose with my favourite southeast wind.
The scene both up the river and down was what only Richmond
upon earth can exhibit; the crowds in those green velvet meadows
and on the shores, the yachts, barges, pleasure and small boats and
the windows and gardens lined with spectators, were so delightful,
that when I came home from that vivid show, I thought Strawberry
looked as dull and solitary as a hermitage. At night there was a ball at
the Castle, and illuminations with the Duke's cipher, etc., in coloured
lamps, as were the houses of his R.H.'s tradesmen.

Thursday morning, 25th

London you may conclude is as deserted as Ferrara, for though I have
been here two days, and supped on Tuesday at Miss Farren's and last
night at Lord Mt Edgcumbe's, I did not hear of one incident worth
repeating.

Madame d'Albany is gone. I believe she made application for some
deficit – I doubt much whether she received even an answer.

Poste restante à Basle en Suisse   Strawberry Hill
                                                    Sept. 11, 1791

Though I am delighted to know that of the thirteen doleful months
but two remain, yet how full of anxiety will they be! You set out in
still hot weather, and will taste very cold before you arrive! Accidents, inns, roads, mountains, and the sea are all in my map!

I have no news for you but a sudden match patched up for Lord
Blandford. It is with Lady Susan Stewart, Lord Galloway's daughter,

contrived by and at the house of her relation and Lord Blandford's friend, Sir Henry Dashwood, and it is to be instantly, that her Grace his mother will scarce have time to forbid the banns.

We have got a codicil to summer that is as delightful as, I believe, the seasons in the Fortunate Islands – it is a pity it lasts but to seven in the evening, and then one remains with a black chimney for five hours. I wish the sun was not as fashionable as never to come into the country till autumn, and the shooting season, and if Niobe's children were not hatched and fledged before the first of September. Apropos, Sir William Hamilton has actually married his gallery of statues, and they set out on their return to Naples. I am sorry I did not see her attitudes, which Lady Di (a tolerable judge!) prefers to anything she ever saw – still I do not much care; I have at *this moment* a commercial treaty with Italy, and hope in two months to be a great gainer by the exchange – and I shall not be so generous as Sir William, and exhibit my wives in pantomime to the public. 'Tis well I am to have the originals again, for that that wicked swindler Mis Foldson has not yet given up their portraits.

Tomorrow my sister and Mr Churchill come to me. By telling you these trifles you may judge how little I have to say. Even the newspapers are forced to live upon the diary of the King's motions at Weymouth. I was told last night that a director of the Bank affirms the two million five hundred thousand pounds in specie have already been remitted or brought over hither from France since their revolution.

I direct this to Basle as it is better my letters should wait for you, than you for them. How I shall rejoice over every stage you make. Adieu! Carissime!

Dorothy Jordan, whom Leigh Hunt held to be the first actress of her day, was no longer young but in her comedy roles was still the adored of the public, 'to hear whose laugh', according to Hazlitt, 'was to drink nectar'. Her London house was in Somerset Street where the Berrys had lived until recently and must often have seen her. Now in a house at Richmond, she was living with Richard Ford whose father was one of the proprietors of old Drury Lane, about to be rebuilt. By Ford she had had three children and called herself by his name and in the search for respectability she hoped he would marry her, but

this he seemed unable to determine upon. Captivated, a shade reluc-
tantly, by the Duke of Clarence, she became his mistress in 1791 and
remained with him at Petersham and later at Bushey Park until 1811,
bearing him another ten children.[27]

Miss Ann Brunton, sister of Louisa, the better-known actress, had
married Robert Merry the previous month.

The Berrys set out from Florence on 17 September on their
homeward journey and now Walpole was in perpetual alarm at their
returning through France. From her account to Mary Berry, Mrs
Damer was constantly at hand to soothe and reassure him. 'His face
changed, and with an expression of much concern', she wrote, [28] *'he*
told me that you was to come through France. On my trying to
comfort him, and saying what I really now in great measure think, he
quite hurt me by suddenly checking himself and saying that "one had
better keep one's ideas and anxieties to oneself". I see that reason will
not do; it is the very thing he cannot bear, and were I to persist, he
would only bottle up all anxieties and grievances and render their
qualities ten times more pernicious by confinement. I mean, there-
fore, to indulge him in his own way, keeping, however, as much as
possible, alarms from him, and giving where I can the most probable
turn to reports to quiet his mind. I have also seen Mrs Buller, who
means to go to Paris in a week or ten days. I am not sure that I shall
venture to tell this to Mr W. He said that his anxieties were more
unsupportable to him in London, for he could not indulge them so
freely as at Strawb.'

Poste restante à Basle   Strawberry Hill
                                            Friday night late, Sept 16, 1791
Yesterday was red-lettered in the almanac of Strawberry and
Cliveden, supposing you set out towards them, as you intended: the
sun shone all day, and the moon all night, and all nature for three
miles round looked gay. Indeed we have nine or ten days of such
warmth and serenity (here called *heat*) as I scarce remember when the
year begins to have grey, or rather, yellow hairs. All windows have
been flung up again and fans ventilated, and it is true that hay-carts
have been transporting hay-cocks from a second crop all the
morning. The setting sun and the long autumnal shades enriched the
landscape to a Claud Lorrain – guess whether I hoped to see such a

scene next year – if I do not, may you! – at least, it will make you talk of me!

The Marquis of Blandford literally married *malgré* the Duchess. The gorgeous season and poor partridges I hear have emptied London entirely, and yet Drury Lane is removed to the Opera House – do you know that Mrs Jordan is acknowledged to be Mrs Ford, and Miss Brunton to be Mrs Merry, but neither quits the stage. My gazettes will have kept you so much *au courant*, that you will be as ready for any conversation at your return, as if you had only been at a watering place – in short, *à votre intention*, and to make my letters as welcome as I can, I listen to and bring home a thousand things, which otherwise I should not know I heard.

Sunday noon

I do this moment receive yours of Aug 29th in which you justly reprove my jealousies and suspicions of your delaying your return, at the moment you are preparing to make such a sacrifice to me, as I am sensible it is – I do not defend or excuse myself – but alas! is it possible not to have doubts sometimes, when I am not only on the verge of seventy-five, but, if I have a grain of sense left, must know how very precariously I retain this shattered frame? Nay, my dragging you from the country you prefer, would be inexcusable, were self my only motive – no, beloved friends, I am neither in love with either of you, nor, though doting on your society, so personal as to consult my own transitory felicity to your amusement. The scope of all I think and do, is, to make your lives more comfortable when I shall be no more – and if I do suffer the selfish wish of seeing you take possession, to enter into my plan – forgive it! But even this theme I must drop, as you have raised a still more cruel fear! You talk uncertainly of your route through France or its borders – and you bid me not be alarmed! – oh! I shall abhor myself, if I have drawn you from the security of Florence to the smallest risk, or even inconvenience – my dearest friends, return thither, stay there, stop in Swisserland, do anything but hazard yourselves – I beseech you, I implore you do not venture through France, for though you come from Italy, and have no connection of any sort on the whole continent, you may meet with incivilities and trouble. If there is truth in my soul, it is, that I would give up all my hopes of seeing you again, rather than have you venture on the least danger of any sort.

Berkeley Square, Monday night, 19th

One thing I must premise, if, which I deprecate, you should set foot in France, I beg you to burn and not bring a scrip of paper with you. Mere travelling ladies, as young as you, I know have been stopped, and rifled and detained in France to have their papers examined. Calais is one of the worst places you can pass, for as they suspect money being remitted through that town to England, the search and delays there are extremely strict and rigorous.

One charge I can wipe off, but it were the least of my faults. I never thought of your settling at Cliveden in November if your town house is free. All my wish was that you would come for a night to Strawberry and that the next day I might put you in possession of Cliveden – I did not think of engrossing you from all your friends, who must wish to embrace you at your return.

Walpole remembered that Milton had been in Florence in the late 1630s and seems to have visited Vallombrosa on that occasion. His well-known lines from Paradise Lost, Bk. I, 302
> *'Thick as autumnal leaves, that strow the brooks*
> *In Vallombrosa. . .'*
made it a kind of obligation for travellers to go there themselves to say they had seen it.

Poste restante à Basle   Strawberry Hill
                                          Sept. 25, 1791

I am sorry you was disappointed of going to Valombrosa – Milton has made everyone wish *to have seen it*; which is my wish, for though I was thirteen months in Florence (at twice) I never did see it – in fact I was so tired of *seeing* when I was abroad, that I have several of those pieces of repentance on my conscience when they come into my hand – and yet I saw too much, for the quantity left such a confusion in my head, that I do not remember a quarter clearly. Pictures, statues and buildings were always so much my passion, that for the time I surfeited myself, especially as one is carried to see a vast deal that is not worth seeing. They who are industrious and correct, and wish to forget nothing left to be seen, but that ugly pigeon-house the Temple of the Winds, that fly-cage Demosthene's lanthorn and one or two fragments of a portico – or a piece of column crushed into a mud wall – and with such a morsel and quotations, a true classic antiquary can compose a whole folio and call it Ionian antiquities! Such gentry do better still when they journey to Egypt to visit the Pyramids, which are of a form which one would think nobody could conceive without seeing, though their form is all that is to be seen, for it seems that even, prints and measures do not help one to an idea of magnitude, indeed measures do not, for no two travellers have agreed on the measures. In that scientific country too you may guess that such or such a vanished city stood within five or ten miles of such a parcel of sand; and when you have conjectured in vain at what some rude birds or rounds or squares on a piece of old stone may have signified, you may amuse your readers with an account of the rise of the Nile, some hints of the Mamalukes, and finish your work with doleful tales of the robberies of the wild Arabs. One benefit does arise from travelling; it cures one of liking what is worth seeing, especially if what you have seen is bigger than what you do see.

The Berrys arrived at Augsburg on 16 October, coming from Innsbruck where the town held 'a sort of German magnificence – wide streets and large uncouth palaces'. From there the drive gave the impression of riding through the most handsome and best-kept park one had ever seen.

In this letter Walpole refers to Mrs Heneage Legge (her husband was the grandson of the 1st Earl of Dartmouth) but was unaware of the real story. Mrs Damer, who had been apprized of the incident, thought it better to keep it from him, aware of his 'fusses, fears, and "jellies"'. What had happened was that having left Florence on 17 September, the very next day the perch (the centre pole) of the Berrys' carriage broke almost in two and they were obliged to get out and sit three hours by the roadside guarding their trunks while people from the nearby village cottage came running with wood and cord with which they and the voiturier *tied it up. Once the carriage was capable of moving, although not strong enough to carry passengers, the Berrys, courier and maid packed themselves with the luggage into two small open carriages and continued to Bologna, reaching there at eleven o'clock at night, having left a servant to come on slowly with the coach. At the gate of Bologna the party was kept waiting for an hour while the keys were fetched from the vice-legate. Next morning the carriage arrived but the best, the only, coachmaker was away. This protracted the Berrys' time in Bologna for a whole week. There they encountered the Legges, whom they had known in Florence, and were probably glad of their company.*

Poste restante à Augsbourg   Park Place

                                          Monday, Oct. 3, 1791

I had exhausted Basle, was at the end of my map, and did not know a step of my way farther, when on Saturday I was so happy to receive two letters at once bidding my pen drive to Augsbourg. I do not wonder at Mrs Legge for liking to accompany you to Bologna, but though my justice can excuse her, I do not love her a bit the better for detaining you two days, for which I am sure of being out of pocket in November. With more days I shall part with pleasure, if, as you seem to intend, you prefer the road through Germany, provided Brussels is quite tranquil.

I trust you have received my letter in which I explained that I never thought of you settling at Cliveden in November. When I proposed your landing at Strawberry, it was because I thought your house in Audley Street was let till Christmas, and I remembered your description (for what do I forget that you have told me?) of how uncomfortable you found yourselves at your last arrival from abroad. A house in which you would be as much at home as in your own, would be preferable to an hotel – *mais voilà qui est fini.* I did and certainly do still hope, that when you shall have unpacked yourselves, shall have received and returned some dozens of double kisses from and to all that are delighted to see you again – or are not, you will give a couple of days at Strawberry, that on the morning of the second I may carry you to and install and invest you with Cliveden. To *that day* I own I look with an eagerness of impatience that no words could convey, unless they could paint the pulse of fifteen when it has been promised some untasted joy, for which it had long hoped and been denied, and which seldom answers half the expectation – and there I shall have the advantage if I live to attain it, for my felicity cannot but be complete, if that day arrives!

As a lover of Gothic architecture, Walpole reports with enthusiasm on his visit to Windsor. Jarvis's painting in the fifteenth-century Chapel was subsequently removed from the prominent position it occupied. The bas-relief represented the attempted assassination in 1786 of George III by Margaret Nicholson who, when offering him a petition as he left his carriage at St James's Palace, drew out a knife to stab him.

Poste restante à Augsbourg   Strawberry Hill
[Forwarded aux soins de M Perregaux   Oct. 9, 1791
banquier, Paris]

It will be a year tomorrow since you set out. Could I have believed that when my clock had struck seventy-four, I could pass a year in such agitations! It may be taken for dotage, and I have for some time expected to be superannuated; but though I task myself severely, I do not find my intellects impaired. Nay, I have some colt's limbs left which I as little expected as my anxieties. I went with General Conway on Wednesday morning from Park Place to visit one of my antediluvian passions – Windsor Castle; and I was delighted and so juvenile, that without attending to anything but my eyes, I stood full two hours and a half, and found that half my lameness consists in my indolence. Two Berrys, a Gothic chapel and an historic castle are anodynes to a torpid mind – I now fancy that old age was invented by the lazy. St George's Chapel that I always worshipped, though so dark and black that I could see nothing distinctly, is now being cleaned and decorated, a scene of lightness and grace. Mr Conway was so struck with its Gothic beauties and taste, that he owned the Grecian style would not admit half the variety of its imagination. There is a new screen prefixed to the choir, so airy and harmonious that I concluded it Wyat's, but it is by a Windsor architect [Henry Emlyn]whose name I forget.

Jarvis's window over the altar after West is rather too sombre for the Resurrection, though it accords with the tone of the choir; but the Christ is a poor figure scrambling to heaven in a fright, as if in dread of being again buried alive; and not ascending calmly in secure dignity; and there is a Judas below so gigantic, that he seems more likely to burst by his bulk than through guilt. In the midst of all this solemnity, in a small angle over the lower stalls is crammed a small bas-relief in oak with the story of Margaret Nicholson, the King and the coachman, as ridiculously added, and as clumsily executed as if it were a monkish miracle. Some loyal zealot has broken away the blade of the knife, as if the sacred wooden personage would have been in danger still.

The Castle itself is smugged up, is better glazed, has got some new stools, clocks, and looking glasses, much embroidery in silk, and gaudy clumsy throne with a medallion at top of the King's and the Queen's heads over their own – an odd kind of tautology whenever they sit there! There are several tawdry pictures by West of the history of the Garter, but the figures are too small for that majestic palace – however upon the whole, I was glad to see Windsor a little revived.

I had written thus far, waiting for a letter, and happily receive your two from Bologna together for which I give you a million of thanks, and for the repairs of your coach, which I trust will contribute to your safety. I have been much diverted by all you tell me thence – the Bolognese school is my favourite, though I do not like Guercino, whom I call the German Guido, he is so heavy and dark. I do not venerate Constantinopolitan paintings, which are scarce preferable to Indian. The characters of the Italian comedy were certainly adopted even from the *persons* of its several districts and dialects. Pantalon is a Venetian even in his countenance; and I once saw a gentleman of Bergamo whose face was an exact Harlequin's mask.

I have scarce a penful of news for you; the world is at Weymouth or Newmarket.

Poste restante à Bruxelles   Strawberry Hill
                                                         Sunday, Oct. 16, 1791
Having no letter, and no direction beyond Ausbourg, this will be an adventurer without credentials, and will take its chance for your finding it at Brussels. Having no other business than merely to welcome you so far, it shall be brief. News I have none, nor will you have missed any by being on the road.

Mrs Jordan, whom Mr Ford declared his wife and presented her as such to some ladies at Richmond, has resumed her former name, and is said to be much at a principal villa at Petersham, which I do not affirm – far be it from me to vouch a quarter of what I hear. If I let my memory listen, it is that I may have some ingredients for my letters,

[125]

and to which you are apprized not to give too much credit, though, while absent, it is natural to like to hear the breath of the day, which at home you despise, as it commonly deserves.

Berkeley Square, Tuesday 18

I came to town suddenly and unexpectedly; my footman John has pawned a silver strainer and spoon, which not being found out till now, as it had been done here, he ran away in the night, and I have been forced to come and see if he had done no worse, which I do not find he has – and I want another footman in his room – I received yours from Padua and Venice last night.

Poste Restante à Bruxelles   Berkeley Square
[Forwarded chez M. Perriguaux à Paris]   Oct. 20, 1791

I think I did tell you that I was come to town on a sudden, one of my footmen having pawned a little of my plate and run away – but I had other motives. I have had for some time a very troublesome erysipelas on my left arm, which I had not only neglected, but had scratched so unmercifully, that it had become a very serious affair. Mr Watson, my oracle, attends my arm, and it is so much better, that, though with my foot on a stool the whole evening of yesterday, I passed it at Mrs Damer's, and stayed there till past twelve – but now comes the dreadful part of the story!

As I rose out of bed Philip told me he would not disturb my rest last night, but before I came home, a messenger had arrived from Strawberry to say that at five yesterday in the evening one of my gardener's men had in my wood-walk discovered my poor servant John's body hanged in a tree near the chapel and already putrefied! – so he must have dispatched himself on the Friday morning on which he disappeared – I had then learnt to my astonishment that he had not even taken away his hat with him, and had dropped down from the library window, a dangerous height! All this it seems was occasioned by the housekeeper, as she always does, locking all the doors below as soon as she knows everybody is in bed – and thus he could not get his hat out of the servant's hall – if poor soul! he did look for it – probably not!

This remain of shame and principle goes to my heart! – happily for me, I had not even mentioned to him the discovery that had been made of his pawning my plate, and Philip and Kirgate had urged him in the kindest manner to confess it on Thursday evening, which he then would not – but a few hours later owned it to the coachman, and told him he would go away. I since hear he had contracted other debts, and probably feared all would be found out – and he should be arrested and thrown into prison – by me I am sure he would not, for I had not even thought of discharging him – but should rather have tried by pardoning to reclaim him for I do not think he was more than eighteen! nay, on Thursday evening after I knew the story, I let him go behind my coach to Richmond as he used to do, and had not spoken a harsh word to him.

I beg your pardon for dwelling on this melancholy detail, but you may imagine how much it has affected me. It was fortunate for me I was absent from Srawberry when the body was found; the corpse was carried into my chapel in the garden. My greatest comfort is that I cannot on the strictest inquiry find that even an angry word had been used towards the poor young man – I may be blamed for taking his fault so calmly – but I know my concern would be aggravated if a bitter syllable from me had contributed to his despair.

I have written all this that you may know the exact situation of my mind, and lest from the abrupt conclusion of my last you should suspect I was ill. The impression of the unhappy accident will wear off, as I neither contributed to it, nor could foresee it nor prevent it.

Aux soins de Monsieur Peregaux,   Berkeley Square
Banquier, rue du Sentier à Paris   Oct. 27, 1791
Nobody could be more astonished than I was last night! Mr C[onway] and Lady A[ilesbury] are in town for a few days, and I was to sup with them after the play at Mrs D[amer]'s, whither I went at nine and found her reading a letter from you saying that you should be at *Paris* today the 27th – I did not know whether her eyes or my ears had lost their senses! I had had no letter from you after your first from Venice, and according to that was reckoning that you would be at Brussels by the beginning of next week – To think you are so near me today gave me a burst of pleasure.

My next surprise, though marvellously inferior, is, that though you have received all my letters, you should still ask Mrs D whether I wish you to land at Strawberry Hill first. I think I had over and over explained that I do *not* wish it – nay, thought it would be very uncomfortable to you, till you had unpacked yourselves, seen some few persons, adjusted your family etc. – nay, if your arrival were known, and that you are not in London, you would be tormented with letters, notes, questions, and after that, be still to rest and settle yourselves. Today I have had the satisfaction of three *letters* at once from you, from Venice, from Inspruck, Ausburgh and in the first of them you say it would be more comfortable to go for the two or three first days to Twickenham. I have told you why I am not of that opinion – nor was, when you misunderstood me – now, unluckily, it would not be very practicable. I have been in town these ten days, being forced to come for a violent inflammation on my arm, for which Mr Watson attends me. It is so much better he has consented to let me go to Strawberry the day after tomorrow for two or three days, where I have left my family, my bills unpaid etc. – and if I did not settle those things before the moments of expecting you, I should be in a confusion very inconvenient and distressing. I shall now finish all my business, return to Mr Watson, and be well and quiet, and fit to receive you, first here in town, and then at Strawberry and have the installation. Be assured that this plan is the best and safest I can form; and as you know how earnest I am to be well at your return, you may be certain I would do nothing to counteract a plan that has been rooted in my head and heart for twelve months.

The Berrys had reached Paris on 27 October, having begun their day at Nôgent at half past four in the morning. Their coach broke down twice on the road but the Hôtel de Bourbon in the rue Jacob was reached that evening and they were satisfied with their accommodation au premier, *consisting of three rooms and an ante-chamber. They were delighted to find their old friend the Swedish Ambassador, Baron de Staël, in the rue du Bac, also his wife the Ambassadress, whom they had known as Mademoiselle Germaine Necker even before her marriage, but 'she was in the height of her passion for Talleyrand', wrote Mary. 'Sup at her house, invited by her husband, who sees us every day. She too much occupied with her passion* de s'apercevoir de mon existence.'

Ten days later they resumed their journey, spending a night in Montreuil on their way to Boulogne. There they found that wind and tide would enable them to reach Dover faster if they sailed from

Calais. Under a full moon through a becalmed sea the Berrys reached Dover on 10 November and, halting at Canterbury, they were at North Audley Street the next day.

To Miss Seton   [Berkeley Square]
                                           Friday one o'clock [Nov. 11, 1791]
Dear good Miss Seton, thank God they are landed! Mrs Damer has sent me word, and my next thought is to make you easy and happy as I am myself – I know no more, for I have no letter yet, but expect one – I have not time for more –

                                Your most obliged humble servant,
                                                           H. Walpole

To Miss Seton   Berkeley Square
                                                             Nov. 12, 1791
Dear Madam, I have but a moment's time to thank you for your letter, and to tell you – not what you know, as Miss Agnes has acquainted you with their arrival, but that your cousins both look quite well, and that Miss Agnes is quite returned to her good looks, though when I pressed it, she could not affirm she is perfectly well; but the great change from what she was thirteen months and a day ago, makes me hope she will be quite recovered after a little rest. I trust we shall all meet comfortably in a few months at Cliveden.
     I am, dear Madam –
                                Your most obedient humble servant,
                                                          Hor. Walpole

The 3rd Earl of Orford died on 5 December; his uncle, Horace Walpole, succeeded to the title as 4th Earl. His nephew had been nothing but a burden and a responsibility, affected at intervals by insanity and surrounded by unprincipled hangers-on. Indeed, Walpole had wondered whether the Norfolk estates might not have been bequeathed elsewhere but his nephew had acted fairly and had left everything to his successor. Though obliged to him for this, Walpole nonetheless found his inheritance overwhelming. Too old and ailing to encompass the journey to Houghton, he had memories of his last visit there many years earlier when he had found nothing but 'confusion, disor-der, debts, mortgages, pillage, waste, folly and madness'. In the wings of the house rooms were rotting with damp and the two exterior flights of steps which rose on front and back of the piano nobile *were exposed to all weathers. Now, twenty years later, dispossessed of the celebrated collection of pictures sold for £40,000 (so it was said) to the Empress of Russia, the staircase on the west side given away to some blackguard friend of its late owner and the park thick with nettles and brambles shoulder-high, Walpole could not face the sight of the dissolution of what once had been a majestic house and fine estate. He could do no more than shut up the house and deal fairly with the estate and its tenants who were now his responsibility. These were affairs with which he was not conversant and having spent twelve months in a fret worrying over the well-being of the Berrys, now with their return, which had promised such enjoyment, he was plagued with unfamiliar business. But a further trouble reared its head.*

The following three letters make sad reading. Regrets, remorse, dignified injured feelings prevail. What had been felicity had turned sour owing to some mischievous journalistic report that self-interest was the foundation of the Berrys' friendship. Also, Mary was always sensitive regarding the loss of what she claimed should have been her father's inheritance. The last letter of this eventful year probably concerns the acceptance by the sisters of Little Strawberry Hill for their lives.

From Mary Berry   [?]Friday night, 12 o'clock, [9 December 1791]
I did not like to show you, nor did I myself feel while with you, *how* much I was hurt by the newspaper. To be long honoured with your friendship and remain unnoticed, I knew was impossible, and laid my account with, but to have it imagined, implied, or even hinted, that the purest friendship that ever actuated human bosoms should have any possible foundation in, or view to, interested motives, and that we, whose *hereditary neglect* of fortune has deprived us of what might, and ought to have been our own, that we should ever after-wards be supposed to have it in view, or be described in a situation, which must mislead the world both as to our sentiments and our conduct, while our principles they cannot know, and if they could,

would not enter into – all this I confess I cannot bear – not even your society can make up to me for it.

Would to God we had remained abroad, where we might still have enjoyed as much of your confidence and friendship as ignorance and impertinence seem likely to allow us here.

Even Cliveden, which sensible as I am to the compliment of settling us near you, I declare I consider as our least obligation to you – if it is always to be foremost in the eyes of the world, and considered as the cause of our affection for, and attentions to you, if our seeking your society is supposed by those ignorant of its value, to be with some view beyond its enjoyment, and our situation represented as one which will aid the belief of this to a mean and interested world – I shall think we have perpetual reason to regret the only circumstance in our lives that could be called fortunate – the only one that I thought happy. Excuse the manner in which I write, and in which I feel. My sentiments on newspaper notice have long been known to you with regard to every one who have not so honourably distinguished themselves as to feel above such feeble but venomed shafts.   Do not plague yourself by answering this. The only consolation I can have is in the knowledge of your sentiments, of which I need no conviction. I am relieved by writing, and shall sleep the sounder for having thus unburdened my heart. Good night.

[Written before Walpole had   [Berkeley Square
received the previous letter]   ? December 11, 1791]
You have hurt me excessively! We had passed a most agreeable evening, and then you poisoned all by one cruel word – I see you are too proud to like to be obliged by me, though you see that my greatest and the only pleasure I have left, is to make you and your sister a little happier if I can – and *now* when it is a little more in my power, you cross me in *trifles* even, that would compensate for the troubles are fallen on me – I thought my age would allow me to have a friendship that consisted in nothing but distinguishing merit – you allow the vilest of all tribunals, the newspapers, to decide how short a way friendship may go! Where is your good sense in this conduct? and will you punish me, because what you nor mortal being can prevent, a low anonymous scribbler partly takes a liberty with your name? – I cannot help repeating that you have hurt me!

My dearest Angel,

I had two persons talking law to me and was forced to give an immediate answer, so that I could not even read your note, till I had done – and now I read it, it breaks my heart! If my most pure affection has brought grief and mortification on you, I shall be the most miserable of men – My nephew's death has already brought a load upon me that I have not the strength to bear, as I seriously told General Conway this morning. Vexation and fatigue has brought back the eruption in my arm, and I have been half an hour under Mr Watson's hands since breakfast – my flying gout has fallen into my foot – I shall want but your uneasiness to finish me. You know I scarce wish to live but to carry you to Cliveden! – but I talk of myself, when I should speak to your mind – Is all your felicity to be in the power of a newspaper? Who is not so? Are your virtue and purity and my innocence about you, are our consciences no shield against anonymous folly or envy? Would you you only condescend to be my friend if I were a beggar? The Duchess of Gloucester when she heard my intention about Cliveden, came and commended me much for doing some little justice to injured merit – For your own sake, for poor mine, combat such extravagant delicacy, and do not poison the few days of a life which you and *you* only can sweeten – I am too exhausted to write more – but let your heart and your strong understanding remove such chimeras – how could you say you wish you had not returned!

I am in the utmost anxiety to know how you do. I dread lest what I meant kindly, should have made you ill. I saw the struggle of both your noble minds in submitting to oblige me – and therefore all the obligation is on my side. You both have made the greatest sacrifice to *me* – I have made none to you – on the contrary, I relieve my own mind, whenever I think I can ward off any future difficulty from you, though not a ten thousandth part of what I would do, were it in my power. All I can say is, that you must know by your own minds how happy you have made mine – and sure you will not regret bestowing happiness on one so attached to you, and attached so reasonably; for where could I have made so just a choice, or found two such friends? What did I not feel for you both? *Your* tears, and Agnes's agitation divided between the same nobleness and her misery for your sufferings which is ever awake, would attach me more to both, if that were possible. Dearest souls, do not regret obliging one so devoted to you – it is the only sincere satisfaction I have left – and be assured that until today, I have, though I said nothing, had nothing but anxiety since your father's illness, so impatient have I been for what I have received but yesterday. Adieu!

If there was any correspondence between Walpole and the sisters in 1792 – and there must have been since Mary and Agnes spent a few months in Yorkshire that summer with their grandmother – it does not appear to have survived. The Berrys were at Little Strawberry, perhaps alternating with North Audley Street when Walpole moved to Berkeley Square. He suffered from attacks of gout during the year but managed, as he said to the Countess of Ossory, to creep about 'and as I can afford a good fire and have a beautiful view from my window, why should I complain?' He had no wish 'to amble to Ham Common and be disappointed of a pastoral at Mrs Hobart's'. Still bothered with lawyers and agents and calculations and financial encumbrances, not proud of being 'the poorest Earl in England', he declared that he had neither sought his present situation nor certainly deserved it should be so bad, but 'I can remain in the state that suited me and that I had chalked out for myself and enjoyed. I cannot help my name being changed; it shall change nothing else.' Determined never to take his seat in the House of Lords, as he would only make himself ridiculous, and having left the House of Commons almost thirty years ago, it was not in the House of Lords that he would 'rise' again, 'I will keep my dry bones for the general review day.'[29]

The only possible advantage Walpole could derive from what had destroyed his tranquillity was that he could 'make his wife a countess and could charge the estate with a jointure of £2,000 a year'. Amused, if irritated, that anyone might seriously consider his marrying he wrote:

An estate and an earldom at seventy-four!
Had I sought them or wish'd them, 'twould add one fear more –
That of making a Countess when almost fourscore.
But Fortune, who scatters her gifts out of season,
Though unkind to my limbs, has still left me my reason;
And whether she lowers or lifts me, I'll try
In the plain simple style I have liv'd in, to die:
For ambition too humble – for meanness too high.

Some talk of this sort occasioned a letter a little while later from Mary Berry to a friend: 'And why should he? when, without the ridicule or the trouble of a marriage, he enjoys almost as much of my society, and every comfort from it, that he could in the nearest connection? As the willing offering of a grateful heart, the time and attentions I bestow upon him have hitherto given me pleasure. Were they to become a duty, and a duty to which the world would attribute interested motives, they would become irksome. Of the world, its meanness, its total indifference to everything but interest, in some shape or other, be assured you cannot think so badly or so truly as I do. "They best" believe "it who have felt it most."'[30]

Writing after her death more than fifty years later, Greville, the diarist, reported that he had gathered from what she said that 'she never herself was quite sure whether he wished to marry her, but inclined to believe that she might have been his wife had she chosen it'.[31]

Except for one letter in the spring of 1793 the correspondence opens in September when the Berrys had gone north again to Yorkshire.

To Mary and Agnes Berry   Tuesday night, 8 o'clock
                                              Sept. 17, [1793]
My Beloved Spouses,

Whom I love better than Solomon loved his one spouse – or his one thousand. I lament that the summer is over, not because of its iniquity, but because you two made it so delightful to me, that six weeks of gout could not sour it. Pray take care of yourselves – not for your own sakes, but for mine, for as I have just had my quota of gout, I may possibly expect to see another summer, and as you allow that I do know my own mind, and when I wish for anything and have it, am entirely satisfied, you may depend upon it, that I shall be as happy with a third summer, if I reach it, as I have been with the two last.

Consider, that I have been threescore years and ten looking for a society that I perfectly like, and at last there dropped out of the clouds into Lady Herries's room two young gentlewomen who I so little thought were sent thither on purpose for me, that when I was told they were the charming Miss Berrys I would not even go to the side of the chamber where they sat. But as fortune never throws anything at one's head without hitting one, I soon found that charming Berrys were precisely *ce qu'il me fallait*, and that young enough to be my great granddaughters, lovely enough to turn the heads of all our youths, and sensible enough, if said youths have any brains, to set all their heads to rights again, yes, sweet damsels, I have found that you can bear to pass half your time with an antediluvian, without discovering any ennui or disgust, though his greatest merit towards you is, that he is not one of those old fools, who fancy they are in love in their dotage. I have no such vagary, though I am not sorry that some folks think I am so absurd, since it frets their selfishness.

Walpole's interest was now focused on the new Duchess of York, who lived mostly at Oatlands Park, the Yorks' house near Weybridge, Surrey. This was built by the Duke after the original royal palace of Henry VIII and Charles I had been completely destroyed by fire following its recent purchase. Leaving her husband to his infidelities in London, the Duchess, no beauty, her face showing a history of smallpox, was popular with those who lived in the vicinity, to whom she showed kindnesses.

The 'Mrs Ankerstrom' to whom Walpole refers at the beginning of his letter is probably Mrs Anderson (Lady Cecilia Johnson's daughter) whom he found unsympathetic with regard to her manner towards the French emigrés. Hard-faced and hard-hearted, he found her parallel in the person of J.J. Anckarström who in March had assassinated King Gustav III of Sweden

For all the protestations Walpole made regarding his dislike of gossip, he nonetheless often referred to the scurrilous True Briton, *a newspaper which for veracity commanded the lowest opinion and for vulgarity had no peer. Information concerning General O'Hara was of personal interest to them all. Following the outbreak of the Revolutionary war he had sailed from Gibraltar and reached Toulon at the end of October, by which time the town with its arsenal and thirty ships of the line had already surrendered to Admiral Lord Hood and his blockading fleet. But it seemed unlikely that with the small contingent of two battalions and a few guns O'Hara would be able to garrison the town. Besides, shortly after his arrival he was wounded and captured and remained a prisoner in France until 1795.*

Tuesday, 3 o'clock
Sept. 24, 1793

You ordered me to write tomorrow, that you may receive this on Friday: I begin to obey you on St Morrow's vigil – a good deal out of humour – not with you – more than I always am, but with that henbelial, Mrs Ankerstrom, and a bit higher too. As the busybody has told me that the Duchess of York talked of coming hither today, I could not help being prepared, though I did not trust to such authority, and had received no formal notice as I had been promised. In short I was ready by noon, my fires lighted, and my whole house made as spruce as beer – You will scold me for having believed what I did not believe, for can any truth come out of Nazareth, I had been told the visit should be made at the end of last week, or at the *beginning* of this – Now pray, ladies, when a week never yet contained more than seven days, by what almanac can its beginning last longer than Tuesday. Wednesday or Thursday may quarrel for the middle – but should it be given even for the former, your argument will not be a jot the better, for here at a good three of the clock, I have received no notice to expect her Royal Highness tomorrow, and which of the three last days are to be created the first, I do not pretend to guess. The sum total is, that I am extremely distressed and kept in suspense, and cannot go to town as I want to do, and yet must wait till I am delivered of my princess.

Today's *True Briton* says Ohara is to command at Toulon – no mortal more fit, but I hope he will not be wanted. The honest men of the convention, who speak truth as conscientiously as Mrs Ankerstrom, have told the Parisians that [General] Carteaux was marching to the relief of Toulon with forty *thousand* men: Captain

Elphinston, who had no very obvious reason for deprecating his own victory, reduces that beaten army to about eight hundred. One may presume that the convention are a little nearer to the truth, when they paint so deplorably the annihilation of their marine by the capture of their fleet at Toulon.

I am impatient for the account of your journey. It rained outrageously yesterday from two to four, and has not been dry this afternoon.

PS. at night. Just as I had begun my dinner, I received a note from General Budé to tell me the Duchess of York was but then returned from Windsor and recollecting her engagement with me, would come tomorrow about noon, if not a very bad morning, and if not inconvenient to me -Padrona – but I shall pray for fair weather, for it will be sad to put off my going to London again.

I tried at my dessert to have eaten your healths in your melon – I hope they are better than it, for it was as hard as a stone and as white: I did not attempt to save the seeds, for I believe they would thrive nowhere but in a quarry.

It has rained again all this evening, I hope instead of tomorrow: I am sitting at home comfortably, writing postscripts to Yorkshire.

The Duchess of York was accompanied by the Duke's secretary for Foreign Affairs, General de Budé, a Vaudois by birth; and Mrs Ewart, herself a Prussian, who had married Joseph Ewart, English envoy to Prussia. To him had been entrusted the task of arranging the marriage of the Duke of York. The Duchess was a great-great-granddaughter of George I and Walpole's explanation of not sitting in the presence of a member of the royal house was that as a child his father, Sir Robert Walpole, had taken him to see the aged King and there had seemed to Walpole 'something about that terrible old gentleman' that caused him to think ever afterwards that it was impossible for him to sit in the presence of his descendants.

To Brompton near Malton,   Strawberry Hill
Yorkshire   Sept 25, 1793
                                          Wednesday 3 o'clock
Everything has gone *au mieux*. The rain vented itself to the last drop

yesterday, and the sun, as bright as the Belvedere, has not had a wrinkle on its brow since eight o'clock this morning, nay, has been warm, and gilded the gallery and tribune with sterling rays. The Thames quite full with the last deluges, and the verdure never fresher since it was born. The Duchess arrived punctually at twelve, in a high phaeton with Mrs Ewart and Budé on horseback. On the steps at the gate was a carpet, and the court matted. I received the princess at the side of her chaise and when entered, kissed her hand. She had meant to ride, but had hurt her foot, and was forced to sit most of the time she was here. We had many civil contests about my sitting too, but I resisted and held out, till after she had seen the house and drank chocolate in the round drawing room, and then she commanded General Budé to sit, that I might have no excuse – yet I rose and fetched a salver to give her the chocolate myself, and then a glass of water. She seemed much pleased, and commended much; I can do no less of her, and with the strictest truth. She is not near so small as I had expected, her face is very agreeable and lively, and she is so good-humoured and so gracious and so natural.

Tomorrow I shall go to Oatlands with my thanks for the honour – and there probably will end my connections with the courts, begun with George the First, great, great, great-grand-father of the Duchess of York – there sounds as if there could not have been above three generations more between her and Adam.

Great news! – how eager Mr B will look! – but it is not from armies or navies, not from the murderers at Paris – no, it is only an event in the little world of me. This morning, to receive my Princess, I put on a silver waistcoat that I [had] made three years ago for Lord Cholmondeley's wedding and have not worn since. Considering my late illness and how many hundredweight of chalk I have been venting these ten years, I concluded my wedding garment would wrap round me like my nightgown – but lo! it has grown too tight for me!

The fire at Cowdray House (built c. 1495-1540) to which Walpole refers left the Tudor house roofless though not a total ruin. The fan vaulting of the porch was a mixture of Gothic and Renaissance detail and was light enough in its design to resemble eighteenth-century work. The interior of the house had decoration of the seventeenth and eighteenth centuries.

To Brompton [Strawberry Hill]
Thursday evening [Sept. 26, 1793]
Don't be frightened; I am not going to send this away this evening, having already sent one to you this morning – but I find I cannot reconcile myself to your absence, unless I am always talking to you, and that is not so comfortable as your talking to me.

I have been at Oatlands this morning, but the Duchess was gone to the drawing room at St James's, as in truth I had hoped she would be, unless prevented by her foot.

The 27 [26] of Sept. 1793, at night
In my disconsolate widowhood I have been this evening with the Cambridges, and I am glad to have, for I have transacted important business with them. George was at home, and he as well as the farrier are decidedly of opinion that Agnes's mare, which is worse for going to London, will infallibly relapse if she sets out for Yorkshire before next Wednesday; and then all riding would be lost during your journey.

That loveliest and perfectest of all ancient mansions Cowdry was on Monday night last totally burnt to the ground in six hours! The Dowager Lady Montagu was at Brighthelmstone, the young Lord abroad, and probably only a few unintelligent servants in the house. It is a grievous loss to us Goths!

This summer, the sweetest-tempered ever born in England, has quite recovered its good humour, and today been enchanting with primeval verdure – I hope it has accompanied you to Brompton – I long to hear of your being arrived there. Good night – I finish without any douceurs; my letters *par ci, par là*, have enough of them, I believe.

Lord Howe, or 'Black Dick' as he was known owing to the tone of his complexion, was an elderly and gallant officer who had seen service since the age of fourteen. Now in command of the Channel fleet, he held the preservation of ships of overriding importance and these he would not jeopardize in winter storms off the Brittany coast. In December he withdrew the battle fleet to the safety of harbour, leaving frigates to patrol the sea.[32]

[Strawberry Hill]
Sunday night, Sept. 29, 1793
Having written to the bone all I had to say, I have let my pen rest for

three days – ay – but why? Not from a fit of idleness, but I have not received your second letter, I expected it yesterday, and your servant [James] expected one too, but neither arrived! He may bear his disappointment as stoically as he pleases; I have no such apathy.

I went to town on Friday to give orders about new-papering and distempering my dining room, and it would be finished in ten days, if there were one tradesman in London that ever spoke truth. In half an hour after my landing, walked into my room General Conway, come only for a single day. In the evening we went together to Miss Farren's, and besides her duenna-mother found her at piquet with her unalterable Earl – apropos, I have observed of late years that when *Earls* take strong attachments, they are more steady than other men.

Rumours there have been for some days and still are, of overtures having been made from Brest to Lord Howe – but his Lordship is not rapid. He moves, like a king at chess at the end of a game, one square inch from Torbay, and the next back again. I do not love to censure men of a profession I do not at all understand, and therefore suppose there are good reasons for his stationary inactivity. Our friend Ohara is certainly made Governor of Toulon. Good night for tonight.

Tuesday morning, 10 o'clock, 1 October

I am glad you approve of our transactions about the mare. James thought last night that she will be able to set out on Wednesday, but he is to call on me after seeing the Cambridge junto.

Adieu! *mes belles voyageuses!*

PS. James is come, and the *savii* hold that the mare may safely go to London on Wednesday and set out for Brompton on Thursday; but *the Infallible* is to be at Twickenham tonight and to decide on the soundity or risk of the journey – but all that you will learn fully from Miss Cambridge's letter to your sister, which she has sent me to frank, as I have.

To Brompton near Malton   Strawberry Hill
                                                     Oct. 2, 1793

James brought me most favourable testimonials of the mare this morning, and Mr George Infallible came afterwards and confirmed the report, and gave very prudent directions, and it was settled that she should go gingerly to London this evening, and proceed to you by easy stages, which may take up to about ten days. All this I determined to notify you today. It was as fine a morning for writing as heart could wish – but trifling away the time reading the newspaper, and finding nothing today to tell your from it, the neat old Lady [Ladies] Murray* came to [see] my house, but before I could begin my tale, hark! a most violent clap of thunder came out of an extempore dark cloud, intended no doubt for the sultry weather in July, or that should have fallen on the French Convention, and such swinging hail and rain, that we could scarce see one another. However, according to the unexampled good-humour of this singular year, it grew fine again. By that time the post was gone, and luckily, for behold I have not a word more to say, and my letter must wait till some good Christian tells me some truth or lie, which you shall have faithfully without addition or diminution.

Thursday night, 3rd

Don't talk of sending me letters not worth a farthing. What are any letters worth but according to the person from whom they come? Do you think that if I had expected last week one of the best letters that Madame de Sévigné ever wrote, and that I had never seen, but had heard it was coming, I should have been wretched for two days, because it was not arrived – pho! don't tell me of letters not worth a farthing – let me but have those I desire, and leave it to me to see the value of them.

To Brompton   Strawberry Hill
                                                Oct. 6, 1793
You are welcome to Scarborough both, and *buon pro vi faccia!*

Before I coin a report for you, I must contradict one: if you should hear in Yorkshire that I am appointed aide-de camp to the Duke of York, you may safely contradict it. It could only arise from the Duchess of York's visit to me; just as the year before you came to Cliveden, your predecessor Sir Robert Goodere literally *told* me that he *heard* that Princess Elizabeth† had been sent to me for two days for the air. On questioning him roundly, I discovered that he had *heard* no such thing, but had conjectured so, on seeing two of the Duchess of Gloucester's servants pass before his door from or to

* Sisters of the 1st Earl of Mansfield.
†Third daughter of George III.

the Pavilions, which ought not to have puzzled the goose's imagination a moment – but thus reports originate.

Home news from Richmond. Your friend Mr Dundas was robbed this morning at eleven o'clock at Cranford Bridge. I asked what was become of Earl Berkeley, who has shot so many highwaymen there near his own house? Dundas happened to tell them he is a surgeon; on which they insisted on his giving them his case of instruments – I suspect they are French surgeons, and will poison the instruments for the first wound they dress.

You see how I labour in your service, though my crops are small. An old Duchess of Rutland,* mother of the late Duchess of Montrose, whenever a visitor told her some news or scandal, cried to her daughter, 'Lucy, do step into next room, and make a memorandum of what Lady Greenwich or Lady M.M. or N.N. has been telling us.' – 'Lord, Madam, to be sure it cannot be true' – 'No matter, child; it will do for news into the country.' It is for want of such prudent *provision pour le couvent* that so many people are forced to invent offhand – You cannot say I am so thoughtless: you receive any morsel piping hot as it comes from the bakers.

One word about our glorious weather, and I have done. It improves every day. I kept the window wide open till dinner-time today, and could do nothing but gaze at the brilliant beauty of the verdure. It is so equal to ordinary Julys that one is surprised to see the sun set before six o'clock. Good night!

To Brompton   Strawberry Hill
                                                              Oct. 10, 1793

I can foresee this will be a dwarf letter in proportion to its predecessors, for I do not know a hapurth of news, and only begin mine to tell you I have just received yours of Sunday last from Scarborough, and it gives me vast pleasure to hear your sister continues to mend, though her mare be not arrived.

To my home gazette I have but one article to add; while it lasted, it was vexatious. The panic – or, blunder-master-general [Lord Onslow] has asked me for a ticket for some French, though it is a fortnight past my exhibitory season [May-Sept.], but said with a petitioning face, 'I think you allow only four at a time' – 'Why', said

*Wife of the 2nd Duke.

[142]

I, 'my Lord, to tell you the truth, I am not so strict about foreigners; they may have but a day or two, and may not know my rules' – in short I allowed him to add to four – give him an inch, and guess how many ells he will take – five, six, seven – and when you have counted seventeen, you will not have exceeded the number! Nanny's cap stood on end! The little parlour would not hold them, the green closet less, the star-chamber still less – and the poor cabinet! I trembled, and so had Nanny, for the moment they were gone, she came running to me, and said, 'Well, they have broke nothing!' Recollect, that these seventeen dozen have passed the whole summer at Richmond, and might have come in detail.

Strawberry Hill
Wednesday morning, 11 o'clock, Oct. 15, 1793
As the summer improves every day this autumn, I have just been at Cliveden, lest it should grow so hot, that I should be tanned if I stayed till November. I went to see the second festoon over Agnes's door, and am glad I did, for it is much too small and much too faint. Kirgate will carry both to the poor painter at Richmond, and have them made to resemble. Cliveden never looked more like paradise, and Mrs Richardson [housekeeper] with all her poultry about her, made a very matron-like Eve.

I have had a letter from the Bishop of Dromore of seven sides of paper, the object of which was, to induce me to add to my *Noble Authors* some meditations by a foolish Countess of Northumberland, and to set me to inquire after a MS tract of Earl Algernon: with neither of which I have complied or shall. The Bishop having created himself a Percy, is gone mad about that family, though the Percys are more remembered for having lost their heads, than for ever having had a head that was a loss to lose.

Thursday morning, 17th, past ten
The safe arrival of the mare is a great codicil to my satisfaction, and with a longer stay at Scarborough, which I beg may be protracted as long as this miraculous season will please to last, I shall hope that you will both be fortified to support a winter campaign in London. I am so conjugal and so much in earnest upon the article of recovery, I cannot think of a *pretty thing* to say to very pretty Mrs St[anhope] nor do I know what would be a *pretty thing* in these days – I might

come out with some old-fashioned compliment that would have been very genteel. Let Mrs St[anhope] imagine that I have said all she deserves; I certainly think it, and will ratify it, when I have learnt the language of the nineteenth century – but I really am so ancient, that as Pythagoras imagined he had been Panthoides Euphorbus in the Trojan War I am not sure that I did not ride upon a pillion behind a gentleman-usher, when her Majesty Elizabeth went in procession to St Paul's on the defeat of the Armada.

You are very kind in being content with my letters uninteresting as they are, for here I learn nothing till it has been mangled in the newspapers, and commonly proved to have been false there.

To Agnes Berry   [Strawberry Hill]
At Brompton   Thursday evening, Oct. 17, 1793
To Miss Agnes Berry,
My sweet lamb,
I rejoice in the arrival of your mare; yet I have still more confidence in the sea air, and shall now be impatient to hear Mrs Seton has joined you at Scarborough, where I hope she will keep you as long as the weather remains tolerable. Absence is charming to lament in ditties of *lovers*, but when founded on the best reasons, it goes to none of *friendship's* tunes – I can quote but one poetic line, that suits my present mood, and to which I hope *you* will bring back the most satisfactory answer.

Rose, what is become of your delicate hue?* Reply: *La voici.*

Whether I am as comfortable as when you are at Cliveden, you may judge by my innumerable letters. Mary cites an authority, that I have not the assurance to adopt: that a man proves his affection to a woman that gives up his time to her: Ah! me! I doubt my being constantly writing to you both, entertains myself much more than it does you two. In short I feel conversing with you, and prefer it to going to Richmond and Hampton Court, which used to be my resources formerly, when I was tired of sitting whole evenings alone – I now return to my letters of the common of two genders.

                                        Friday morning after breakfast
The coach has just brought me from Park Place a grove of lavender

*John Byrom, from the *Spectator*. October 1714.

plants for you, of which Mrs Damer had given me notice. My gardener [Vickers] is gone to distribute them about Cliveden, which I hope next summer will be as odoriferous as Mount Carmel. They have brought to my recollection the tag of an old song that I learnt in my first babyhood, that I am sure has not been in my head these threescore years and ten, but suits incomparably with my second infancy:

> Rosemary's green, diddle diddle, lavender's blue;
> If you'll love me, diddle, diddle, I will love you.

Were Mrs Stanhope to know what *pretty things* I say to my wives, I believe she would not covet such a superannuated *galant* – but you will not expose our curtain-*douceurs*!

This is a hors-d'oeuvres, and so shall go away – adieu both!

To Brompton   Berkeley Square
                                   Wednesday, 3 o'clock [Oct. 23, 1793]
I am just arrived and most unluckily can find nobody that can give me any certain information on anything, especially on what I am infinitely anxious to know, the fate of the Queen of France! The *True Briton*, before I came away, had told me she had been tried, acquitted, and massacred by the mob – my servants, whom I have sent about to learn what they could, bring me word, that she was tried on the 15th and executed on the 16th – I am so wretched for her, that it will be a kind of relief to know that she is dead and at the period of her miseries – the most dreadful that ever human being suffered for so long a term!

To Brompton   Berkeley Square
                                                   Oct. 24, 1793
The horrible tragedy of the Queen of France is but too true! Our royal family put off going to the play last night, and the Queen has no drawing-room today as was appointed. I do not know any of the shocking circumstances. Now the protracted martyrdom is completed, I shall be curious to learn nothing of that bloody and atrocious nation but its punishment – indeed they seem to meditate it themselves, and to intend to lay it waste – it is fit for nothing but a

desert inhabited by wild beasts – I expect *Marshal* Conway* in town today; he was to have kissed the Queen's hand presently, but will find himself disappointed.

The Marshal has been here [but] had left me, stepped back to tell me before he had got out of the Square, the Prince of Wales whom with his blindness he did not know, but took for his nephew Lord George [Conway], stopped him, took him by the hand and wished him joy, telling him, an officer is just arrived from the Prince of Saxe-Coburg [who] has completely defeated the army of the fiends – the *True Briton* said so this morning – but who dares believe anything under a Prince of Wales? Oh! I should be transported, if I could in a moment forget the Queen of France – but grief and joy cannot so soon mix, and her sufferings will long lie heavy at my heart.

Berkeley Square
Oct. 25, 1793

I have abjured nonsense, and now I think I shall renounce my senses. In this romancing age it is not safe to believe anything *under a King*. I observe, it is the universal usage to say, *search for truth*, which implies, that is – or was, a simple individual, extremely concealed, and who was either never found, or died a virgin and left no progeny. We did not know who was the Adam to that Eve, the father of lies, but as the marriage was never solemnized, it must be his bastards who have stocked the globe. Those imps have misled me, who have been one of the fools in *search of truth*, to pester you with daily letters for this last week – not so much even for the sake of sending you events, as to contradict the falsehoods I had too impatiently dispatched, from eagerness to communicate with you any momentary pleasure I tasted. I must now lower your victorious sails, and recall the Prince of Coburg's laurels. It is certain that they were most generally believed all yesterday, not only by the source of my information, but by very cool reasoners; and a brother of Lord Mornington was cited as the express – he was come, but was messenger of nothing and early this morning the Flanders mail is arrived, and has not brought a leaf that would cover a silver penny.

Well, I disclaim gazetteering The worst news of all, the death of the Queen of France, is true – the particular horrors I do not know –

*General Conway had been appointed to the rank of field-marshal.

Louis and Antoinette are butchered – Catherine Slayczar and Prussian Frederic live and triumph! – It is a pity they are not King and Queen of France; then the sovereigns and the nation would be properly adapted – Well! I will endeavour to remove these horrible images which haunt my imagination and will talk only within my own little sphere.

Last night I supped with the first Marshal (thank my stars it was not with the second [Duke of Gloucester] on the new list) at my sister's [Lady Mary Churchill] – besides her and her husband, her daughter Sophia, Lady Englefield and Sir Harry. The son was most importantly instructive. Her I am always glad to see, and was particularly so last night, as she has so lately left you two. She said she had left you both very well, and as a proof, that she had seen you at a ball – the evidence did not entirely convince me. I have known you both go to balls when not remarkably in health – the proof grew still weaker, when I came home at twelve and found your letter of the 21st in which you do not speak so sanguinely of your sister's looks – but your constant anxiety about her is apt to make you think her worse than she is.

I found my room quite finished and clean and smug – but I have found the town so totally empty, that I shall return to Strawberry tomorrow; and nobody's Bible oath shall make [me] believe any news again, till St Thomas who was no giddy credulous person, assures me he has had digital proof of the fact. Adieu!

Strawberry Hill
Tuesday, Oct. 29, 1793

I cannot satisfy you nor myself in half we want to know about the most interesting of all events – and my greatest astonishment consists in the execrable monsters having let enough be known to consecrate Marie Antoinette to immortal glory, and devote Paris and all its fiends to the horror and detestation of posterity.

The last days of that unparalleled Princess were so superior to any death ever exhibited or recorded, that for the sake of her glory, I think, unless I could restore her to happiness, to her children, to her untainted friends, and could see her triumph over the murderous mobs that have massacred her, I would not revive her, if I could. When did there ever exist such august simplicity! What mind was ever – I will not say, so firm, but so perfectly mistress of its own thoughts and intentions; that could be attentive to every circumstance, and distracted by none? Think of all that was comprehended in that question to the monsters called her counsellors, but certainly allotted to her as defamatory spies, 'Had she assumed too much dignity, as she passed to her trial, for she had noticed one of the furies, who said, "How proud she is"?' It proved her unaltered presence of mind, and that she was ready to condescend, if it would better become her. And then recollect the length of her sufferings, her education, exaltation to happiness and supreme power, her sudden fall, the disappointments she had met, the ingratitude and treachery she had experienced, the mortifications and insults heaped on her, and studiously, maliciously aggravated for five years together, the murder of her husband, the miseries of and terror for her children; the total deprivation of all decent comforts, and perhaps the greatest cruelty of all, not to have had one friend – but a thousand times worse, to have been at every moment in the hands of the most unfeeling jailors, sum up all this mass of woes, and perhaps thousands more of which we never heard, and then see this phoenix rise superior to hosts of torturing spiteful fiends, and hear her pronounce the most sublime word that ever passed through human lips – when *they* (I have no adequate epithet for them) had declared sentence, and asked her, what she had to say, she said, *Rien*. Too calm, too sensible, too collected, and unshaken, she was above fear, indignation, and solicitation, and accountable only to herself. Her invincible patience was all that appeared, and that was a negative, but as unvaried as all her illustrious virtues, and great qualities, on which rancour and persecution have not been able to fix a speck of stain – Let history or legend produce a similar model!

These are the effusions of my heart – not dictated by the impulse of the moment, but the result of my cool reflections of three days. I trust them in perfect confidence to your honour, and exact from the fidelity of your friendship that you will not communicate nor read them to any mortal but your father and sister, nor let this paper pass out of your own hands, nor suffer a tittle of it to be transcribed. I like that you two should know my sentiments on all important topics, but I extend this confidence not a jot farther. I firmly believe every word I have asserted, because all the facts come from the barbarians themselves – but as I cannot be positively sure they are true, I will not

Strawberry Hill from the south east.

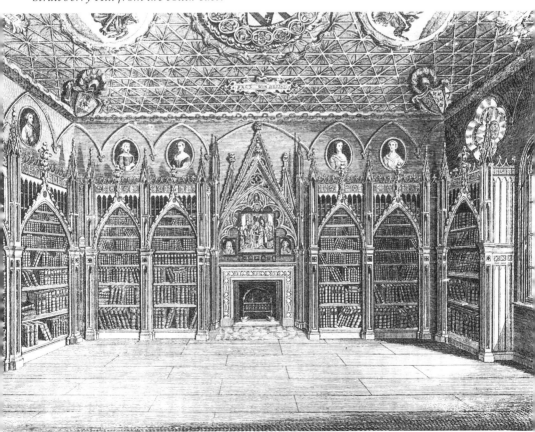

The Library at Strawberry Hill.

Little Strawberry Hill.

Mary and Agnes Berry, by Zoffany.

Mary (left) and Agnes Berry: miniatures by Mrs Foldsone

The Misses Berry, *by Paul Sandby.*

Horace Walpole, by George Dance.

Mary Berry, by Hon. Mrs Damer.

after breakfast, and in his study

before dinner, when drest, and in the Cabinet

after dinner, and in the Gallery

Horace Walpole:
caricatures by John Carter.

Horace Walpole, by Sir Thomas Lawrence.

place my veracity on a possibility of having been misinformed – and therefore I depend on your not committing me by showing my letter – I repeat it earnestly, *to nobody but your father and sister*, and beg you will assure me that you have not. I do not mind your reading trifles out of my dispatches, though certainly calculated for nobody but you two – but this letter I do most seriously restrain from all other eyes.

Strawberry Hill
Nov. 7, 1793

I often lay the eggs of my journals two or three days before they are hatched. This may make some of my articles a little stale before you get them; but then you know they are the more authentic, if the echo has not told me to unsay them – and if a Prince of Wales drops a thumping victory at my door as he goes by, you have it hot out of the oven – though, as happened lately, not half baked.

In the meantime it is provoking to hear of Catherine Slayczar sitting on her throne and playing with royal marriages.

Our weather remains unparagoned: the elms are evergreens. I a little regret your not seeing how beautiful Cliveden can be on the 7th of November – ay, and how warm. Then the pheasants, partridges and hares from Houghton that you lose: they would have exceeded Camacho's wedding, and Sancho Panca would have talked chapters about them. I am forced to send them about the neighbourhood, as if I were making interest to be chosen for the united royal burghs of Richmond and Hampton Court – but all this is not worth sending – I must wait for a better *bouche*.

When you return to London, if you spy from Highgate a vast edifice peeping over the shoulder of St Paul's, don't imagine that the Pope has sent St Peter's over hither to secure it from French atheists. No, it is the new Temple of Venus in Drury Lane. I assure you that Lord Derby told me a fortnight ago that he had seen it that morning from Westminster Bridge towering above all the buildings but St Paul's. They say the frontispiece of the scaffolding is a most beautiful sight.

November 10th

I have neither heard a word, or had a word to say these three days. Victories do not come every tide like mackerel or prizes in the Irish lottery. Yesterday's paper discounted a little of Neapolitan valour, but as even the Dutch sometimes fight upon recollection, and as there was no account yet of O'Hara's arrival at Toulon, I hope he will laugh or example *loro Signori* into spirit.

You will wonder at my resuming my letter, when I profess having nothing to add to it; but yours of the 7th is just arrived, and I could not make this commenced sheet lie quiet in my writing box; it would begin gossiping with your letter, though I vowed it should not set out till tomorrow. 'Why, you empty thing,' said I 'how do you know but that there may have been a *Gazette* last night crammed with vast news, which as no paper comes out on Sundays, we shall not learn here; and would you be such a goose as to creep through Brentford and Hammersmith and Kensington, the bells may be drinking some general's health, and will scoff you for asking whose? Indeed you shall not stir before tomorrow. Moreover, no posts sets out from London on Sunday nights and you would only sit guzzling – I don't mean you, Miss Berry, but you, my letter, with the clerks of the post office, who might be tempted to make some improper liberty with a matrimonial sheet. Patience till tomorrow.'

I am not so consentful about going to town myself yet. We have had some rain, even this last night, but the weather is fine all day and quite warm; I believe it has made an assignation with the Glastonbury Thorn, and that they are to dance together on old Christmas Day. What could I do with myself in London? All my playfellows are here, and I have no playfellows left there! Lady Herries's and poor Mrs Hunter's are shut up. Even *the one game more at cribbage* [Lady Ailesbury] after supper is on table, and which is not my supreme felicity though accompanied by the Tabor and Pipe,* is in the country – or to say all in one word, North Audley Street is in Yorkshire. Reading composes little of my pastime either in town or country. A catalogue of books and prints, or a dull history of a county, amuse me sufficiently.

Monday morning, 11th

If the newspaper does not bring me something fresh for you presently, this limping letter must set out with its empty wallet.

Mrs Piozzi is going to publish a book on English synonyms – methinks she had better have studied them, before she stuffed her travels with so many vulgarisms!

* Two old ladies so-called by Walpole.

To Brompton   Strawberry Hill
                                     Thursday, Nov. 14, 1793
                                              At night

I have been with the Cambridges, and saw him and both sons: the
hens were at roost, and did not appear. George had just heard that
Egalité is actually beheaded; comfortable news for the doctors of his
sect, who may see that no crimes are a protection. Well! there is
another atonement to the King and the Princesse de Lamballe; and no
cordial to Madame de Sillery and Pamela Fitzgerald.

You will perhaps ask why I am still here in the middle of Novem-
ber? because in any other year, such a day as this fourteenth of
November would have been thought very fine and warm in the end of
August. I remember that at Florence they used to boast of their
Stagione di San Martino – well, to be sure the mornings were very
clear and bright, but as cold and sharp as Greenland.

                                           Friday noon

I must close my letter, for I have none from you, nor is even the
newspaper come yet – but what signifies whether the *True Briton* or I
confirm or postpone the execution of Orleans? – Stay – the paper
arrives and says he is dead – Ah! and so is a happy beauty at the top
of her prosperity, Lady Westmorland. I am sorry for her. I knew her a
little by seeing her so often with my niece Lady Waldegrave, and liked
her good-humour as well as admired her great beauty – but there is
no moralizing more on change of fortune after the enormous excess
of it in the case of the Queen of France! Adieu!

To Brompton   Tuesday morning
                                           Nov. 19, 1793

My own motions are undecided yet. I was to have gone to Hampton
last Saturday evening – but it rained so hard and was so foggy, that I
did not choose a voyage over the [Hounslow] heath. Sunday was as
bad, and I resolved to go to London on Thursday; but yesterday and
today have fallen on their knees and beseeched me to stay a week
longer, promising to be as fine as it has been these six months, and so
indeed they are, as soft, and of a rich golden colour, over all the trees
that Golconda is not more magnificent.

Mr Berry I see grows impatient for news, but I know nothing
specific: the *True Briton* is not come in, and I dread it, expecting

nothing but murders and massacres. Of Orleans's exit I know no particulars; nor am I curious about so foul a wretch.

Ohara is arrived at Toulon. If it can be preserved, he will keep it.

Known as 'The Charming Man' by Walpole and his friends, Edward Jerningham, versifier and playwright, had his The Siege of Berwick *produced at Covent Garden to moderate critical reaction.*

A small force under Lord Moira had been assembling and by December the expedition sailed without sufficient stores or armaments. On reaching St Malo they were unable to land as the western Royalist insurgents had been driven out.

The wealth of Robert Child, of Child Bankers & Co., and of Osterley Park, had descended to his only child, Sarah, wife of the 10th Earl of Westmorland. With her death in November, her daughter, Lady Sarah Fane, later the wife of the 5th Earl of Jersey, and distinguished as a leader of society, inherited a vast fortune.

To Bransby Hall, Yorkshire   Strawberry Hill
                              Saturday, Nov. 23, 2 o'clock, 1793

My jaunt to town seemed at first to have been barren indeed: I called at Mrs Damer's, she was gone to the play with the Marshal her father – then to the Churchill's – then to Mrs Buller, not at home; then to Miss Farren; found her and La Signora Madre only. Things mended at night: I had been told in Sackvill Street that Mrs Damer would probably bring her parent home to supper and she did. Soon after arrived – oh no! I have jumbled the two evenings – on Thursday there were only father and daughter; it was last night that the latter had collected the rest for me, who were my niece Sophia, Mrs Buller and her son 'Mistress Buller', and the Charming Man; and we had a pleasant supper. I congratulated the Charming highly on the success of his tragedy, and on his prologue which I had seen in the papers and like; the epilogue they say is still better. All this puts him in great spirits.

Well! but do I say nothing of the war? What cares Mr Berry how many visits I made and found nobody at home? He had rather I had gone to the coffee-house – patienza, my good Sir. Tomorrow Lord Moira is to sail with a great force for the coast of France – St Maloes is supposed the object, but no doubt that has not been told. He certainly carries ten thousand men, and 400 *émigrés* from Jersey. What fleet, military stores, etc., the papers will tell you, I cannot, who neither love details, nor remember them. Most anxious I shall be, and most zealous I am for the event – yet I am not sanguine. Lord Moira's behaviour is noble; he offered himself for this service some months ago – and he has not, since his father's death, less, with the estates of Huntingdon, than £18,000 a year – oh! but it is a joke to talk of a great fortune – the whole property of the Childs vests now in Lord Westmorland's eldest daughter; and Dent, Child's partner, says before she is of age (and she is not above six) the savings will be above a million, though Osterley and the seat in Staffordshire [Upton, in Warwickshire] are to be kept up at the great expense as in Mr Child's life – the shop pays £25,000 a year – I am glad the expense will continue as the money will circulate – but I hope Catherine and the king of Prussia will not attempt a partition of the property.

Madame d'Arblay [Fanny Burney] has written a pamphlet for the French clergy: I sent for it in town and then forgot to bring it with me – I shall wait with patience till I go back, for Mrs D says it is a mere nothing.

Sunday night, 10 o'clock

There is a strong presumption that Lord Howe has taken six or seven French men-of-war of the line. My heart takes joy on the first, and my head will on the second, if confirmed; for they are in different compartments, my heart presiding over *home* affairs, and my head over foreign. *Voici* the marrow of the rumour. A lieutenant arrived yesterday at Admiralty House from Lord Howe, who learning that part of the Brest fleet had sailed to meet and convoy their West Indiamen his Lordship, twenty-six strong, had set out post, and had actually got between the French and their coast, and last night and this morning all London was expecting a second dispatch, at least this evening – all I can do *here* is to listen for the ringing of the bells – they do not ring yet.

Well, now for your letter, which in compliment to your curiosity I postponed answering, till I had tapped Lord Howe.

Our weather it seems still continues better than yours; yesterday was as mild as April ought always to be, and today is better than most English Junes. The leaves all went at once, being of so rich a hue, the garden looks like the country of El Dorado.

I will send you no more victories of Lord Howe, till he sends them himself: in what a hubub have we been kept – ay, and still are, even since this day sennight, when we were told he was catching six of the Brest fleet. Every moment we expected to see him sailing into St James's with six French men-of-war tied to his chariot's wheels, and dragging their West India fleet in tow. Then came an account from two of his own squadron that they had left him actually boxing with two French ships, and then – and then – a dead silence – not a cockboat as big as you can see from Dover Cliff has come in with a syllable for five days! All the town has been running about, asking, guessing, conjecturing and spreading imaginary reports – 'Any news of Lord Howe? – What! no news yet!' – Well! this morning a Danish or Dutch ship has told somebody, who has told everybody, who have told the *True Briton*, who has just told me, that Lord Howe has taken five men-of-war, and will be here with them presently – if they come by here, before this must go to the post, you shall know – if not, you must scold the east wind, they say, or learn what you can from Jacobin newspapers, who will not tell you a word of truth as long as they can help it – I must go talk of something that interests me more than random rumours.

My Agnes I know does not love writing, yet methinks I should like now and then to see a line from her dear hand, were it but in a postscript. The volumes I send you are my great occupation – my poor lame fingers have no great delight in the business, especially as the principal agent, the fore one that is actually moving the pen, has actually a fit of chalk, for which the surgeon has been dressing it this morning; but as it does not confine me at home, for I supped at Mrs Damer's last night with the Duchess of Richmond, Lord Derby, the Farrens and shall go to Lady Lucan's this evening to meet Mr [Edmund] Burke and Mr [Edward] Gibbon, I will not indulge its unwillingness, though I plead it to any other occasional correspondent and employ Kirgate – but I really should be ashamed to dictate even to him all the trumpery that I write to you, because I write to you two just as I should talk – the only comfortable kind of letters.

As soon as we *find* Lord Howe, we shall transfer our anxiety and curiosity to Lord Moira. An English captain of a sloop, who was one of the 250 prisoners of ours that were transferred from Dinant to St

Maloes before they were sent away to Guernsey, has deposed before our Cabinet that complaining of the badness of the bread with which they were fed while confined at the latter, the chief of the guard said, 'You are not worse treated than we ourselves,' and showed him a black loaf, composed half of sand.

                                        Half an hour after three
I have this moment seen a person who has just been at the Secretary's office, where they know no more of Lord Howe than the man in the moon – or perhaps not so much, for there they say all *lost* things are reposited – so I will go and be dressed, and you must satisfy yourselves with being sure that you know as much as all London. Adieu!

Lord Howe's perambulations invite an almost comic appeal. Walpole has taken Addison's Cato, *v.i. as indicative of the doubts and uncertainties of the public. Walpole was to go to the theatre twice within a week; on this present occasion it was the excellent low comedian who drew him to the Little Theatre in the Hay. Ten years later John Bannister would be manager of Drury Lane Theatre. Elizabeth Pope, one of the foremost of English actresses, was acting in Jerningham's play; Harris was the chief proprietor of Covent Garden.*

The Comte de Coigny, an émigré since 1792, had been an inspector of cavalry in the French army.

                                        Berkeley Square
                                    Wednesday, Dec. 4, 1793
I begin my letter that I may have it ready to send away the moment I shall have anything worth telling, which I certainly have not yet. What is become of Lord Howe and Co. you may guess if you please, as everybody is doing –

                    'I am weary of conjectures –'

but shall not end them like Cato, because I take the fate of a whole fleet a little more likely to come to a solution, than doubts in metaphysics; and if Lord Howe should at last bring home two or three French men-of-war, one would not be out of the way to receive them. In the meantime let us chat as if the destiny of half Europe were not at this moment in agitation.

I went on Monday evening with Mrs Damer to the Little Haymarket to see *The Children in the Wood* [a 'musical entertainment'] having heard so much of my favourite young Bannister in that new piece, which by the way is well arranged, and near being fine. He more than answered my expectation and all I had heard of him. It was one of the most admirable performances I ever saw; his transports of despair and joy were incomparable, and his various countenances would be adequate to the pencil of Salvatore Rosa. Bannister's merit was the more striking, as before *The Children in the Wood* he had been playing the sailor in *No Song, No Supper*, [also with music] with equal nature. I wish I could hope to be as much pleased tomorrow night when I am to go to Jerningham's play, but there is no Bannister at Covent Garden!

On Sunday night I found the Comte de Coigny at Lady Lucan's. He was to set out the next morning with Lord Moira's expedition as *a common soldier*. This sounded decent and well – but you may guess that he had squeezed a little Frenchism into his intention, and had asked for a vessel and some soldiers to attend him – I don't know whether he has condescended to go without them.

Just as I had written the above, a ridiculous accident happened. The postman brought me a letter, directed as he thought to me, the predominant feature of which was *Berkeley Square* with my name not quite so distinct. I opened and found another within, for *Lady Orford*, so plain as I thought, that though my surprise made me look at it again, I still saw nothing but to *Lady Orford*. You know my extreme stupidity when I have taken anything into my head or my eyes – I had no more doubt of having seen *Lady Orford*, than if I had written those words designedly myself. The next step was to conclude that this was some joke, and that *you* was the person meant: I tore it open, and though in the second line stood Lady *Oxford*, so strongly had my fancy taken possession of me, that though the letter consisting of four sides of congratulations on her Ladyship's recent marriage, I could perceive nothing but a dull joke, as I still supposed it, till in the fourth page appeared *Lady Oxford* in still larger letters than all the rest – I have no excuse for my blunders, but that on both directions the *x* was so ill marked, or rather only half of it, that it looked on reinspection more like an *r* than an *x* and being coupled with Berkeley Square, where Lord Oxford does not live, it appeared indupitably designed for me; nor indeed did Lord Oxford [5th Earl] whom I never saw, nor ever heard mentioned, and whose late marriage which I think I did see in the papers, but did not in the least recollect, come into my head. I bundled my blunders with a million of humble excuses to their Lordship and Ladyship – but I wish the man would have a house in London, or I am very capable of being in the scrape again, as I seldom remember to read a direction, nor can treasure up in mind I don't know whose colts or weddings.

Sophia came to me just after I sent my packet to the post – had she arrived half an hour earlier, it would have been very unlike me to imagine that the letter to Lady *Orford* was wit of hers, and that she came to see what effect it had? I am very glad I did not make that mistake too – I fear I should not have been so indifferent about it.

Thursday noon

Yesterday came a letter to the Admiralty from Penzance notifying that Lord Howe had taken five of the Brest squadron – but this intelligence is derived through so many somebodies, that handed it to somebodies, that I am not much inclined, except by wishing it true, to believe it. However, the wind is got much more to the west, and now we shall probably not remain much longer in total darkness.

Three o'clock

Another account is come with the same story of the five captive French men-of-war, and so that reading is admitted – but for my part, I will admit nothing but under Lord Howe's own hand – it is tiresome to be like the scene in Dryden's *Amphitryon*, and cry one minute 'Obvious, obvious' – and the next, 'dubious, dubious.' Such fluctuability is fit only for the stockjobber – Adieu!

To Post Office, York   [Berkeley Square]
Wednesday [Friday], past 11
at night, Dec. 6, 1793

That there may have been such persons as King Arthur, and the Wandering Jew, and Lord Howe and his fleet, I will not take on me to deny; yet as history is silent on what became of them, I will not easily credit their re-existence I know I have been told late this evening that signals of a fleet have been seen off Plymouth, supposed to be Lord Howe's; but as it also supposed that he had no French captures with him: I don't see why this should be imagined, unless more is known than has come to my knowledge – and there I must leave this mystery till tomorrow.

I went last night to the Charming's tragedy, and most sincerely found it much superior to my expectation. The language is very good; there are pretty similies and allusions, no bombast, nothing low, and the *ordonnance* well contrived. It seldom languishes. Mrs Pope plays admirably, and was extremely applauded; the men do not shine, but the whole was well received, without a single murmur against any part. Well! there have I been twice at the play this week! I confess I felt very comfortably this morning, knowing I was not to go [to] the play again tonight. I had not the least difficulty in getting in or out of either theatre, nor was fatigued; but I do not like exhibiting my antiquity in public: it looks as if I forget it.

Monday morning

This letter though begun three days ago, will clear up no mystery, for no news yet from Lord Howe. All we know is, that he did not get up with the five French ships, for they escaped him and are returned to Brest. You may perhaps expect as little from Lord Moira, the French having had time to guard all the coast, and the Royalists of La Vendée, though they have twice again very lately beaten the Republicans, being retired to the Loire. Not a tittle do I know of other news of foreign or home consumption.

Past one

I this moment received the double letter from dear both but it is the hour when my coffee-house generally opens, and I expect to be interrupted, and have heard nothing to add within this half hour. My Agnes's letter is exactly like her modesty about her own drawings, always deprecating herself; but I am not blind to the merit of her pencil or pen, as I was to the letter for Lady Oxford, who I am told is not yet so* – had I known the marriage not yet solemnized, I should have been still more persuaded that it was levelled at one of you.

You bid me direct to the post office at York – hark – somebody knocks! It was the Duchess of Gloucester, and she has stayed till it is so late, I must hurry and finish, only that I cannot forget what it is so important for me to ask – you bid me direct to York till I direct my coachman to Audley Street – why?

Are you to arrive in a balloon? Are you to stop nowhere? You

*She married in 1794.

tell me to expect you on Wednesday or Thursday sennight, but by not mentioning on what day you are to set out, nor how long you propose being on the road, can I guess how long I may direct to York? I am to sup in Sackville Street tonight and will learn, if I can, greater certainty – Well, the middle or end of next week (for I will allow for accidental delays) will I trust put an end to difficulties of correspondence, and to correspondence *by letters*! Adieu.

[Berkeley Square
Dec. 13, 1793]

You will not wonder at my dullness about the time of your setting out and of the *gîtes* you are to make on the road; you are used to my fits of incomprehension – and as is natural at my age, I believe they increase.

If I believed Lord Howe's success too rapidly, you have seen by all the newspapers that both the ministers and the public were equally credulous from the collateral channels that imported such assertions – Well! if you have been disappointed of capturing five or six French men-of-war, you must at present stay your appetite by some handsome slices of St Domingo, and my plentiful goblets of French blood shed by the Duke of Brunswic, which we firmly believe, though the official intelligence was not arrived last night (Thursday). His Highness, who has been so serene for above a year, seems to have waked to some purpose.

The Conways are in town for two or three days, they came for Jerningham's play: Harris had at last allowed him the fourth night, and he had a good night. You will wonder perhaps that I have tumbled to tittle-tattle, and not dropped a syllable on Lord Moira and Toulon: in fact I know nothing positive about either, and am very sanguine about neither.

Saturday, Dec. 14, 1793

I am glad this is to be the last of my gazettes: I am tired of notifying and recalling the articles of news – I hope I send you no more falsehoods – at least you must allow it is not on bad authority. If Lord Howe has disappointed you, will you accept the prowess of the virago his sister, Mrs Howe? As soon as it was known that her brother had failed, a Jacobin mob broke her windows, mistaking them for his – She lifted up the sash, and harangued them; told them,

[159]

that this was not the house of her brother, who lives in the other part of Grafton Street [No. 8]; and that she herself is a widow, and that *that* house [No.12] is hers. She stilled the waves, and they dispersed quietly.

The Berrys were home and the correspondence for that year ceased.

To

MY PEN

on the cessation of our correspondence by her return

Here rest thou, faithful servant of my heart!
With thanks I quit thee, though rejoic'd to part.
Thou kind one, hast a tongue to absence leant,
And almost chear'd regret into content,
For while each thought of mine thou has conveyed,
A pen still kinder has each note repaid;
And thus, while distance urg'd its tyrant laws,
Our converse scarce appear'd to feel a pause;
Yet now thy freedom I with joy restore,
And thy fond service hope to ask no more.

To Miss B.

O.

There are no letters between the correspondents in 1794 until Eastertime when April saw Walpole in London recovering from many weeks of illness and the Berrys, at Little Strawberry Hill, were extolling the numbers of nightingales. At the end of the month they spent a short time in North Audley Street, probably to help restore Walpole's spirits. His strength was not wholly repaired but he had felt able to join an evening at Mrs Damer's. Bertie Greatheed, poet and author and an old friend of Mr Berry, was to be there. A friend too of Mrs Siddons, who in 1788 had acted in a rather unsuccessful play by him at Drury Lane. She was pregnant now with her seventh child (born in July) but was to play Lady Macbeth on Easter Monday, 21 April, in the newly opened Drury Lane Theatre.

The important news was that the Allies' campaign had opened in April, France having declared war on Britain and Holland at the end of January. By the French invasion of Belgium and their opening of the Scheldt to commercial traffic under opposition of all treaties, Britain recognized the danger to her own vital interests and was herself preparing for war. The West Indian campaign still showed all the signs of success. Martinique, St Lucia and Guadeloupe fell to the British forces by May but the French reinforcements reconquered some of their possessions.

Mrs Piozzi's British Synonymy *was published now.*

[Berkeley Square]
Thursday evening, April 16 [17], 1794

I am delighted that you have had such good weather for your *villeggiatura*. The sun has not appeared here today; yet it has been so warm, that he may not be gone out of town, and only keeps in, because it is unfashionable to be seen in London at Easter. All my evening customers are gone except Mrs Damer, and she is at home tonight with the Greatheds and Mrs Siddons and a few more, and she had a mind I should go to her. I had a mind too, but think myself still too weak: after confinement for fourteen weeks, it seems formidable to sally forth.

I have heard no novelty since you went, but of more progress in Martinico. The *Gazette* arrives, and little of Martinico remained unconquered; the account is one continued panegyric on the conduct of our officers, soldiers and sailors, who do not want to be driven on, by cannon behind them and on both sides. A good quantity of artillery and stores is taken too.

I have run through both volumes of Mrs Piozzi. Here and there she does not want parts, has some good translations and stories that are new, particularly an admirable *bon mot* of Lord Chesterfield, which I never heard before, but dashed with her cruel vulgarisms. I have picked out a motto for her work in her own words, and written it on the title-page; 'Simplicity cannot please without elegance.' Now I think on't, let me ask if you have been as much diverted as you was at first? and have not two such volumes sometimes set you o'yawning? It is comic that in a treatise on synonymous words she does not know which are and which are not so. In the chapter on worth, price, value, she says, 'The worth even of money fluctuates in our state', instead of saying in this *country*. Her very title is wrong: she does not even mention synonymous Scottish words, it ought to be called not *British* but *English Synonymy*.

[Berkeley Square]
April 21, 1794

You are most kind indeed in offering to come to town for me, but you certainly shall not. I repented sufficiently of having dragged you from Italy, though my most urgent reason was my impatience to install you at Cliveden. I will not inveigle you thence, when the verdure, blossoms and weather are in perfection.In this country we should always take summer by its forelock, though it may claim its waiting, like the Groom of the Stole, out of the regular course: we may have no more sunshine before our faithful October. I can force myself to go out in an evening if I will; I was at Mrs Damer's last night and stayed till they went to supper, and was not fatigued. There were her parents, the House of Argyll, the Greatheds, Mrs Hervey and the Charming Man – and not a spoonful of news. Today I have seen nobody yet, but it is only one o'clock, and I have been airing in my coach as far as Fulham.

The Marshal bids me tell you that however proud you may be of your nightingales, they have as large a colony at Park Place.

Walpole, now back at Strawberry Hill, had left the Berrys in London and was able to report to them that the Duke of York, having been given the command of the cavalry, had gained a victory against French forces at Le Cateau. There was also his interest in gaining information regarding Gibbon's unpublished manuscripts following his death in January; and this was more easily come by in London. However, he would soon be there himself and hoped for a glimpse of Mary after she had heard Mme Banti give a performance at the King's Theatre (Opera House). This Italian soprano was making her début *in Bianchi's* Serimaride *after her recent return to London.*

After this letter there is a three-month gap in the correspondence. The early summer was spent by both households at Twickenham; Mary made a short expedition to Oxford in July with Mrs Damer where evidently Nuneham Park's Palladian mansion did not detain her, and then returned to Park Place. Agnes had gone to Cheltenham with a Mrs Lockhart.

Strawberry Hill
May Day, 1794

I will come out of town ten times to my going thither once (as a tutor at Cambridge said to his pupils scolding them for leaving their chambers and studies so often and going out of college) if it brings such good luck and good news. Yesterday as I got into my coach, I received the extraordinary *Gazette* without a mouthful of success. At night John has been in Twickenham and heard that a courier had galloped through the village as fast as he could, considering that he was loaded with a stack of laurels that he was carrying to the Duchess of York to make bonfires at Oatlands – I knew not for what, till on my breakfast table just now I found your welcome letter and another from Marshal Conway confirming the great victory, the prodigious number of cannon taken, our small loss, and the capture of the French General [Chapuy].

As I have bushels of May, though no milkmaids as you are not at Cliveden, I shall make a garland for myself, and as I cannot yet dance, shall sit and hear the nightingale sing its country dance as I did last night.

I shall be glad to hear what you have learnt of Mr Gibbon's MSS; but that will not be before Saturday – though the verdure is not brilliant from want of rain, I do not think of returning sooner. That evening I conclude you will go to hear the Banti – but perhaps you may call for a moment just before dinner; I shall scarce be in town much earlier, as I propose calling on Lady Di on my way, for I am so delighted with being here again, that I do not like to lessen my term. Adieu!

To Agnes Berry	Strawberry Hill
Posthouse at Cheltenham	July 31, 1794

The longer I know you, my sweet Agnes, the more I find new reasons for loving you, as I do most cordially. You threatened not to write and I have already received a charming letter from you: and now as you never disimprove, I am confident you will let me hear from you sometimes, though I will not be exacting. I shall hear accounts of you from Mary, for you cannot help writing to one you have constantly talked to ever since you was born. Your father and sister arrived soon after seven yesterday evening; I did not, though that was the time they had fixed, expect them so soon, concluding they would be pressed to stay longer at Park Place, and would be frail.

I have received no letter, nor have I a tittle to tell you, but that I dined at Hampton on Tuesday – in the evening came a whole cacklehood from the Palace.

Your sister is as much delighted with Oxford as I expected she would be, struck with profound respect for Blenheim, as was fit, but not a quarter so delighted with Nuneham as I am –

Your pussy is enchanting; with all the graces of her kind, she has all the sense of a dog; she literally comes when I call her, though above stairs, follows me wherever I go without being called, and meets me when I come home – Still I shall wean myself from her, as it is time for me to do from everything – if I can. I say nothing as a conclusion from myself, for I trust all my actions and all my letters tells you how much I am Yours

O.

The Berry family were about to leave for a month of sea air at Broadstairs but meanwhile there was renewed commotion over brigands and highwaymen still to be encountered on Hounslow Heath and thereabouts. Abroad, news was worrying but life went on equably enough at Strawberry Hill.

Prospect House [Strawberry Hill]
near Broadstairs Sunday, September 21, 1794
I begin my journal today, though only the eve of its departure, and though I have nothing new to tell you from Europe or from Strawberry Hill, but much from the circumambient district, for the marauders have begun their courses again. A young Mr Digby, who lodges in Twickenham, was, with another gentleman in a post-chaise robbed at *one o'clock at noon* by two footpads on the heath just beyond Whitton. The son of the malster here by the post-house, ditto

[164]

robbed by ditto – but on inquiry this happened at Kennington Common, where they are more apt to be hanged than to rob – however I shall grow uneasy when you return.

Ten at night

Yesterday was most tempestuously windy, but today has been warm and fine, and I trust you have had a pleasant journey.

Maugre banditti, I have been at Lady Bute's door this evening, but she was not well enough to see me; and I returned with my purse and watch in my pocket. I beg of you both to return as revived and looking as fresh as Agnes did from Cheltenham, and then I shall not lament my involuntary widowhoods, for I do not wish, as Lady Wishfort* says for any iteration of nuptials, nor to have an opportunity of expressing myself like a tender husband of whom I have just been reading, who set up a tomb for his wife with this epitaph, 'Joan le Feme Thomas de Frowicke *gist icy, et le dit* Thomas *pense de giser aveque luy.*' You see folks were not so delicate in that age as we are, though to *sleep* with the departed would have been even a more scriptural phrase, and more in the style of our good ancestors, *qui n'entendaient pas raillerie en tout,* as the French have done in late years. Good night, *sans raillerie, le feme Marie et le feme Agnes de*

Horace de Orford

Monday morning

In the new edition of history of highwaymen, for Mr Digby and Co, robbed in a post-chaise by two footpads, read, robbed, as he was walking alone on the heath, by two highwaymen. As truth lies at the bottom of a well, the first who dip for her, seldom let the bucket low enough.

To Prospect House   [Strawberry Hill]

Wednesday, Sept. 24, 1794, near one

I have received your long letter from Prospect House [near Broadstairs] and thank you most kindly for it, but I cannot answer it now for the Churchills are here and in the room while I write; it has rained heavily ever since breakfast, and they can neither go out in their chaise which they had ordered, nor into the garden, and just as I

*In Congreve's *Way of the World.*

am going to begin my letter, the newspaper came in, and he has been reading it aloud to us paragraph by paragraph half of which are full of bad news, of retreats of our army [towards Nimeguen], of the capture of our Mediterranean fleet by the French, and what I think as bad as anything in Europe, of the King of Prussia having been forced to raise the siege of Warsaw. Before I could digest half of this, he came to a sale of milch cows – I don't mean the King of Prussia, nor that we are again one of his milch cows, but Mr Churchill who wants some for Lewisham and has been reading of them to his wife, till I have not a clear idea left, but about your bad post-horses, and your liking your new residence, at which I rejoice. Canterbury I know by heart. It was the chief fund of my chimney-pieces, and other morsels.

Mrs Damer's removal from Sackville Street to 8 Grosvenor Square, nearer both to Berkeley Square and North Audley Street, was naturally of interest enough to Walpole.[33] *Unfortunately, its being a corner house, he felt he would suffer the curiosity of the passers-by (from two sides) as he made his descent from his carriage, the infirmity of age being now his lot.*

Meanwhile there was a good deal of place-seeking to be part of Princess Caroline of Brunswick's entourage on her arrival in England as the future wife of the Prince of Wales. In the event it was Lord Malmesbury who was sent to escort her from Brunswick. Lady Jersey, the Prince's supposed mistress, was assigned as one of her ladies-in-waiting while Lord Cholmondeley took up the appointment as Lord Chamberlain after the marriage.

News from the Berrys in Prospect House, North Foreland, on the Kent coast, a house which Lord Cholmondeley compared to Athens's Temple of the Winds, was of gales and cold weather and Walpole likened their discomforts to those portrayed by John Rich in his celebrated pantomime transformation scenes in which he always played Harlequin. The Berrys' house stood on the foremost piece of land jutting out into the sea which formed the isthmus between Margate, a small watering-place barely two miles to the north, and Broadstairs, a considerable hamlet still closer, to the south. Ramsgate lay slightly beyond still, to the south. Close by, Kingsgate, so-called for having been Charles II's landing place in 1688, presented a curious though not altogether displeasing impression.[34] *On ground*

*open to all the elements, the first Lord Holland had indulged his
fancy and his wealth by erecting several buildings on the cliff top.
These were in a variety of styles, ranging from a castle for stabling
horses complete with portcullis in the manner of Edward I in Wales,
to a large villa representing Tully's Formian villa on the coast of
Baiae, graced with a noble portico in the Doric order. Another
imitated an ancient monastery, embracing cloisters, while adjacent
stood a strange edifice, a high-soaring tower in the style of Roman
architecture and so shaped that it had been compared to 'a chamber
candlestick'.*

*The very small circular miniature of Anne of Cleves, wife of Henry
VIII, and the ivory box 'turned like a Provence rose' of which Wal-
pole writes, are in the possession of the Victoria and Albert Museum.
Only the miniature is on display.*

*Walpole closed his letter on Michaelmas Day, the feast day of St
Michael, when it was customary to feast on goose.*

Strawberry Hill

September 27, Saturday night, 1794

I have been in town, as I told you I should, but gleaned nothing worth
repeating, or I would have written this morning before I came away.
The Churchills left me on Thursday, and were succeeded by the
Marshal, who dined and stayed all night. I am now alone.

I went yesterday evening to Mrs Damer, and had a glimpse of her
new house [8 Grosvenor Street] literally a glimpse, for I saw but one
room on the first floor, where she had lighted a fire – that I might not
mount two flights, and as it was eight o'clock and quite dark, she
only opened a door or two and gave me a *cat's-eye* view into them.
One blemish I had descried at first – the house has a corner arrival
like her father's – ah me! who do not love to be led through the
public. I did see her new bust of Mrs Siddons [as Melpone], and a
very mistressly performance it is indeed – apropos, Miss Farren is
missing. She is known to have landed last Sunday – not a word from
her since, which makes one – aye, and two, fear that she is ill on the
road.

From Mrs D I went by my sister's where I found Sophia, Lady
Englefield, Mrs and Miss Egerton and Mr Falkener, played at cribbage with them and sat by while they supped. This is not only the

[167]

whole of my private history, but of the world's too, so far as it had informed me, except that Lord Southampton does not go to fetch the future Princess of Wales, precedents having sworn that by their books it is clear that it must be her chamberlain, though she has none before she is she; and he, they say, is to be Lord Pembroke – a very good choice. Lady Worcester, Lady Weymouth, and Lady Parker, are kissing the public's hand for the Bedchamber, and the two first will probably kiss *tout de bon* – of the third's chance I know nothing.

I was diverted a few days ago with a paragraph in the *True Briton*, which, supposing that the Prince is to reside at Hampton Court, said that as there is a theatre and a tennis court in the Palace, Twickenham will not want a succession of company even when the *venerable* Earl of Orford shall be no more. I little thought I was as attractive as a theatre or a tennis court, or served in lieu of them. Pray, Lady Leah and Lady Rachel, venerate your Methusalem!

I wish you had seen Canterbury some years ago, before they whitewashed it, for it is so coarsely daubed, and thence the gloom is so totally destroyed, and so few tombs remain for so vast a mass, that I was shocked at the nudity of the whole. If you should go thither again, make the cicerone show you a pane of glass in the east window, which does open and exhibits a most delicious view on the ruins of St Austin's.

Sunday night, 28th

I have received another letter from dear *Mary* on the 26th, and here is one for [?from] sweet *Agnes* enclosed. By her account of Broadstairs, I thought you were at the North Pole – but if you are, the whales must be metamorphosed into gigs and whiskies, or split into them, as heathen gods would have done, or Rich the harlequin. You talk of Margate, but say nothing of Kingsgate, where Charles Fox's father scattered buildings of all sorts, but in no style of architecture that ever appeared before or has since, and with no connection with or to one another, and in all directions – and yet the oddity and number made that naked, though fertile soil, smile and look cheerful -

I wish on your return, if in good weather, you would contrive to visit Mr Barrett's at Lee, it is but four miles from Canterbury. You will see a child of Strawberry prettier than the parent, and so executed and so finished! There is a delicious closet too, so flattering to me! and a prior's library so antique, and that does such honour to Mr Wyat's taste! Mr Barrett, I am most sure, would be happy to show his house to you, and I know if you tell him that I beg it, he will produce the portrait of Anne of Cleve by Holbein in the identic ivory box turned like a Provence rose, as it was brought over for Henry VIII. It will be a great favour, and it must be a fine day, for it lives in cotton and clover, and he justly dreads exposing it to any damp. He has some other good pictures, and the whole place is very pretty, though retired.

Monday, September 29

PS. If this is not a long letter, I don't know what is. This, which is St Goose's day, or the commemoration of the ignoble army of martyrs, who have suffered in the persecution under that gormandizing archangel St Michael.

From Mary Berry   Prospect House
Sunday night, September 28, 1794

I did not suppose that the Prince of Wales was likely to become your *successor*, in anything, till the newspapers told me so.

The storm has at last ceased here, and we have seen one fine calm day, which I assure you appears to great advantage on our boundless prospect. We are at Rams*gate* in the morning, which is, of all the *gates* in this neighbourhood, by far the prettiest I think; and since dinner have walked to one of Lord Holland's strange would-be Gothic buildings at Kingsgate. We are so far both from the two metropolises of Margate and Ramsgate, that having as yet had no inducement strong enough to take us out three miles in cold dark nights, we have spent every evening at home and alone, except last night, when we dined at Broadstairs, our nearest town, with a Scotch Lord and Lady Balgonie, people who we never visited before; but as they belong to [Fife] the county in Scotland to which we *ought* to have belonged, and have been very civil to us, we wished to be the same. Your *favourite* Lord Galloway, was one of the party, and I have got a headache today by dancing Scotch reels with him and one of his daughters. Mr Parsons, that high priest of ennui is in this part of the world; and I meet every day hundreds of other faces that I know, in our airings of a morning; but we are so *penitus toto divisos orbe* at this North Foreland that they can none of them trouble us. Mrs Fitzherbert is at Margate driving away sorrow in a phaeton and four, and the Duchess of Rutland at Ramsgate, being *driven after* by a man of the name of Devisme, or Devel, who, without knowing her, professes the most ardent passion for her, and literally follows her wherever she goes. His carriage is always at the tail of hers; when she stops, he stops, and when she goes on he pursues. You may guess what a noise a circumstance of this sort must make in a place like this, where the man, who seems to be not at all well known, has acquired the name of *Malvolio*.

Monday morning
And the finest morning that ever was seen – bright sun, calm air, and smooth sea; we mean to be out as much as possible to enjoy it. Farewell, and let us hear from you very soon.

A plot had been devised by two young apprentices, and one other, to assassinate the King at Windsor. The plan was then changed and the action was to have taken place at the theatre but the men were apprehended before any damage was done.

Designs by Wyatt for a large palace in medieval style situated at the northern end of Kew Gardens on the edge of the river, just south-west of the Dutch House, were recorded in 1794. This castellated structure was to replace the nearby White House in which the King and Queen had lived for twenty years. Begun in 1802, it was demolished, uncompleted, in 1827.

[Strawberry Hill]
September 29, 1794, 3 o'clock
Codicil to my letter of this morning
Yes, it is very true – the plot, and it is not true that Lord Cholmondeley is at Cowes, for he was in this room at one o'clock, and confirms the truth of the intended assassination of the King by a poisoned arrow through a reed, and it was to have been on the terrace at Windsor yesterday sennight, but the arrow was not ready – so you see murder is not dead with Robespierre. The Duchess of Gloster has been here till this moment, and my letter must wait till tomorrow, for the post is gone.

Lord Cholmondeley came to acquaint me that the Prince of Wales had sent as express for him, and told him, that being on the brink of marriage, he should set him and Lady Cholmondeley at the head of his family; and as yet had named nobody else – so perhaps my report of Lord Pembroke is not true. The Duchess says Lord Southampton does go for the Princess – I tell you what I hear, but answer for nothing; I have no more right to know the truth than the rest of the world, who do not care a straw whether what they tell be truth or not. Lord Cholmondeley heard yesterday from Townshend, the fac-totum of the police, that he himself seized the two assassins, and is in chase after a third; and the Duchess had heard of the plot too. Every-body has affirmed for this last week that the King is building a superb palace at Kew and has begun pulling down houses – reduced to a simple fact; a couple of rooms are erecting there for Prince Ernest [Duke of Cumberland].

Lord Cholmondeley told me what touches me much more! He once hired Prospect House, and says it is a single house and the very Temple of the Winds, and that he once rose out of bed thinking a troop of them were come to eject him. I hope they will give *you* warning, without filling a bill; and I am afraid to mention it, lest you should think me impatient to bring you back – not in the least – go any whither, where you can be safe – but do not be blown into the chops of a French privateer!

Eleven at night

I have been at Lady Douglas's, where the Mackinseys, Onslows, and everybody agreed in the reality of the plot. The known criminals are three young apprentices, two of them are in custody. The plan was to raise a riot in the playhouse to occupy attention, and during the confusion, to shoot the King. A watchmaker, who was employed on the fabrication of the dart, discovered the design – I pretend no far-ther intelligence yet.

Strawberry Hill
October 1, 1794

My letters are continually giving themselves the lie; but I have warned you, when I tell you news, *to wait for the echo*. This is a favourite proverb with me, but I except Prospect House out of my injunction, for when the wind blows there I beseech you not *to wait for the echo*, but to descend to the plain.

The assassination plot here is universally believed, and no doubt had deep root. The three young English apprentices were not likely to

[171]

have had zeal enough of themselves to meditate royal murder: it tells me that our Jacobin clubs having been checked by the seizure of so many of their instruments, have been working underground. I wonder what diabolic sacrament they have invented to bind their devotees.

I have received your Sunday's dispatch, and begin this answer before dinner against tomorrow, lest I should be interrupted then. Where is Lord P[aget] that he leaves the whole coast open to Malvolio! and so you have Mrs Fitzherbert! I suppose our Countesses, especially the latest, are now thinking on, or ordering their robes, since Mrs F has waived her claims to *Ich Dien*.

I went to Bushy this morning, and not finding Lady Guilford, returned to Cliveden to look after your new plant-shed. It is quite finished except glazing, and the garden is as trim as that in Milton's *Allegro*, and much prettier, though not so immortal.

Lady Bute I doubt is going; it will be *very inconvenient to my Lord Castlcomer*, for her house you know was my resource in winter evenings. I have outlived almost all my acquaintance of my own century, or the remainder are grown too young again ever to be in their own houses, unless when they expect half the town, and that at midnight. I came into the world, when there were such seasons as afternoons and evenings, but the breed is lost! and if any of them did exist, they would be of no more use than an old almanac. I believe Hannah More herself will soon be obliged to keep saints' night instead of saints' days.

Ten at night

Well! well! well! and so at last I fib, when I think I am most sure of my veracity. Two officers from London this morning, who say the plot is now disbelieved in town, and that nothing will be made out – no! Then I am sure the ministers have acted sillily in publishing it, before they were certain of their ground. I have a mind to send you no more news, for what can one believe? and yet what can I do? I had rather write what others invent, than be forced to invent myself. Pussy and I have no adventures: now and then a little squabble about biting and scratching, but no more entertaining in a letter, than the bickerings between any husband and wife.

Goodnight! I am disgusted with the falsehoods I have told you, and am not at all in humour to add to the number – you may as well rely on the daily papers, and dispense with me as your gazetteer.

Thursday morning

The *True Briton* is not arrived, but I have had a note from the Pavilions with a letter to be franked, and as the Duchess [of Gloucester] tells me nothing new, I suppose there is nothing.

I cannot tell how your weather is on Mount Ararat. October but just shows those marks of green old age that become so beautiful a summer, like that good sort of old man whose economy begins to take a tinge of gold.

From Mary Berry   Prospect House
                                        Wednesday morning, Oct 1, 1794

We shall certainly not be blown away from you, for it has been the finest calm, clear weather for these last three days at the Prospect House, that can be conceived, and the sea is so covered with our vessels, of all sizes, from seventy-fours to fishing boats, that you have as little chance of getting rid of us by a French privateer; though at this instant, from my window, I can clearly see that hostile coast. With a glass I can discern several high buildings near the coast, the situation of a village, and a windmill; and at Ramsgate they say they have seen the tricoloured flag flying in a camp near Calais.

With respect to our return, you are exactly as I could wish you – very anxious to get us back, but not at all displeased at our staying a little longer while the good weather lasts.

Lord Cholmondeley, in spite of the bad character he gives the Prospect House, inhabits the next house, within fifty yards of it, in just the same exposed position, where he is expected to return tomorrow evening. The little boy, Lord Malpas, who has continued here, is as fine a stout, healthy child as you ever saw, and the image of his father. That Lord Cholmondeley is to be put at the head of the Prince's family is really news, as everybody has been anxiously making out lists of his household, and Lord and Lady Cholmondeley were in none that I have either made or heard made, though I think them perfectly proper people for such a situation, and only wonder nobody thought of them before. We say *at Broadstairs* that Lady Sutherland is to go over with Lord Southampton to fetch the princess, in which case, I should suppose, she must be intended to continue in her household. Much as attendance on princes and places at court are laughed at and abused (by those who can't obtain them), so desirable do I think any sort or shadow of occupation for women, that I should think any situation, that did not require constant attendance, a very agreeable thing.

What a strange business is this plot of assassination! But I cannot help thinking it will be found never to have gone further than the mad heads of these three or four poor apprentices, led astray by their nonsensical and pernicious doctrines they hear in their clubs and societies, and pushed on and encouraged by *much more* profligate villains, who would willingly make use of their feeble arm to create a confusion, which, in some way or other, they suppose (and perhaps too truly) they could turn to account.

I am sorry that you *would*, and did, see Mrs Damer's house before it was ready to be seen, for fear that from seeing nothing well but its only defect (the corner entry), you should take one of your sudden prepossessions, which you say yourself (though in *all* cases I won't allow it) totally deprives you of future judgment.

The Greatheads are returned to Margate, and we are going to dine with them tomorrow. This is our first *gaiety*, for, except our dinner at Broadstairs, we have spent every evening at home and alone. But the rides and drives here in fine weather are really charming and almost infinite for the country, though not without trees, is so perfectly open and unfenced and unditched, that one may steer to almost any part of the Island with a compass in hand, without meeting the smallest obstacle to turn you half a yard out of your course. The unaccountable *colony* of buildings at Kingsgate exactly answers your description. Altogether they are an ornament to an open country, though separately they are one worse than another. But is is really very odd that any man should have had the rage of building so much, and in so many different styles, without *ever deviating* into any one ever seen before, or worthy to be seen again. Mr [Thomas] Coutts at present inhabits the large house – the Italian villa as it is called – the front of which is in much purer taste than many Italian villas; but I should think the very large pediment and colonnade not projecting, but sunk *into* the house, must make it a bad and inconvenient dwelling. If the weather should be fine when we leave this, and we find it compatible with our journeying with our own horses, we will certainly go and see Mr Barrett's, in which case I shall beg you to advertise him of our visit, that we may not be taken as swindlers come to steal his Anne of Cleves, or to see his house under false pretences.

I have nothing but a letter from Mrs D., just setting out for Goodwood. Farewell, then, for the present, and let us hear from you soon,
for I like your letters when you have nothing to say, almost better
than when you have much.

*Walpole read into Mary Berry's last letter a sense which she did not
mean to convey and one that she was far from entertaining herself.
But it gave vent to one of the most agitating apprehensions of Walpole's mind which it took several letters to assuage.*

[Strawberry Hill]
Saturday, Oct. 4, 1794

I have been writing to Mr Barrett, but cannot help adding a word on
a passage in your letter on which I had determined to meditate till
tomorrow – but lest you should think that you can drop a word or hint
a wish that does not make an impression on me, I must add a few lines,
though I have scarce time. To my extreme astonishment you speak
with approbation of a place at court! Is it possible *you* should like one?
or can I assist such a wish? Interest I have none upon earth anywhere,
nor if I had, would condescend to employ it for anyone but for you and
your sister. I have been rummaging my head, and can see no glimmer-
ing but one: My telling you of Lord Cholmondeley perhaps led you to
think I might try through him – for *you* I would – Maid of Honour I
can scarce induce myself to believe you would submit to: Bedchamber
– Woman you may perhaps mean – destined they most probably are by
this time – but if you have such a wish, it shall not fail through my
neglect – therefore make me an immediate answer, and a direction to
him, if you wish I should write to him.

From Mary Berry   Prospect House
                                                                      Oct. 5, 1794

My dear friend –
   Your letter, which I have just received, would make me laugh, if
your kind affecting attention to my *every supposed* wish was not
much nearer making me cry.

The sentiments I expressed in my last with respect to places at court were merely general, and occurred to me from having heard them laughed at and abused by those to whose idleness and insignificance no court could add. Your letter first suggested the possibility of their application to ourselves, and at the same time a probable means of success. But as for myself, I feel to belong so entirely to the two or three people in this world in and by whose affection, friendship, and society I alone support a sickly existence, than *any* situation that in any degree separated me from them, were it that of the Princess herself, instead of that of her attendant, would by me be shunned as a misfortune. As to my sister, I trust I shall see her happily established in a respectable marriage, the best and most desirable of all settlements for a young woman.

I know you are aware, and do me the justice to feel, how little the native pride and independence of my mind has ever in any circumstances been swayed by motives of interest, and *that* from principle, and not from any romantic contempt for the goods of this world, or of ignorant sensibility to their advantages. You cannot wonder, therefore, that I should sometimes cast an anxious thought towards the possibility of my sister's feeling, in more advanced life, the evils of a narrow fortune, to the thoughts of which it is not without effort that I have accustomed myself.

I am writing in a hurry for the post of today, but I think I have said enough to convince you how exactly my sentiments are your own on this subject. I wish I had said or *could* say enough to satisfy my own heart with respect to *you* – to your offering that interest which I know you not only never prostituted to power, but never condescended to employ even for those who had every claim upon you, except those of the heart.

While I retain *these*, be assured your *interest* will be a sinecure with respect to my further demands upon it. Farewell.

From Mary Berry   Prospect House
                                      Monday, October 6, 1794
My dear friend,
I feel not to have said half enough to you in my hurried letter of yesterday, and yet I know not in what stronger terms to express your total misapprehension of my meaning. Can you possibly conceive me

a *Bedchamber-Woman*? dawdling away my time in waiting-rooms and stuck up with people who might probably as heartily despise me as I should them – No, my dear friend, my attendance shall be of a very different sort, and the willing homage of a grateful heart to a character which courts could never either captivate or corrupt. I should not think it necessary again to mention the subject, because I am sure a moment's thought will convince you what must be both my own and my sister's ideas upon it in every light, but that I know how difficult it sometimes is to erase first impressions from your mind.

It blew last night what the sailors call a *capful of wind* after several perfectly calm days, and we have just heard the melancholy tidings that two small vessels were wrecked between this and Ramsgate. These incidents are so common on every coast that they make but little impression except upon us inland people. And when do you turn your faces inland again? I hear you say. Why, certainly the beginning of next week, or sooner, if the weather should become bad, for all the comfort and amusement here depends upon the weather – a vile situation for climate, you will say. I have made a sketch of Prospect House for you, that you may yourself judge of the snug retreat we have been inhabiting. Lord Cholmondeley's house, much as he abuses the situation, is within fifty yards of ours, and much civil parley had taken place between us. They have with them a Mr Lee, an old acquaintance of ours, who the other day gave us a long account of all the particular civilities that accompanied the Prince's interview with Lord Cholmondeley and his desiring him and Lady Cholmondeley to be at the head of the new household. He says Lord Cholmondeley declined going to fetch the Princess, which the Prince wished him to do, because during the time of his embassy he must be considered as receiving orders from and acting under the ministry, with which he wished to have nothing to do – and made a sort of proviso for the future freedom of his political conduct and sentiments. This is attempting to *thread a needle*, which I should think he will find impossible.

We are going to the play at Margate with the Greatheads to see *Hamlet* acted by gentlemen, and very *gentleman-like* acting I daresay it will be, but I expect to be much amused. Mrs Siddons left this very day after we called upon her, so that we were none the better for her neighbourhood.

Strawberry Hill
Tuesday, October 7, 1794

Your answer, which I own arrived a day sooner than I flattered myself it would – I wish it *could* have told me how you passed the storm of Sunday night! has not only relieved me from all anxiety on the subject, but has made me exceedingly happy, for though I mistook you for a moment, it has proved to me that I had judged perfectly rightly of your excellent and most uncommon understanding. Astonished as I was no doubt while I conceived that you wished to be placed in a situation so unworthy of your talents and abilities and knowledge, and powers of conversation. I was *of* a court myself, but from my birth and the position of my father could but, for my first twenty years, know much of the nature of the beast; and from my various connections since I have seldom missed farther opportunities of keeping my acquaintance even with the interior. The world in general is not ignorant of the complexion of most courts, though ambition, interest and vanity are always willing to leap over their information, or to fancy they can counteract it – but I have no occasion to probe that delusion, nor to gainsay your random opinion that a court life may be eligible for women – yes, for the idle ones you specify, perhaps so – for respectable women I think much less than even for men – I do not mean with regard to what is called *their character*, as if there were but *one* virtue with which women have any concern – I speak of their understanding and consequential employment of their time – In a court there must be much idleness even without dissipation – and amongst the female constituents, much self-importance ill founded, some ambition, jealousy, envy, and thence hatred, insincerity, little intrigues for credit, and – but I am talking, as if there were any occasion to dissuade you from what you despise and I have only stated what occasioned my surprise at your thinking what you never did think at all.

Still, while I did suppose that in any pore of your heart there did lurk such a wish, I did give a great gulp and swallowed down all attempts to turn your thoughts aside from it – and why? Yes and you must be ready to ask me how such a true friend could give in to the hint without stating such numerous objections to a plan so unsuitable for you? – Oh! for strong reasons too. In the first place, I was sure, that, without my almost century of experience, your good sense must have anticipated all my arguments: you often confute my desultory logic on points less important, as I frequently find – but the true cause of my assenting, without suffering a sigh to escape me, was, because I was conscious that I could not dissuade you fairly, without a grain or more of *self* mixing in the argument: I would not trust myself with myself – I would not act again as I did when you was in Italy – and answered you as fast as I could, lest self should relapse – yet though it did not last an hour, what a combat it was! What a blow to my dream of happiness, should you be attached to a court – for though you probably would not desert Cliveden entirely, how distracted would your time be! – but I will not enter into the detail of my thoughts: you know how many posts they travel in a moment when my brain is set at work, and how firmly it believes all it imagines – besides the defalcation of your society – but enough – I conquered all these dangers – and still another objection rose – when I had discovered the only channel I could open to your satisfaction, I had no little repugnance to the emissary I was to employ – Though it is my intention to be equitable to him, I should be extremely sorry to give him a shadow of claim on me – and you know those who might hereafter be glad to conclude that it was no wonder they should be disappointed when gratitude on your account had been my motive – but my cares are at an end – and though I have laboured through two painful days, the thorns of which were sharpened, not impeded by the storm, I am rejoiced at the blunder I made, as it has procured me the kindest and most heart-dictated and most heartfelt letter that ever was written, for which I give you a million thanks. Forgive my injurious surmise, for you see that though you can wound my affection, you cannot allay its eagerness to please you at the expense of my own satisfaction and peace.

Having stated with most precise truth all I thought related to *yourself*, I do resume and repeat all I have said both in this and my former letter and renew exactly the same offers to my sweet Agnes, if she has the least wish for what I supposed you wished. I can swallow my objections to trying my nephew as easily for her as for you; but having had two days and a half for thinking the whole case over, I have no sort of doubt but the whole establishment must be completely settled by this time, or that at most if any places are not fixed yet, it must be from the strength and variety of contending interests; and besides the new Princess will have fewer of each class of attendants than the Queen, and I shall not be surprised if there should already be a *brouillerie* between the two courts about some or many of the nominations. And though the interest I thought of trying was the only one I could pitch upon, I do not on reflection suppose that a person just favoured has favour enough already to recommend others. Hereafter that may be better; and a still more feasible method I think would be to obtain a promise against a vacancy, which at this great open moment nobody will be thinking of asking, when the present is so uppermost in their minds – and now my head is cool, perhaps I could strike out more channels, should your sister be so inclined – but of that we will talk when we meet.

Eleven at night

Our footpads seem dispersed – I believe they no longer met with game; our old does took the alarm and kept close in their burrows. I have been in their warren in Richmond for the last two evenings; so they will have no claims on me when you return. Good night! I reserve a morsel of my paper in case of having anything to answer – Methinks my whole time is employed in writing to you or in being frightened about you – Pray come back, that I may have time to think on other people.

Thursday

I have received the second letter that I expected, and it makes me quite happy on all the points that disquieted me, on the court, on the tempest, and I hope on privateers, as you have so little time to stay on Ararat, and the winds that terrify me for you, will I trust be as formidable to them; above all I rejoice at your approaching return, on which I would not say a syllable seriously, not only because I would have you please yourselves, but that you may profit as much as possible by change of air. I retract all my mistake, and though perhaps I may have floundered on with regard to A, still I have not time to correct or write any part of it over again – besides, every word was the truth of my heart, and why should you not see what is or was in it?

[Strawberry Hill]
Tuesday October 14, 1794

I am rejoiced you have been at Mr Barrett's, though it will have made Strawberry sink in your eyes, Lee is so purely Gothic, and every inch of it so well finished. I am still more glad that your visit thither, instead of hurrying on, has not made you risk Shooters Hill and Black Heath – Well, I hope that on Thursday all my alarms will be at an end, and that I shall neither dread tempests, nor privateers, nor highwaymen. Come and enjoy your own balcony and little conservatory, and a friend, who hopes to see you looking much better for your expedition, and Agnes as charmingly as she returned from hers, and who always wishes to have you both pleased, though your absence always fills him with fears of one sort or other.

Strawberry Hill
October 15, 1794

I can bear disappointments cheerfully when it is for your health or pleasure; I consult both, and do not allow myself to reason against your reasons. If you call the weather settled, I will call it so too. It is enough that you can amuse yourself where you are – your liking to stay longer contents me.

I shall be glad to hear your opinions on Lee, and am pleased that I contributed to your seeing it, both for your sakes and Mr Barrett's, to whom I owe the greatest gratitude for his too great partiality to me.

[Strawberry Hill]
October 17, 1794

I had not the least doubt of Mr Barrett's showing you the greatest attention; he is a most worthy man, and has a most sincere friendship for me, and I was sure would mark it to any person that I love. I don't guess what your criticisms on his library will be; I do not think we shall agree in them, for to me it is the most perfect thing I ever saw, and has the most the air it was intended to have, that of an abbot's library, supposing it could have been so exquisitely finished three hundred years ago: but I am sorry he will not force Mr Wyat to place the Mabeuse over the chimney, which is the sole defect, as not distinguished enough for the principle feature of the room. My closet is as perfect in its way as the library, and it would be difficult to suspect that it had not been a remnant of the ancient convent only newly painted and gilt – my cabinet, nay nor house, convey any conception; every true Goth must perceive that they are more the works of fancy than of imitation.

I believe the less that our opinions will coincide, as you speak so slightingly of the situation of Lee, which I admire. What a pretty circumstance is the little river! and so far from the position being insipid, to me it has a tranquil cheerfulness that harmonizes with the house, and seems to have been the judicious selection of a wealthy abbot, who avoided ostentation, but did not choose austere gloomth – I do not say that Lee is as gay as a watering-place upon a naked beach.

I am very glad and much obliged to you for having consented to pass the night at Lee; I am sure it made Mr Barrett very happy – I shall let him know how pleased you was – and I too for his attentions to you.

The mass of politics is so inauspicious, that if I tapped it, I should not finish my letter for the post, and my reflections would not contribute to your amusement, which I should be sorry to interrupt, and which I beg you to pursue as long as it is agreeable to you. It is satisfaction enough to me to know you are happy; it is my study to make you so, as far as my little power can extend; and as I promised you on your condes[cen]sion in leaving Italy at my prayer, I will never object whatever you like to do, and will accept, and wait with patience for any moments that you will bestow on

Your devoted
Orford

The winter, climatically mild, had done little to induce Walpole to London. Having outlived most of his friends and since all the hours for sociable intercourse had been recast, he preferred Strawberry with his devotees at hand to summon at will.

Only one letter survives for the first part of 1795. The Berrys were at Twickenham and Walpole in London was able to provide them with a piece of news. In August they made their yearly peregrination, this time to Cheltenham.

[Berkeley Square]
Tuesday morning, [April 7, 1795]

The Princess Caroline [of Brunswick] arrived at St James's on Sunday at three o'clock – nor do I believe that Mrs Fitzherbert would forbid the banns, for she has taken Marble Hill, and proposes to live very platonically under the devout wing of Mrs Cambridge.

Mr Churchill and Lady Mary, who were at Lewisham, went to Greenwich and saw the Princess show herself at a window and bow exceedingly to the people, as she has since done at St James's, till the Prince shut the window and made excuses at her being fatigued. Everybody speaks most favourably of her face as most pleasing, though with too much rouge; she is plump, and by no means tall. The marriage is not till tomorrow.

Cheltenham, August 1785. Could anything have seemed more harmless? Yet, if Walpole had known then of the romance that was blossoming, sincere and passionate on Mary's side, it would surely have left him unhinged. For there was Mary, with father and sister, taking the waters, needing a change of air (for one or other of them was of an invalidish nature), and there too was General O'Hara, newly released from two years' imprisonment at the Luxembourg in Paris. As yet his name is not mentioned by Mary and Walpole writes serenely of the arrival of Lord and Lady Mendip; of Lady Diana Beauclerk and Dorothy Jordan. And, amusingly, of the pregnancies of the Prince of Wales's wife and of his mistress, Lady Jersey. A few days later he tells of a regimental water party seen from his closet where stands Mrs Damer's terracotta bust of Mary, made earlier in the year.

Post-house at Cheltenham   Holbein Chamber, Strawberry Hill
                                 Wednesday evening, August 19, 1795
The Mendips are expected tomorrow – and we shall be as lively as soups, and removes and entrées and pools at cribbage set to clarionets can make us. Moreover I shall learn for your edification all that the corps diplomatic knows or is ordered to dispense – as from another quarter I shall be informed how all the princes and princesses in Europe do – can I miss you, when my time may pass as merrily as if I were at the Diet of Ratisbone?

Today you have had charming weather for travelling – not sultry for certain, and not a drop of rain. The corn I hope you found most levelled: the papers talk of such prodigious plenty, that one would imagine there were danger of our being devoured by wheat and barley and that the farmers and Jacobins would raise a clamour on that score!

Wednesday night

I have been with Lady Di and *voici* what I heard. Nel of Clarence plays Ophelia tonight at Richmond. Miss Hotham has issued cards for a tea on Friday – I have not received one, though last year she *swore* by me; but this has not noticed me – I shall not break my heart. And here is a *bon mot*, though not perfect enough for the Berryana. It seems it has been reported that of the two pregnancies at Brighton the greatest is a tympany, and the biggest a dropsy. 'What', says W. Fawkener, 'is the Prince still between wind and water?'

Strawberry Hill
August 22, 1795

Though I persuaded you to go to Cheltenham, and am happy you are there, I little imagined I should rejoice at your *not* being here; yet I do, at least I did yesterday, when we had an outrageous storm of thunder that would have frightened *you* terribly; I thought it directly over the blue room, it was so near that it did fall on Davenport's field over against the round tower and reduced a shock of corn to powder. Lady Cecilia (her first visit since her return) was with me, and though so apt to be frightened out of her senses when not in the least alarmed, was not at all dismayed, for she was frying Lady Jersey, and had no leisure to be terrified.

Mrs Ankerstrom has dined with the court of Orange. Her mother no doubt is laying roundabout plans for being invited, and then will say they made the first overtures – and she will succeed, for Nixon is appointed apothecary to their household and will be to pimp for her.

Yesterday just as I had breakfasted in my closet where your bust is, I saw the Kingston Fencibles pass by on the river; they were standing in rows on a high platform in a western barge with colours and music; they saluted my castle with three guns – unluckily I had no cannon mounted on my battlements to return it – then they gave Mrs Osbaldiston seven, who I suppose was standing in her garden on the shore and repaid the compliment with seven bowls of punch, and perhaps had invited company for the *spectacle*, as she did when she imagined the Queen was to come in a barge to breakfast with me.

August 25, 1795

I do not grow at all reconciled to your absence; *pis-allers* are the worst *allers* in the world, and when the coach comes to the door at eight o'clock and it is not to carry me to Cliveden, I grow peevish.

Of news I have not heard a tittle. On *Sunday* as it was a most comely evening, I returned the anti-divine Cecilia's visit, concluding she would be on the terrace of the Palace sidling towards the Oranges – and I had guessed rightly. Then I called on Mrs Garrick, and to my surprise was for the first time in my life let in, though uninvited. She met me at the door and told me she had an hundred head of nieces with her – and in truth so I found; there were six gentlewomen, a husband of one of them, and two boys. An elderly fat dame affected at every word to call her *Aunt* – however they were quiet enough, and did not cackle much; and even the lads were tame, and did not dare stare at my limping skeleton, as I expected, and which I do not love to expose to giggledom.

Berkeley Square
Wednesday after dinner, August 26, 1795

Here I am, with no earthly whither to go, but to my sister's at supper-time – then why should I not go on writing to you, which I like better than anything when I am not with you, especially as I have some nothingly scraps to send you.

Mrs Molyneux, grandmother of the present late-Princess of Wales [Mrs Fitzherbert] is dead – they call it *suddenly*, though she was above ninety years of age before this impromptu came into her head.

The Courts of Brighthelmstone furnishes the idle of this town with their chief topics of conversation. Mr Tyrwhit, a favourite of no ancient date, is gathered to his numberless predecessors, for having roundly lectured Lady Jersey on her want of reverence for the *legal* Princess, and the poor injured lady had no way to escape but by inventing a swoon, in the height of which came in the Prince. Miss Vanneck is come away furious also, on never being asked to play at cards; nay she was desired for her *amusement* to bring her spinning wheel into the playroom, where I suppose she banged and bungled the instrument. The Jerseys are to have the house of their son-in-law Lord William Russel, which was his Grandmother Bedford's in Pall

Mall – still *harping* on Carleton House – don't mention these *oui-dires* (for the truth of not one of which I will be responsible) on the Steen or Pantiles of Cheltenham, which I repeat merely to divert you without caring a straw about the dramatis personnae. My next paragraph was printed at the bottom of the play-bills at Richmond last week, that Mrs Jordan would not perform, as it was the birthday of his R.H. the Duke of Clarence – no, to be sure she could not, for the Prince of Orange was to dine with him, and she did the honours at the head of the table – no, the Princesses were not there.

Miss Hotham is to have another tea on Friday and has sent me a card for it. I shall be exceedingly unwilling, and have not promised, for I have heard that on Monday she had Miss Tag, and Miss Rag, and Miss Bobtail, and I suppose will have as many next time.

The weather is as gorgeous as in the Summer Islands – I hope you have your full share of it. The verdure is luxuriant from the snow of the winter and the rains of the summer – it is a pity we must buy fine autumns so dear! Methinks when the Parliament brought the months eleven days forwarder, it should have ordered that the commencement of summer should not date till after the deluges of St Swithin.

Goodnight for the present – all I have been saying will keep cold for two or three days.

28th, eleven at night

Well, I have been to Miss Hotham's in a bright but most chill moonlight – the assemblage was not so ungain as I expected, for though there were some of the clan of the Bobtails, there were several I knew, as the Guilfords, Mount Edgcumbes, and a few more; I played with Lady Cecilia, Lady Guilford and Mr Sutton; and Mrs Sutton with a thousand civilities invited me to Moseley for Tuesday next, and I will certainly go, as they are of your acquaintance.

By 2 September Walpole had heard of O'Hara's presence at Cheltenham but bore the information with equanimity. In a letter of delightful trivia, Mrs Sutton's house was, if anything, of greater interest to him as were the elderly ladies staying at what was once Alexander Pope's villa, a short distance downstream from Strawberry Hill and now belonging to Lord Mendip.

Charles O'Hara, the illegitimate son of Lord Tyrawley, fifty-five years old to Mary's thirty-one, had knocked about the world a good deal. He had been appointed captain in the Coldstream Guards; as brigadier-general he was with Cornwallis at Yorktown, Virginia, earned mention in despatches, and was imprisoned but later released with an exchange prisoner. As major-general he had returned to England but finding himself in pecuniary difficulties had gone abroad; in Italy in 1784 he had met the Berrys in Rome.

A handsome man, well set up, and at home in society, he had nevertheless a touch of roughness which led him to entertain friends with scandalous gossip, even to hinting of his own triumphs with the celebrated beauties of Europe. He was a bon vivant, universally popular, out to enjoy life. Of his looks in 1791 we have Walpole's own comment: 'His face as ruddy and black, and his teeth as white as ever'; his eyes were very dark and 'his appearance, indeed, was of that striking cast, which once seen, is not easily forgotten'.[35] Equally his temper had been described as 'most frightful and ungovernable'.

Such a man seems an unlikely choice for the recipient of Mary's devotion. Perhaps it was his virility, so different from the fastidious connoisseur, antiquarian, man of fashion and of delicate health with whom she had spent so much of the last seven years. Perhaps as long ago as that first introduction in Rome he had raised her sympathetic response. At Cheltenham he quickened her interest and touched her heart. 'Old Cock of the Rock' he was called by the military serving in Gibraltar, [36] but this presumably Mary did not know any more than she knew that he had mistresses in Gibraltar, probably waiting his return, for he had now been appointed there as Governor and his departure was close at hand.

At the end of August he had been at Park Place to mourn with Lady Ailesbury and Mrs Damer the death of his old friend Field-Marshal Conway, who had died very recently. From there he went to Cheltenham, and to Mrs Damer, her close friend and confidante, Mary was soon making known her attachment. Mrs Damer, who knew O'Hara well, though not intimately, was apprehensive lest 'the qualities of his heart, which I have ever thought excellent, may be obscured, his sensibility and natural good sense weakened, by long habits and intercourse with a base world, alas! I know not'.[37] Walpole was to know nothing yet and, surprisingly, Agnes suspected nothing, too occupied perhaps with her own uncertain attachment between herself and young Mr Ferguson, of Raith, the son of the very man who inherited her great-uncle's wealth (having

[187]

changed his name accordingly), which in the Berrys' reckoning should have gone to their father. This sad little romance floundered and finally failed.

Post Office at Cheltenham   Strawberry
                                                            Sept. 1, 1795
I am resolved to correct my hand, for my writing has grown so small and so close, that I myself could scarcely read over my last letter, and though your eyes are fifty years younger, I believe you found difficulty to decipher it. At present I have so little to say, that I had better make my alphabet as tall as Jerningham's, though I have not his happy faculty of making every sentence a *double entendre*. Mercy on us if he and Sophia [Walpole] were to correspond! They would have occasion to use an expression of Lord Bacon's, *to speak without fig-leaves*. Some say *the Charming* will succeed Tommy Tyrrwhit. I wish with all my heart he may! He will not offend by lecturing his old friend Madame de Main*tenant* [Lady Jersey].

After all his vast profusions Lord Moira's expeditions are given over, and he is retired to Donnington Castle, carrying with him his first aide-de-camp the Duc d'Angoulême, son of Monsieur, who is gone to tap another attempt on Bretagne. How those two *rejettons* of the Plantagenets and Bourbons will sympathize on their vanished grandeurs! This is all I know beyond the next milestone.

                                                                    2nd
I was last night at Mrs Sutton's: there was not an inundation of people, as I feared, chiefly Hampton courtiers and its excrescences Dutch and French; there was a little music, a Miss Broadie sung and played, and so did another man, and there was a large supper, at which I left them. The situation seems handsome, the house extremely pretty and in very pure taste – there is a lovely little gallery painted in treillage, rather prettier than a paper of that gender, which I have seen somewhere or other, I forget where. Mrs Sutton's own landscapes, as far as I could judge by candle light, seem very good – I like her herself and her husband too, he is the civilest of men. I recollect the terror I felt last Christmas when you was to return from a ball there at three o'clock in the snow – I had concluded you was to ferry – and had quite forgot the bridge at Hampton Court – you know I sometimes have such inveterate distractions!

[188]

This far I have written before breakfast, but though I have received your Monday letter, I could not finish mine, for I had promised Mrs Doiley to show my house to her Mrs Sloane and a dowager – Miss Agar who is at Pope's, and they being old women who do not live at the brink of fashion, they came in sunny time, and not three hours after it was pitch dark, as fine ladies would have done, who hope to be immortal by always being too late for every diversion they may be supposed to like.

I am delighted that you have got Ohara. How he must feel his felicity at being at liberty to rove about as much as he likes! Still I shall not admire his volatility if he quits you soon. I am sorry he thinks Lady Ailesbury so much changed – yet how amazing it would be, if such a loss as she has had made no visible impression! a husband who living and dying seemed to have thought only of her!

Don't measure your letters by mine; I wish to amuse your idle moments but not to misemploy them – and it is fit that your youth should be confined to the entertainment of your great-grandfather? Let me babble. but don't reply.

Strawberry
Sunday night, Sept. 6, 1795

I sent two letters today, one for your father, the other for your sister, and two to Audley Street which I received by the post – but none from myself, for I had not a morsel of news in the house, and this letter perhaps will wait for a supply: our region is quite dry, unless I were to send to the scandal-pump at Hampton Court, with which you like to deal as little as I. In our village I suppose I am thought grown very sociable unless they suspect the true cause, for I call every now and then (at my *vacant* eight o'clock) on the few I do visit: last night a second time at the foot of the Bridge [the Cambridge family], where indeed they are very zealous about Clivedenists. I am a little tired of the clan at Pope's, of the formality and cribbage, and formality again! T'other night there was an Irish miss, who is thought a prodigy in music, and indeed she did belabour the harpsichord as if it had no more feeling than a kettledrum!

I sent the Udneys half a buck: they wanted me to partake it, which luckily I declined, and well it was I did, for they had invited that surfeiting flatterer Lady Elgin, and such a hogshead of sweet sauce would have overloaded any stomach that has not a royal digestion – not that I have escaped, for alas! she is there still, which I not knowing, went thither this evening and fell into her mouth – Oh! how she crammed me with all that the Queen and Princesses has said to *her* about their breakfast here, and how they every day recollect something new that they admired – I fear I did not offer her to come and see how *she* would like the house. Mrs Leneve formerly advised me never to begin with civilities to people I don't like, for, said she, you soon let them see that, and then they were more offended than they would have been by coolness at first. You will bear me witness that I did not snuff up the Countess's incense kindly the first time it was offered to me.

Tuesday morning

Here is your letter, and I like all it tells me, that you have chained your General to your car. I like your jaunts and that they answer so well. I suppose you will advertise me when I am to change my direction, though unless the public is more prolific of events than it has been for this last week, Twickenham is not likely to provoke me to write soon. Adieu!

Post-Office Cheltenham   [Strawberry Hill]
Tuesday evening, September 8, 1795

This is a mere codicil of business to my morning's letter. I have been to survey the works at Cliveden. Imprimis, the new road is not begun. Nobody, they said, had received specific orders, about it. I specified them to purpose. Chapman [the builder] was there, and imagined there was to be a double ditch and rail – no such thing – a simple path of gravel for a coach: what a fright would more be from Agnes's balcony.

The two [new] rooms are covered in, the scaffold will be struck tonight. I clambered to the top of the stairs and peeped in, though the steps are not placed yet; they will be pretty chambers, and each will have a *closettino* to its own self.

Mr Berry's rick is almost finished.

I found poor Muff bad – not with his eyes, but his back very mangy. I have ordered him to be entirely clipped, and dipped at the powder mills. As the letter to the gardener only affected to have been wafered, but came open, I looked to see whether I could expedite any orders – I found that your favourite gardener is leaving you – I asked wherefore? He replied the wages are too low – pray suspend that decree, if you wish to keep him – I think I could accommodate that impediment.

I have given orders for a new gigantic ice-house, that you may not want a profusion, if there should ever be such a *feel-omenon* as a hot summer.

While Walpole's letters are full of local matters telling of how he had entertained Lady Guilford and her son-in-law Sylvester Douglas (later Lord Glenbervie) to dinner; that the daughters of his niece, Laura Keppel, had been indifferently brought up; that George Hardinge at Ragman's Castle was hoping to get himself invited to dine so as to bring a party to see over Strawberry – while these unexceptionable communications were being reported to Cheltenham, Mrs Damer at Park Place was carrying on an animated correspondence with Mary, chiefly on the subject of O'Hara, full of observations, sympathy and sentiment but occasionally digressing about her own ills – how, for instance, a tendon of her leg affected by inflammation might well have ended in lameness for life, 'inevitably and irretrievably', had it not been for the efficiency of the application of a poultice. Her letters (there are none from her correspondent) give some idea of Mary's indecision of mind but it is difficult to know whether Mrs Damer's effusiveness helped. 'How much I wish a speedy decision', she wrote, 'for I quite dread the influence of an anxiety I, God knows! feel for you, and with you, on your mind', and 'I am sure you know that painful state of existence when one is battling and battling with anxiety, that one may not be quite overcome, tho' to conquer one knows it is quite impossible.'[38] And then in the garden, poor Mrs Damer was being devoured by gnats, 'My knee, tho' as I said appearing much to mend daily allows me nothing deserving the name of a walk, and sitting out with a book or musing, is a pleasure almost totally spoiled by the odious gnats, and various insects that so sting and maul my vulnerable skin that if I sit in one place for ten minutes, I come home in a perfect fever.[39] A suspicion that Mary may have heard something of O'Hara's less honourable proclivities finds some substance in a passage of one of Mrs Damer's long letters: 'I read doubts of your fears of a woman, tho' his reason and judgement, as well as his heart, whisper to him how very superior such a woman is to those with whom he has been hitherto connected in any way. Once united, your character must inspire him with perfect security on all rational subjects, and other subjects will find their excuse in a heart like yours.'[40]

The letters never ceased and the time of O'Hara's departure drew nearer.

Strawberry

Sept. 10, 1795

The postman at Cheltenham may growl as much as he pleases, or make as ill-natured glosses as he has a mind, on my writing to you almost every day: as long as your servant fetches the letters from the office, what has the man to do but receive them? If Kirgate, who is forced to put my letters into the post so very often, were to complain, and demand an increase in wages, I should not wonder, though since my press has stopped, he has scarce anything else to do – or if you, the greatest sufferer of all, were to lament being obliged to read such heaps of insipid scribbles, it would be no marvel; but till I receive some remonstrance of that kind, I shall persist to the last drop of the next fortnight. I trust I am still in a free country, and not in one where everybody that is below me is much above me, and has a right to tell me what I shall not do, when I have nothing at all to do, and when, as at this present writing, no mortal can take upon himself to say that I am doing anything at all.

Having thus confuted the postman and asserted my natural liberty as a peer of England of being as foolish as I please, I come to the next important article of my present life, which is very necessary for you to know, or you would be entirely ignorant of one trifling event of my actual existence. The house of *North and by Douglas* dined here today, and I could not get a soul to meet them: I sent to the Mount Edgcumbes, but they are gone this blessed day, he to the Mount and she to Norfolk, while the Dowager is merrymaking with Lord Cardigan in Northamptonshire. I invited the Mother Ankerstrom [Lady Cecilia Johnstone and her daughter-in-law, and they also would not come; so not being able to make up a party for Lady Guilford, she and her younger daughters went after tea to Pope's to visit Mrs Arch-Cashel who by the way is created Lady Somerton, for Irishwomen turn to peeresses as easily as the figurantes at the opera who from shepherdesses in the first dance, are changed in the next to graces and goddesses – so being left alone on my own shore, what could I do, but fling myself into the Thames or write to you? – Now you see and rue the consequences of leaving me by myself in this depopulated region! Another danger is, that if you don't return soon, I shall be devoured by venison, and hares and partridges and pheasants from Houghton: I am forced to water all my neighbourhood with game – to Lady Anne [Connolly] I shall be supposed to be making court for a legacy, though it is only gratitude for the large cabinet of gold and silver medals which she insisted on giving to me, and which I was so overjoyed, when authorized to send it back to her.

Saturday morning, 12th

Thank all the stars in which I have any friends, for bringing me yours of Thursday last at this instant when I had not had a word to say, nor could have made out the semblance of a letter, had I not had this antecedent piece ready cut and dried in my writing box, though as you justly say, when my pen gets a drop of ink in its eye, it cannot help chattering (to *you s'entend*) as fast as Miss Hotham.

If you have gulped enough of the fountain, though I fear not, nor conceive that water can work miracles in three weeks, I like your journeyings about and diverting yourselves with sights. Of Sudeley Castle the principal point to tell you is, that there is a print of the beautiful chapel, in which but few years ago was found the tomb of Catherine Parr, the castle then belonging to her last husband Admiral Seymour, and as I am descended from her by her first [second], I would you had been advertised to say a mass for your great-grandmother.

I do not wonder Madam K[eppel] ordered the windows to be shut when the weather was sultry – it was to display her dignity, or to increase the volume of her noisy voice which she always exerts for the same reason. I wish *they* [and her daughters] had been gentlewomen, and then they would not have always aimed at being princesses.

The out-pensioner of Bedlam G. H[ardinge] whom I hoped I had offended in the spring by refusing him a plenary indulgence, wrote to me last night to *dine* with him on Tuesday next with the Archbishop of Cashel – I knew this was to imply '*my* cousin is Lord Lieutenant' – Accept I did not, however as it showed good humour, I sent a very civil sorrowful fib in return and pleaded having engaged company myself for that day. You know I never enter into dinner-parties that have a round of consequences. Adieu!

The Berrys had left Cheltenham to stay with a friend near Andover in Hampshire and would shortly be on their way to Park Place where Walpole was to join them on 26 September, staying three days and returning together to Strawberry. Mary's mind must have been in turmoil and after this visit Walpole would have had some recognition of what was passing behind his back. Lady Ailesbury, who was packing up Park Place prior to selling it, may have, by a look or a word, dropped a hint. Mrs Damer, always to the fore, suggested that he 'does not choose to see, and none, they say, so blind'.

That Mary loved O'Hara with passion there is no doubt, and though latterly the indecision seems to have lain with him, an engagement was entered into, O'Hara proposing an immediate marriage so that she might sail with him to Gibraltar. This last she felt unable to agree to: her father and sister, so helpless without her efficient and guiding hand, Agnes's unresolved attachment, and the dread of telling Walpole were the formidable impediments. To these obstacles Mrs Damer rebounded by observing that if she paid attention to Walpole's selfishness it ('the vile weed') 'must grow stronger, and that, you may depend on it, it will, and increase by indulgence; were you to sacrifice all your best days to come and your whole existence to him, there would be no end to his encroaching fancies'.[41] Perhaps Mary visualized a long engagement, such as was common, or else she would join him after some delay or at his next home leave.

In a letter of 15 October from Mrs Damer[42] she must have now been satisfied that her lover was sincere in his affection:

October 15, 1795

O'H spoke to me of you as if himself with openess and confidence. All that he said was expressive of passion, softened by the tenderest care and concern for you, which the cool voice of reason and good sense made but the more touching to me. I think by all he has said, and by his whole conduct, that I can plainly perceive he yet scarcely

[194]

will allow himself to trust entirely to what his *heart* tells him he need not doubt, and to what, if he knew your character as I do, his *reason* would tell him he *could* not doubt; but unaccustomed as he must be to sentiment, tenderness and affection so expressed, so blended with truth, candour and sincerity, I cannot wonder if all should seem to him still like a flattering dream he dares not trust.

At Quarley near Andover   [Strawberry Hill]
                              Friday night, September 18, 1795
I mean this shall meet you at Mr Coxe's on Sunday, and am quite happy that you have had and have such a posthumous summer for your travels. Today has been the phoenix of days, so bright, so clear, so soft, and warm enough to be called hot by the courtesy of England. I am obliged to the weather too for furnishing me with a beginning, for the trade of correspondence is low indeed!

The emigrants of Richmond are beginning to return. The dowager Mount Edgcumbe is arrived at her son's villa – These scraps are all I can sweep together – were you to be absent another fortnight, I should be reduced to have recourse to Hampton Court to learn what all the inhabitants of the neighbourhood have had for dinner every day this week.

                                                     Saturday morn
Oh! thank you, and so does my letter, for it was quite exhausted, and here is yours of 17th to set in going again. Yes, I will certainly come to you at Park Place but I will allow for accidental delays and will not be there myself till Sunday the 27th or Monday 28th if I hear that you have met with any *remora* [obstacle] – not by your cold I hope – but how can it last in this celestial weather, which ought to operate all the miracles in Pope's *Messiah* – ought – I don't say does, for though I am certainly lame enough for a marvellous experiment, I am so far from finding I can

                    Leap exulting like the bounding roe*

that last night I was near tumbling headlong down Lady Di's steps, as I got out of my coach, but her footman caught me in his arms – Well! today is yesterday's twin. The cream was actually turned this morning at breakfast – what a phenomenon on the 19th of September!
*From Pope's *Messiah*.

[195]

I wish every *Jacobiterian*, that would lay waste the face of this beautiful rich country were to taste a few – not a quarter, which would be too many for one human being to wish to another, of the horrors that General Ohara beheld in France – and where excess of reformation has now produced a system of despotic impudence that surpasses even the triple partition of Poland! Adieu!

Between Walpole's last letter and the next of 4 November, Mary had taken leave of her betrothed. On 20 October O'Hara had heard of his immediate departure.

General O'Hara to Mary Berry[43]   Tuesday morning
                                                   [October 20,] 1795
The arrangements for the protection of the Mediterranean ships are made and they are under orders to sail immediately. Come to town this evening, that I may see and press you to my breast as often as possible before I leave you. Some excuse for this sudden coming to London must be made; suppose you say Mrs Damer wishes to see you before she goes to Goodwood. Her house is ready, but I think you would be better, from being less observed, at home.

That evening they met to take their faithful farewells and Mary was left with the agonizing uncertainty whether or not she had made the proper sacrifice and whether O'Hara would recognize it as such.

Mary Berry to General O'Hara[44]   Twickm
                                      Saturday morning Oct. 24, 1795
After three or four hours of broken slumber, I wake to the melancholy certainty of a long uncertain and painful absence. My dear friend, I find my mind much less strong than I believed it and yet, in submitting to this absence, I *think* I am doing right, I am *sure* I am consulting the peace and happiness of those about me and not my own. I think you will hereafter love me better for knowing me capable of a sacrifice, which you cannot now doubt how much I feel, and my future happiness (if there is any in store for me) will be

unsullied by the idea of having anticipated it at the expence of the feelings of others – but in the meantime you are gone and I am here, and my mind is not yet in a state to derive much comfort from cool reasoning. I feel now as if there were fifty things I should have liked to have said to you which my extreme and painful oppression prevented last night, and would, I am convinced still prevent, were you at this instant by my side. One idea, however, has so often occurred to me that I will mention it – as in every *possible* future event and circumstance I shall always be proud of your affection and sentiments for me, I beseech you in case of illness, or any danger, to send me if possible some token or assurance that you thought of me to the last as you do at this moment. Writing this has been a relief to me. Let me hear from you from Portsmouth as soon as you can, I beseech you.

Still at Portsmouth owing to an unfavourable wind, O'Hara wrote to Mary:

General O'Hara to Mary Berry[45]   Portsmouth
                                        Tuesday, Oct. 27, 1795
I am fully sensible, my Dearest Mary, that your letter ought, if I was a reasonable Being, to afford me much relief and comfort; but every moment of my existence proves, too forcibly for my peace, that comfort will be a stranger to my breast when absent from you, for I cannot, like you, from the imperfection of my nature, derive fortitude sufficient to sacrifice my own to the happiness of others. The delicacy of a mind and sensibility of heart like yours are alone equal to such a task, and tho', I assure you with much truth, I believe you are right, it will be in vain for me to profit by an example.

As I always, and ever shall, act without reserve, in every possible circumstance of my life that may affect you, and under the full persuasion that your confidence is as unbounded as mine, – open your heart to me, be the consequences ever so injurious to my happiness, for you must know me but little, if you suppose me capable of putting your peace of mind in competition with my own. Your flattering sollicitude (Mary, your tenderness undoes me; how very strange that what should soothe and comfort can at the same time excite such

[197]

excessive anguish) *'that I should give you in the event of illness or danger, some token that my sentiments respecting you continued the same as at present'* makes too deep an impression for any language to express; would my heart was in your breast, for that alone could make you sensible of the tender and affectionate regard of my dearest Mary's faithful friend

Cha. O'Hara

I must give up, I fear, even the hopes of seeing you before I go, for Admiral Waldegrave shewed me a letter this afternoon from Admiral Cornwallis intimating that, tho' the wind was contrary, if the weather should moderate, he should endeavour to sail.

Farewell, farewell.

On 29 October, still in harbour, O'Hara was asking Mary to date her letters correctly, for she seemed to do so not knowing what she was about – 'je prends déjà le ton de mari.' This gives the impression that Mary was suffering a nervous crisis, added to which – or so wrote the indefatigable Mrs Damer – 'Poor dear Ag, I really do pity her, but I do really pity you, for I had a specimen yesterday morning when she came to me of what you have to go through, and of the little comfort (hard as it seems to say it) that she can on any occasion ever be to you. I mean nothing in particular, only her way of taking up things, her hurry, fidget and confused ideas.'[46]

General O'Hara to Mary Berry[47]   Portsmouth
Saturday, Oct. 31, 1795

Here I am, my Dear, Dear Soul, and here am determined to remain, for I cannot venture to see you again. This self-denial, you are fully convinced, must cost me much, but our meeting to part again afflicts and strikes too deep to be often repeated. Let the pleasing reflection that when we meet again it will be for life, comfort and support us thro' the anxious, tedious hours of our separation.

I believe to have recommended your consulting our friend wither you should, or not, mention to Lord Orford our proposed connection. Upon reconsidering the matter, I would by no means have you think of it, for you owe to his affection, his friendship and the very flattering distinction he has long, constantly and most pointedly shown you, every degree of attention and gratitude, and consequently to keep from him as long as it is possible, the knowledge of an event that, separating you, will overwhelm him with sorrow, and disappointment and defeat all his views and only substantial comfort he enjoys and probably wishes to live for. (My dear Mary, thou art a most extraordinary creature.) In my opinion, the proper time to break it to him will be when you are at the eve of quitting your Father's house for mine, and that communication must be made by yourself. It will be childish in you, and not treating him with the deference and confidence I trust he deserves, to employ any body else. I think I see you pale and trembling, thy dear delicate frame shook to pieces, hesitating what to do; and when I put myself in your place, I feel most forcibly that upon this occasion your emotion must be great, and that reflection, when I consider the cause that agitates you, makes me see my dearest Mary in a point of view of all others most interesting to my heart.

Lord Orford will for his own sake, as well as yours, receive your information kindly. You must, however, be prepared possibly for some sudden, peevish animadversions upon your marriage, some dictated by friendship, and others by resentment. Be that as it may, he has a claim upon your patient hearing, and possibly you may profit from the many truths he will lay before you, drawn from his long experience of the world. He will endeavour to prove what with him admits of no doubt, the excessive folly of burning incense at any other shrine but those of *Wealth* and *Birth*. Poor me, I feel humbled to the dust when I think of either; and when he has talked himself out of arguments, which, *à coup sûr*, will not be till out of breath, preserve a respectful silence, for you will plead in vain to a judge who, being so very differently composed as yourself, it is perfectly impossible you should understand each other.

The Noble Earl takes glitter, show and precedency – all very good things in their way as appendages, but not commanding features – for his guide. Thy sober, chaste mind builds its happiness (God forbid it prove delusive) upon being the comfort, the support, the warm disinterested friend of a Man who has nothing to give but reciprocal feelings. With all the respect and deference I really have for Lord Orford, and making every reasonable allowance for the claim he has upon your gratitude, if he really is your friend, unwarped by selfish considerations, he ought to rejoice at an event you contemplate with

[199]

pleasure, and he ought, from his knowledge of you, to think you perfectly competent to judge for yourself what are the qualities you wish the Man to possess to whom you give your Person and dedicate your time for life.

Having now, my dear Mary, disposed of your *Peur, tant bien que mal*, that I know weighs heavy on you, my next care (for I consider myself already wedded to you, and bound to share all your troubles and anxieties, which I do du fond de mon coeur), is to soothe your throbbing breast with respect to your Father, Sister, and your other self [Mrs Damer] – they must know, as they do not understand either of us, that when you are mine, you will be as much theirs as ever you was, and as they are all independent Beings, they may be with us as much as they please.

God bless and preserve you in the same sentiments you now experience for your truly affectionate and sincere friend,

Chas. O'Hara

During the delay in Portsmouth harbour there is no mention of Mary going to see O'Hara, chaperoned by Mrs Damer. Is it too much to suspect that now he knew the love affair was over (it coloured the whole of Mary's future life), he had already suited himself with a mistress or two to sail with him to Gibraltar? A line in Lord Houghton's biography of the Misses Berry gives a slant on the matter: 'General O'Hara, under the influence which, it is said, accompanied him to his post, broke off the engagement ....'[48]

It was not till 11 November that O'Hara sailed for Gibraltar. In the first day or two of November Mary was already at Park Place desperately in need of Mrs Damer's understanding and sympathy. By Walpole's letter of 4 November it is clear that he is aware, perhaps not of the strength of Mary's affection for O'Hara or of their engagement, but that he himself is being relegated to a lower place. Mrs Damer, writing one of her lengthy letters from Grosvenor Square, admitted that she could not be sorry that he 'shows his most unfair crossness to you now, because I know it is there and exists in his breast. I do not from your account feel uneasy at his indisposition, and I am sure that when I think of what his dinners are, and how he eats them, I wonder he and his cat are not sick together every day for their dessert.'[49] (In such wounding ways as these, Mrs Damer indicated her jealousy of Walpole's devotion to Mary; it must have been of solace that Mary turned to her as confidante.)

To Park Place   [Strawberry Hill]
                                    Wednesday, November 4, 1795
You commanded me, mighty princess, to write to you, and I said I write best when I have nothing to say – no flattery to the moments when I have anything to relate – however, were the case so, this letter would be perfection!
                                                  Thursday, 5th
You! – you are no more a judge of what makes a good letter than Dame Piozzi, who writes bad English when she ought to be exactly accurate, but mistakes vulgarisms for synonymous to elegancies – hear the oracle Lear

Nothing can come of Nothing – speak again –

So I will, when I really have anything to say – at present, not finding the inpsirer Nothing very procreative, I shall only tell you that I have a little gout in my right foot, and though I had ordered the coach for Cliveden last night, I could not go, though I am easier today and think it will not be a fit, but I shall propose to my Agnes & Co. to come to me.

To Park Place   [Strawberry Hill]
                                    9 o'clock, [November] 6, 1795
A storm is *something*, and in a village a big event, and I have now a wherewithal for writing. We had a tremendous tempest of wind this morning before 5 o'clock; it did not wake me till the close, though it has done me mischief. It has levelled the two tall elms in the meadow beyond the clump of walnut trees, and snapped two others short in the grove near the terrace; it ripped off the tiles from the corner of the printing-house, Kirgate rose in a panic. It demolished some large trees in the angle of the common, and threw down one of the vast elms before Hardinge's door; but it fortunately fell towards the river, or had crushed Ragman's Castle, and perhaps some of the inhabitants. At Lord Dysart's [Ham House] it has felled sixteen trees, which I suppose will only improve the prospect, which he always

[201]

made keep its distance. Havoc too I hear is made in Bushy Park – other distant mails are not yet arrived -

Saturday

Good morrow. One of our bricklayers, who is at work on *our* new icehouse, says there has been a great slaughter of chimneys in London, which I conclude will raise the price of smoke like everything else; and two houses have been blown down, but as truth does not know where, it was probably her toad-eater Mrs *Theysay* who told her so.

Strawberry Hill
November 22, 1795

The night you left me, I went to Cambridge's to advance my £50 for the potatoes for the poor here. He told me a curious circumstance, that the great elm which fell into the Thames at Marble Hill in the late hurricane, killed several fishes. It is new for gudgeons to be knocked on the head by a tree in their own element.

As Mr C. was peroring to me, I did not hear his boy who entered at nine to tell me my coach was come, so I trespassed half an hour on the prayers – I did not stay till one in the morning as with you at Teddington – I think I should have found out the length of the time – indeed I did now wonder that nine o'clock came so slowly, and did ring the bell – however old Cherrytrees was very goodhumoured and gracious about my having entrenched on the canonical hour.

Strawberry
November 24, 1795

My own story will be very brief. Being a very fine evening, I did go last night to Lady Juliana [Penn]. There was one large bouncing woman that I wish you had seen – she was all in the reigning white, but with an ample stream of blood-coloured ribband flowing from her chin to what would have been her knees, had they not spread like t'other side, so that she seemed to be a large carcass of hog into which a butcher had just stuck his knife.

There I heard of the conquest of the *Cape of Good Hope* – I always direct myself to believe in good omens and never in bad, so this is of the propitious side. It will keep up the credit of our navy a little, which has been sadly hurricaned – and we shall have many

[202]

trinkets to go to market with at the Peace – yet I had rather we had taken one seaport in France than all the Capes and Corsicas in the ocean.

My former old gardener, who lives near the church and is superannuated, t'other day in a feverish delirium flung himself out of a window thirteen feet from the ground, and yet was but little bruised.

Mr Coxe comes to me tomorrow to read some more chapters of my father's life to me – I am exceedingly pleased at its being undertaken by so very able a hand – but I shall wish it not to be published till I am gone. As there will not be a sentence of my writing in it, though I have given him some information, I should be sorry to have a tittle imputed to my partiality, though I religiously told him nothing but the truth. Even when he consulted me on his memoirs of my uncle, I said to him, 'Though I acknowledge that I had the strongest reasons for having great prejudices to my uncle, I will not suffer those prejudices to influence me in what I shall say to you of him' – and indeed I believe you will not find in Mr Coxe's account of that man one hint of the injuries he did me, of which I have told you, nor of his base ingratitude to his brother in regard to the descendants of the latter – but keep all this part of my letter to yourself at present.

The last letters of the year speak mainly of illness: Mary in North Audley Street suffering from some ill-defined trouble, possibly a collapse from fatigue and strain, causing anxiety to Walpole and the main reason for his fidgets, until he too underwent a severe attack of gout lasting some two months. 'From the little finger of my left, through all that hand, wrist and elbow, I am a line of gout,' he wrote to Lady Ossory in mid-December. It would have been at the end of this year (1795) or else at the very beginning of the the next (as Mary told a friend eleven years later) that she confessed to Walpole that in a few months (as she then thought), she 'was to leave him for a still dearer friend and a nearer connection, and satisfied with having acted up to the most scrupulous, the most romantic ideas of the duties of friendship', she had indulged herself 'in all rational hopes and fair prospects which seemed then open to her still enthusiastic mind. Alas! Alas! all too soon cruelly crushed, and since levelled with the dust.'[50]

[Strawberry Hill]
December 3, 1795

The note your father has brought, gives me great comfort by telling me your pain is gone. Your headaches return so very frequently, that I apprehend there must be some latent cause in your constitution, and that I am earnest to have explored and discovered, that antidotes may be applied. I cannot be easy while I apprehend perpetual returns.

[Strawberry Hill]
Sunday, December 6, 1795

It will be impossible for me to be in town before Tuesday, and I must want the sight of you for a day longer. I shall certainly come on Tuesday, for I have various threats of the gout, both in the left wrist and foot, yet as neither is swelled or inflamed I do not apprehend it will be a fit. I suppose you will think I have stayed too long in the country and caught cold – which is far from being the case. The weather has been soft as in the beginning of autumn, and I have not been out of these two rooms since Wednesday morning last. I hate to trouble others with complaints of natural infirmities, and perceive how sensibly I decay, I like much to be much alone, and care not how few I see, except the very, very few that I really love.

There are no letters between Walpole and Mary at the beginning of 1796; presumably they were all much together at Strawberry Hill. Three letters only exist from Mary to O'Hara; the first is of touching domesticity.

Mary Berry to General O'Hara[51]   [c. January 1796]

Setting to work with a pen, ink and paper and an Arithmetic upon the plan of life you at first proposed, my dear friend, I find, as indeed I told you at the time, that it would cost much more than you had any idea of, and much more even than the funds of which you then supposed yourself possessed. But upon a smaller scale (on the accuracy of which from my experience in my father's house I think you may depend) I have made out a plan which, I am persuaded, includes every comfort necessary to a small establishment in London upon the only footing that you and I should like any establishment – that of order and regular expence, not of pinching economy and pitiful savings of which I am as incapable as yourself, *c'est tout dire*. You who are perfectly unacquainted with the details of an Establishment in this town, will, I daresay be astonished at the expence of every article. I have taken them up at their present high price, and made such a liberal allowance upon most of them that I think we should never exceed and might sometimes be within the mark; but upon a less sum, that is to say, at less than the rate of this sum per annum, I don't think you could possibly live comfortably to yourself in London. I mean seeing agreeably all those friends who should prefer a neat plain dinner or supper, and *our agreeable society* to a French Cook and dull company.

You will see I have cut off all *your* extravagances, your saddle horses, your separate carriage, and one of your men-servants; and yet I have not reduced my calculation within the limits you prescribed; but I have to observe that our expences whether we were in the kingdom of Gibraltar, visiting the Pyramids, or on any other travelling scheme whatsoever would everywhere be considerably less than established in London, – and that whenever you find such establishment inconvenient or imprudent, I shall be the person most eager to break it up and most willing to accompany you to any other part of the globe. I must tell you, too, that upon my father's talking to me upon the subject of affairs, which he has done since we parted, I find him quite unwilling that I should be a burthen to you, and determined that every thing I can have from him shall belong to you as soon as I do myself.

Enough upon the subject of money, on which I know we both think much alike. I am aware of all it advantages, take all it procures, and know how little it can be done without; but *the more* or the *less* never made happiness, and when weighed against the real satisfactions of the heart is not (even to the sober eye of reason) a feather in the scale.

[Enclosure]
One pair of job horses inclusive of coachman's wages
   for eight months of the year   125. 0. 0.
Annual repairs to carriage about   25. 0. 0.

Two men servants at £20 a piece	40. 0. 0.
An Upper man at the wages of	55. 0. 0.
Wages of 4 women servants, a housekeeper, a cook under her, a house maid and a lady's maid	58. 0. 0.
Liveries for the 3 men servants and the coachman	80. 0. 0.
House rent and taxes	200. 0. 0.
Coals	50. 0. 0.
Candles	25. 0. 0.
Beer	25. 0. 0.
Wine	100. 0. 0.
Housekeeping, at the rate of £10 a week or £40 a month	480. 0. 0.
	£1263. 0. 0.
To you	800. 0. 0.
To me	200. 0. 0.
	£2263. 0. 0.

There were other letters, several from O'Hara, now lost, probably destroyed. From a reference Mary made to one of hers of early April it is apparent that she had already grave doubts of his conduct. Had she perhaps heard that he had taken up with two women in Gibraltar by each of whom he had, or would have, children? O'Hara's letter, probably destroyed, to which the following is a reply, must have been the most devastating blow and, couched in a manner in which he placed the blame on her, wounding in the extreme.

Mary Berry to General O'Hara[52]   April 27, [1796]
All my doubts are at an end. – You have at last thought fit to speak a language which no prepossession can mistake, nor no indulgence palliate. – I have now received your letters of the 26th February and 30th March. Make yourself perfectly easy. – Your having *'consented to become my husband'* as you are pleased to express yourself to Mrs D. will entail none of the evils you so much dread.

My last letter of the 4th April will have shown you my unwillingness to believe and my determination not to admit, the only interpretation your long silences and the very improper style of your letter could bear, till sanctioned by yourself – that sanction you have at last fully and completely given in two letters whose *least* faults are their being a farrago of *inconsistencies* and *contradictions*, both with regard to *me* and *yourself*. – They are expressed in terms which I believe were never before used to any *Gentlewoman*, not to say any woman of common sense and common spirit. – They have, however, *completely* done their business, yet so persuaded have you chose to be (from what part of my character I am perfectly at a loss to guess) that, whatever your conduct, *I am determined to marry you*, that I fancy you will hardly now believe your own eyes or my assertions. You desire *me* to be explicit and to be serious (as if *I* have ever been otherwise) but I shall now be explicit in your *own words*, which as they are generally very extraordinary ones, may perhaps (to yourself) be clearer than any others. I do then '*indeed suppose, and verily believe that you have recourse to a thousand falsehoods and imaginary apprehensions merely as a cover to disguise the real cause, you having altered your mind and not meaning to marry.*' Even supposing your intentions with regard to marriage were not really altered, then your conduct towards me for these last six months has been such as '*justly to have forfeited my good opinion with all its inevitable consequences, – my affection and esteem.*'

My frank, open, honourable nature would have preferred and given you credit for a more immediate, a more decided and a more *Gentlemanlike* avowal of a change in your sentiments; it would have spared me many months of cruel anxiety, and when I had ceased to consider you as a lover, your character would to me have remained inviolate as a friend. You have chosen it otherwise so fare you well, and if ever in future you feel the want or require the comfort of a sincere, intelligent, affectionate friend, remember the *pains* you took to eradicate sentiments which you will then no longer mistrust and of which no power on earth but yourself could have robbed you. Farewell.

April 29th

In your letter of the 27th March you talk to *me* of keeping *you* in doubt and uncertainty – to *me*, who, till the receipt of your last letters, had no more doubt of becoming your wife than she has now of having nothing more to do with the man who can bargain for tyranny beforehand, and would accept of that being for his wife who he found would patiently submit to ill-treatment.

The distress Mary felt over her broken love-affair would have been obvious to those who cared for her and the extract that follows (all that remains) implies that she had disclosed the whole of her story to Walpole.

From Mary Berry   May 19, 1796
But let me assure you (though I trust you know me too well to doubt it), that whether in or out of spirits, happy or otherwise, every new occurrence of my life only seems to give me fresh instances of your consoling friendship, to increase my confidence in it, and to convince me that I may flatter myself with having inspired *one* sentiment at least as lasting as it is rare. Farewell.

Since the day of her marriage to the Prince of Wales, Princess Caroline had suffered from his hostile treatment. Her vulgarity and want of personal cleanliness had increased his distaste but as his association with Lady Jersey was well-known and was condemned by the public, their sympathy for the time being was with her. On the first occasion of her visit to the opera house, Bianchi's Antigona *was given; a second visit followed when the audience again applauded her presence.*

Meanwhile the Prince had paid £2,100 for a year's lease of The Grange, the Drummond family's shooting box at Northington, Hampshire (not yet the Barings' great neo-classical house it was to become in the next century). His stay there was for no more than the month of June during which time the Jerseys were frequently present. When Walpole had visited The Grange in the middle of the century he had remarked on the stairs and cupolae'd corridor as being 'models of the purist and most classic antiquity'.[53]

[Berkeley Square]
May 30, 1796, 3 o'clock
A million thanks for your letter, though with my poor unwriting hand I don't think I can have time to answer a quarter of it before the post departs. I have had people till this instant and Kirgate is not at home.

The scene at the opera on Saturday was much stronger than even the papers represent it. The Princess first retired, but the D. of Leeds persuaded her to stand up and curtsey – she did and then all the house rose, and then every woman as well as men, in every part clapped incessantly and repeated it – and it was well *two* other persons were not there [the Prince and Lady Jersey], as insults were loudly declared to be intended, and on their not appearing, 'God save the *King*' was called for and sung, with the same view. Their Majesties were not there.

My fingers are too bad to suffer my writing more, and I [am] sure you will forgive your

O.

Walpole was unable to accompany the party of 5 June to the Royal Academy Summer Exhibition on Joseph Farington's invitation; his limbs were so weakened by months of suffering from gout that he could scarcely stand without the help of two servants. Mary and Agnes Berry, Mrs Damer and Lysons joined Farington at the Academy and Mary admired one of the artist's landscapes.

Berkeley Square
June 2, 1796

I hope the post will bring this to you before you set out tomorrow, which I do not write so much to answer your letter, which I might have delayed for a day, as to remind you, that you must return tomorrow, if you mean to go to the exhibition on Sunday with Mr Farington, who lives at *No. 35 in Charlotte Street Rathbone Place* – I speak very disintrestedly, for I am sure I shall not be able to accompany you, as my leg is not yet well.

I did not suppose you could send me my commissions on Monday, it was so tempestuous, that nobody who had not a rage for going abroad at the very moment she had proposed to do anything, could have taken it for a day suited for a jaunt into the country; much less was it one for your crossing my lawn.

The crisis ripens, the universal applause was repeated on Tuesday at the opera, but nothing offensive heard. I think *her* appearance was well advised; her absence would have fallen on her husband and been imputed to him; to suppose that she sought popularity would have offended nobody but him, which at this moment could not have made the case worse. He is said to be gone to the Grange for a month – Lady J[ersey] removed three days ago to her daughter's new house, and her new child is dead, will probably move farther, for her present position is not tenable.

Recollecting the loss of the Houghton collection of pictures to Catherine of Russia, Walpole in other circumstances would have acquired one of the eight pictures which Richard Westall RA exhibited at the Royal Academy that summer. This was Hesiod Instructing the Greeks, *commended by the critics. The second to which he referred was* Sappho Chanting the Hymn of Love.

[Berkeley Square]
June 25, 1796, in the evening
George Nicol brought me yesterday two of Mr Westall's pictures that were in the Exhibition. I was astonished. Were the Houghton collection mine now I should be glad to have the Hesiod in it; it is by far one of the finest compositions ever painted in England, the groups are so finely detached, and there is still so much harmony in the whole, a favourite object with me (though I am not deserving to be the principal one), that I should not haggle long about its great price of £150, though, being in water colours, I fear it may be changeable. The figure of Sappho in its companion is beautiful beyond description and a few of the other figures are very good too; but there are some large detached masses, some of great light and some of great shade, which destroy the unity of the whole, which I think are rarely to be found in such a given space. There! I am tired, besides having nothing more to say.
PS. Newer news of last night.

It was affirmed to me that the King had written to Lady Jersey to dismiss her, and to forbid her appearing at Carlton House. I did not believe a syllable of it – nay, I do not and shall not yet. However, I think I may venture to advise you to be ready to change part of your creed by Tuesday next, when, as great secrets of state will not keep three days, any more than positive resolutions, *moi qui n'opine pas, opine*, that you may chance to hear the contents of a letter, or perchance see a copy of it in the newspapers, from an affectionate father-in-law to a tender daughter-in-law, acquainting her with the dutiful submission of the prodigal son, who *[consents]* to the removal of the mote out of his lady's eye – further, this deponent saith not.

On 16 July, the date of the following letter, Mary had received one from O'Hara dated 20 June. She replied immediately and with her letter ends what we know of her engagement and of her cherished hopes for the future.

Mary Berry to General O'Hara[54]   Twickm
July 16, 1796

Alas, my dear friend, how have you trifled and *doubted* away both your own happiness and mine! – I have this moment received your letter of the 20th June.

The high opinion, the confidence and the affection which you know I have so long had for you when considering you merely in the light of a friend, still assures me that what you say in your letter is strictly true or at least what you believe to be so. And as far as I am able to comprehend your real meaning and wishes from your letter; it is this: – That your *intentions* with regard to me have never altered, but (to use your own words) *'when separation gave you time to reflect and see what would be probably the result of our marriage considered on the serious side'*, such doubts and fears of our mutual happiness arose in your mind as you thought necessary to communicate to me. Remember it is not of *this* I complain: on the contrary, you know my principal reason for objecting to our marriage before you left England was that it might be sanctioned by reflexion, but the moment that reflexion, made it appear to you in a different light, the moment such doubts and fears took possession of your mind, that moment you should have decidedly and openly owned *your* altered feelings, instead of only starting injurious doubts which your always making to originate in *my* sentiments instead of your own, together with the frequent levity of your style, have alone thus long deceived me both as to your conduct and your real wishes.

My constitution and character does not like yours *'urge and press me on with giant steps upon every occasion'*. On the contrary,

[211]

obliged from my earliest youth not only to think for myself, but to think for those who ought to have thought for me, I have learnt to make giant steps in nothing but thoughtfulness and precaution. I had given the subject of our union my most serious consideration in every point of view in which *I* could place it, before I agreed to it, and before we parted. No separation would then have made any difference in my opinion till I was convinced it had altered yours, but the instance this was the case to have concealed it from me would have been treachery to my all-confiding affection and sacrificing every real principle of honour to a phantom that would have made us both miserable. All I have to complain of is that you did not sooner explain yourself in clearer and less offensive language, and did not continue for months together writing to the being who, by your own account, you still continued to love, letters whose style, arguments, and general import deceived not only my partial judgement but that of my father, that of my sister. Can you *possibly* think that those people, all warmly partial to you, should unite in wilfully misunderstanding and misconstruing your letters, if they had been in any respect such as reason and affection should have dictated to a person in my situation, at such a distance, and who always addressed you with the perfect, unbounded confidence and affection which she always felt for you? Can you, I say, think this POSSIBLE? And yet in your letter of to-day you still continue to talk of *your* having been '*so ungenerously and unhandsomely misconstrued.*'

What then remains for me but, while I acquit you of any dishonourable charge in your *intentions*, to lament, which, believe me, I do heartily, an obstinate wrong-headedness which in despite even of your own wishes will ever prevent your judging fairly of my character – to lament that the false and profligate ideas which I know you entertain of women in general, and which I have so often and so seriously combated long before I thought myself at all concerned in your opinion, should have so pervaded your sentiments and so falsified your view of every individual, as even to prevent your warm and excellent heart indulging in its natural and unbiased feelings towards those best formed to understand and sympathize with them? Sincerely I do pity a disposition which I know must inflict upon itself *almost* as much pain as it has given me, for your natural good sense will often, for a time, get the better of these vile prejudices, and you will then feel that while they deprive you of every thing that can give rational comfort, they supply nothing in its place but unavailing precautions, useless doubts, and ungenerous sentiments.

You say you are '*certain it will be in vain to plead against prepossession and prejudice as strongly taken up as mine appears to be.*' You see I have neither '*prepossession*' nor '*prejudice*', and that the moment you speak seriously, I seriously acquit you of any change in your *intentions*; but how can I acquit you of what you nether own nor attempt a justification of – your various and repeated misconceptions and want of confidence in my character? How can I acquit you of eternally construing the frank, unaffected dictates of my affection for you into a determination of marriage of *any sort*, and an eagerness for *this* in particular, which in the very next sentence, perhaps, of the same letter, you declared it impossible for me to like or wish? Tell me how I can acquit your *understanding* of all this, for your heart, I still believe excellent – and I may still have the comfort of thinking of you as I did six months ago.

I have still a high value for your friendship and good opinion, both of which I *feel* I deserve, but I will never purchase either by the baseness of saying I regret a conduct guided throughout by the calm dictates of the sincerest and most rational affection for you, tempering the consideration ever due to oneself; a conduct which I am certain, were you an unprejudiced spectator you yourself would be the first to approve. When you talk of '*the tone of harsh and bitter invective with which you have been treated*' I have only to conclude that you weigh your *own* words as little as you do those of others. I shall cease *endeavouring* to convince myself that the O'Hara with whom I have been corresponding is the same warmhearted, rational, affectionate O'Hara with whom I parted in October. Farewell.

He would never fade from her memory and she would always claim that had the separation not taken place 'I should never have had to complain of him nor he to doubt me'. When in Paris in 1802, seated in an opera box with Lady Stuart de Rothesay, the British Ambassadress, she heard someone say that the Governor of Gibraltar had died in office, she fell senseless to the floor.[55] In his will of 1800,[56] domiciled at Ewhurst Common, Surrey, he bequeathed to his 'loving wife' Sarah, all his silver, furniture, china, 1,799 guineas, all other effects and estate including 'prize money which I am entitled to or interested in on account of the capture of sundry little ships off the Island of St Helena'.

Very much later, when Mary was past eighty years of age, she opened the packet of letters which she had kept since her parting with O'Hara. Before closing it up she added a note:[57]

This parcel of letters relate to the six happiest months of my long and insignificant existence, although these six months were accompanied by fatiguing and unavoidable uncertainty, and by the absence of every thing that could constitute present enjoyment. But I looked forward to a future existence which I felt for the first time, would have called out all the powers of my mind and all the warmest feelings of my heart connected and supported by a being, who thoroughly knew my character and but for the cruel absence which separated us, would never have for a moment doubted, that we should have materially contributed to each other's happiness. These prospects which satisfied at once both my heart and my understanding served me to pass cheerfully a long winter of delays and uncertainty, by keeping my mind firmly riveted on their accomplishment. A concatenation of unfortunate circumstances – the political state of Europe making absence a necessity, and even frequent communication impossible – letters lost and delayed – all certainty of meeting more difficult – questions unanswered doubts unsatisfied. All these circumstances combined in the most unlucky manner, crushed the fair fabric of my happiness, not at one fell shock, but by the slow mining misery of loss of confidence, of unmertited complaints, of finding by degrees misunderstandings, and the firm rock of mutual confidence crumbling under my feet, while my bosom for long could not banish a hope that all might yet be set right. And so it would, had we ever met for twenty-four hours. But he remained at his government at Gibraltar till his death, in 1802. And I, forty-two years afterwards, on opening these papers which had been sealed ever since, receive the conviction that some feelings in *some* minds are indelible.

M.B. Oct. 1844

Among these papers was an account of a dream,[58] *dreamt in old age,*

*that she was 'walking with Mrs Damer by a southern shore, young
again and married to General O'Hara'. She was perfectly happy – so
happy that she prayed to die 'before this beautiful vision of life fades,
and fade it must from my senses'.*

*Numbered in months the early dream had lasted barely nine, but
the recollection of happiness in her love for O'Hara was a life-long
memory.*

*Soon after writing her last letter to O'Hara, Mary went to Bognor,
relying on change of air and scene to restore her shaken constitution.
She diversified her stay with a visit to Goodwood House. Mrs Damer
was also there, the Duchess of Richmond being her own half-sister.*

*William Gerard Hamilton had acquired the sobriquet of 'Single-
speech Hamilton' by his celebrated maiden speech as Member of
Parliament for Petersfield in 1775. Thereafter he was to hold other
prominent appointments.*

[Entirely in Kirgate's hand]   Strawberry Hill
                                                August 9, 1796
I have just received such a long letter from you of the 6th that if I
attempted to answer it with my own hand, I should be two days
engraving it.

You may be assured that Lady J. does not go to Brighton, nor any
of the connection, or disconnection. Mrs Lisle is commissioned to
search for a villa for her mistress, which she has not yet found. The
Countess drives about in a plain coach without arms.

I have little faith in an invasion at present, the unparalleled spirit,
activity and cleverness, of our seamen will not tempt the French
sailors much to embark; they may attempt to run in a few vessels here
and there into open coasts of the three kingdoms, and they do give
out that they will try one more campaign against us, *corps à corps*.

Have you heard of Single-speech Hamilton's mad will? He bequeathed the landed estate to [the third] Lord Egremont, and ten
thousand pounds to the young Lady Spencer, and then said, he was
very sorry that both land and money had been entailed by his father,
and that he only made the bequest to show his kind disposition
towards them.

The Duchess of Devonshire has been in great danger of losing her
sight, by catching cold very indiscreetly; they have saved her eyes by

[215]

almost strangling her with a handkerchief, and forcing all the blood up into her head, and then bleeding her with leeches.This is all I have to tell you, but a few words on myself. I take the air every morning in my coach, and sit an hour out upon the lawn, and crawl a little about between two servants; and do think I have gained a grain of strength.

Most of the neighbourhood is dispersed; the House of Orange, (which is nothing to me) are gone to Nuneham, Oxford, and Blenheim. The Murrays to make a visit somewhere for a fortnight. The Mackinzeys to Brighton, for his rheumatism: The young Mounts are upon their mountain.

By his celebrated miniature of Mrs Fitzherbert in a large hat, Richard Cosway leapt to fame and with the Prince of Wales as his patron he became a very popular miniature painter. The death of a beautiful daughter and only child, contrary to Walpole's speculation, afforded him deep grief.

Fanny Burney (Madame D'Arblay) had published her third novel, Camilla, *in five volumes, this year.It had not elicited much praise from Walpole who nevertheless thought 'her talents wasted in the folding of muslins', but her father, Dr Burney, was proud of his daughter's success. Owing to ailing health she had resigned her employment as second keeper of the robes to Queen Charlotte and had married Count D'Arblay, a French émigré.*

The properties Walpole recommended to Mary's attention were all in Sussex; Uppark and Petworth House were late seventeenth century, Stansted, seventeenth and eighteenth.

[Strawberry Hill]
Tuesday, Aug. 16, 1796

Though I this morning received your Sunday's full letter, it is three o'clock before I have a moment to begin answering it, and must do it myself, for Kirgate is not at home. First came in Mr Barrett, and then Cosway, who has been for some days at Mr Udney's with his wife; she is so afflicted for her only little girl – the man Cosway does not seem to think that much of his loss belonged to him: he romanced with his usual vivacity. Next arrived Dr Burney, on his way to Mrs Boscawen. He asked me about the deplorable *Camilla* –

alas! I have not recovered of it enough to be loud in its praise. I am glad however to hear that she has realised about £2,000 – and the worth (no doubt) of as much in honours at Windsor, where she was detained three days, and where even Mons. Darbelay was allowed to dine.

I rejoice at your bathing promising so well. If the beautiful fugitive [Lady Jersey] from Brighthelmstone dips too, the waves will be still more salutary.

[The rest of the letter is in Kirgate's hand.] I like your going to survey castles and houses.

Wednesday after breakfast

I resume the thread of my letter. You had not examined Arundel Castle enough, for you do not mention the noble monuments in alabaster of the Fitzalans, one of whom bragged of having married Adelizia, widow of Henry I. In good sooth, they were somewhat defaced by Cromwell having mounted his cannon on the roof to batter the castle, of which, when I saw it, he had left little but ruins, and they were choked up by a vile modern brick house, which I know Solomon [11th Duke of Norfolk] has pulled down, for he came hither two years ago to consult me about Gothicizing his restoration of the castle. I recommended Mr Wyat. There are other splendid seats to be seen within your reach: as Petworth, and Standstead, and Uppark.

As Agnes says she has promised I should give you an account of a visit I have lately had, I will, before anybody comes in. It was from a Mr Pentycross, a clergyman schoolmaster of Wallingford, of whom I had heard nothing for eight and twenty years, and then having only known him as Blue-coat boy from Kingston; and how that happened he gave me his account last week. He was born with a poetic impetus, and walked over hither with a copy of verses by no means despicable, which he begged old Margaret to bring up to me; she refused, he supplicated, at last she told him, that her master was very learned, and that if he would write something in the learned languages, especially in French, she would present his poem to me: in the meantime, she yielded, I saw him, and let her show him the house. I never heard his name again till this winter, when I received a letter from him from his place of residence, with high compliments of some of my editions, and beseeching me to give him a print of myself, which I did send to him. In the Christmas holidays he came to town for a few days, and called in Berkeley Square, but it was when I was too ill to see anybody. He then left a most humble and modest letter, only begging that some time or other I would give him leave to see Strawberry Hill. I sent him a note by Kirgate, that should he come to town in the summer, he should certainly see my house. Accordingly, I let him know that if he could fix any day in this month I would give him a dinner and a bed. He jumped at the offer, named Wednesday last and came. However, I considered that to pass a whole day with this unknown being might be rather too much. I got Lysons the parson from Putney to meet him; but it would not have been necessary, for I found my Blue-coat boy grown to a very sensible, rational, learned and remaining a most modest personage, with an excellent taste for poetry, for he is an enthusiast for Dr Darwin; but, alas, infinitely too learned for me, for in the evening, upon questioning him about his own vein of poetry, he humbly drew out a paper with proposition forty-seven of Euclid turned into Latin verse, I shrunk back and cried, 'Oh dear Sir, how little you know me! I have forgotten almost the little Latin I knew, and was always so incapable of learning mathematics, that I could not even get by heart the multiplication table as blind Professor Sanderson honestly told me, above three-score years ago, when I went to his lecture at Cambridge.' After the first fortnight, he said to me, 'Young man, it would be cheating you to take your money, for you never can learn what I am trying to teach you.' I was exceedingly mortified, and cried; for being a Prime Minister's son I had firmly believed all the flattery with which I had been assured that my parts were capable of anything. I paid a private instructor for a year, but at the year's end, was forced to own Sanderson had been in the right.

To Bognor   Strawberry Hill
                                                             August 24, 1796
Bathe on, bathe on, and wash away all your complaints: the sea air and such an oriental season must cure everything but positive decay and decrepitude – on me they have no more effect than they would have on an Egyptian queen who has been embowelled and preserved in her sycamore *étui* ever since dying was first invented and people notwithstanding liked to last forever, though even in a pyramid.

In short Mr Huitson [his surgeon] has teased me so much about jumbling my relics, that I have aired them every morning [remainder in

Kirgate's hand] in the coach for this fortnight, and yet you see I cannot write ten lines together! Lady Cecilia lets me call on her at twelve and take her with me, and yet I grow tired of it, and shall not have patience to continue, but shall remain I believe in my mummyhood.

Here is a letter for you from Hannah More, unsealed indeed, for chiefly *à mon attention*. Be so good as to tell her how little I am really recovered, but that I will hammer out a few words as fast, that is, as slowly, as I can to her in return.

Ignorant of what the immediately preceding letters between the correspondents contained, it is only possible to guess at the meaning of Walpole's letter of 7 September in which he reproaches Mary for writing of 'future absences' after the close of her unhappy love-affair. Had she perhaps told him in blunt terms that she had sacrificed her happiness for his sake in refusing to accompany O'Hara to Gibraltar as his wife and that in future she intended to absent herself as she pleased? But, in turn, her communication to him, judging from Agnes's continuation, seems to indicate that she had written in response to a letter from Walpole, accusing her, perhaps, of preferring to stay with others to being his companion at Strawberry Hill. Possibly he had seen her engagement to O'Hara as a betrayal of his own devoted friendship and condemned her for not valuing it at its true worth. By 9 October he had recovered his spirits and Lord Glenbervie reported that he and the Misses Berry 'came in the evening. Lord Orford is so lame as to be carried in and out by his footmen, but when rested was particularly cheerful and full as usual of anecdotes'.[59]

To Bognor Rocks   [Strawberry Hill
                                                    Sept. 7, 1796]
Can you wonder at a heart so affectionate as mine being wounded by some (I am willing to hope, unmeant) expressions in your last letter? Mortified as I have been in finding so little return of a friendship that had been the principal occupation of my whole life, and conscious of having no address, felicity, or arts of attaching those whom I have most wished to please and decayed in spirits and in every agreeable light, I naturally dread being grown a burden to those whom I

chiefly cultivate. The short time I can expect to enjoy my satisfaction, has made me still more apprehensive of those dear moments being abridged; and though I had both friendship and command enough of myself to conceal my chagrin, when I learnt that I was to be deprived of half of my chief blessings for a time that to me would be forever! yet I was too little on my guard, when I heard in the same breath of the danger of losing you being lessened, and yet of *future absences* which might precede what I had most dreaded, and might anticipate even the few days that still be mine!

What I may perhaps have felt more acutely still, was the expression to which I feared I had given cause by *officious importunity*. My jealous affection was alarmed at being told of the *rational* attention and care paid to you by another – it may have been more *rational* – mine I am sure has been incessant and unbounded – It will not lessen – but it shall not be so troublesome.

[Continued by Agnes] I have just been over to our poor old friend and found him finishing his last sentence with great pain and difficulty. The general sense of it will, I am sure, satisfy you as to his affection, and the last phrase which I objected to, you must pity and forgive. I had said so much to him the other day, that I had nothing left but to regret the pain he had given you, and I really believe he is in *some degree* ashamed of it himself, and he particularly begs that you will say no more on the subject in your letters, as he writes with such difficulty and cannot employ Kirgate.

I shall follow your advice about a manservant, but, indeed, I am myself deadly sick of a fine gentleman. Lady Englefield wrote me word of one she has seen, who she thinks worth my seeing, though she fears after William's magnificence I may not think him well-looking enough. I am to see him on Friday morning, but certainly will not fix till I have had time to think about it and give you some account of his appearance – though I should like to have settled before you come home to be plagued by them. As to William, he has offered to stay as long as we please, but I don't wish to be obliged to him in any way. I have had a long talk with Sally, who offers to do her best as cook, and we are very good friends, but she very quietly told me that she never intended to *stop with us the winter,* for it was very *lonesome* and she had *stopped* long enough, etc., etc., – and as I find it would be quite vain to ask her to stay, I shall say no more to her, but look out for another before we leave the country as she is willing to stay till then –

[Berkeley Square]
Thursday, December 15, past noon, 1796

I had no account of you at all yesterday, but in Mrs Damer's letter, which was rather better than the preceding. I am grown a dull old tabby and have no 'quips and cranks and wanton wiles' left.

The House of Commons sat till half an hour after three this morning, on Mr Pitt's loan to the Emperor [of Austria] when it was approved by a majority of above two hundred. Mr Fox was more temperate than was expected; Mr Grey did not speak; Mr Sheridan was very entertaining: several were convinced and voted for Mr Pitt, who had gone down determined against it. The Prince came to town t'other day ill, was blooded twice, but has now a strong eruption upon his skin, which will probably be of great service to him. Sir Charles Blagden has been with the Duchess of Devonshire, and found her much better than he expected. Her look is a little altered; she suffers but little, and finds herself benefited by being electrified.

I have received a compliment today very little expected by a superannuated old Etonian. Two tickets from the gentlemen of Westminster School, for their play of Monday next. I excused myself as civilly and respectfully as I could, on my utter impossibility of attending them. Adieu! I hope this will be the last letter I shall write before I see you.

It was to be his last letter to his dear Mary Berry. A frame weakened by lengthy attacks of gout could scarcely withstand a 'consuming fever which came to increase his general debility.' [60] *Having lost its elasticity and having no employment, artistic or literary, to occupy its attention, his mind wandered while blame and complaints to those nearest to him in affection were perpetual. During these weeks the Berrys, now at North Audley Street, were constantly by his side. At the beginning of January 1797 Lord Glenbervie, that intelligent, scholarly, vain, that most welcome-in-society Lord Glenbervie, recorded in his diary: 'I found at Lord Orford's the two Berrys, the eldest with her eagle eyes and manner – if not to threaten, to command. Agnes more mild if less beautiful.'* [61]

Mary Berry takes up the account of Walpole's last days:

When not immediately suffering from pain, his mind was tranquil and cheerful. He was still capable of being amused, and of taking some part in the conversation; but during the last weeks of his life, when fever was superadded to his other ills, his mind became subject to the cruel hallucination of supposing himself neglected and abandoned by the only persons to whom his memory clung, and whom he always desired to see. In vain they recalled to his recollection how recently they had left him, and how short had been their absence; it satisfied him for the moment but the same idea recurred as soon as he had lost sight of them. At last nature, sinking under the exhaustion of weakness, obliterated all ideas but those of mere existence, which ended without a struggle.

A merciful death brought him peace on 2 March 1797.

Epilogue

Walpole's funeral took place at Houghton church eleven days after his death. He lies there in the family vault, the last of Sir Robert Walpole's sons, and the best known.

His will was generous to the Berry sisters. To them he left Little Strawberry House, its grounds and furniture and to each the interest for life of £4,000. In addition to these bequests he left a wooden box marked with an 'O' to Mr Berry, containing his literary papers, published and unpublished, for a new edition of all his works. It was well understood that Mary, in fact, would be the editor. For a year she laboured at her task, scrupulous and persevering, till in 1798 the *Works of Horace Walpole, Earl of Orford*, were published in five volumes. In the next century she edited and published further letters of Walpole as well as works of her own. Her comedy in five acts, *Fashionable Friends*, written in December 1793, was produced at Drury Lane in 1802, but failed to attract.

It has been generally said that throughout the rest of her life – she lived till 1852 – Mary Berry never recovered from her tragic disappointment in the loss of O'Hara's love. Not only the wound remained but also the recollection of the few happy weeks in Cheltenham when she thought herself beloved. However, in 1795 during this unfortunate period, she met Thomas Hope of The Deepdene, as yet unmarried, of Scottish origin and Dutch descent, a patron of the arts and a collector, wielding enormous artistic influence. At the beginning of the next century, and possibly in 1805, a year before Hope married his beautiful but empty-headed wife, Mary endeavoured to marry him. Thomas Hope had confided in Maria Edgeworth in 1819 when she was in England, of Mary's 'courtship of him – disappointment – anger and quarrel' with his future wife.[62]

Agnes's one chance of marriage seems to have been a pallid enterprise. There had been an 'understanding' between her and her cousin Robert Ferguson, of Raith, son of William Berry who had changed his name on creeping into his uncle's affections and appropriating what the Berrys had always contended should have been their inheritance. The uncertainty of her sister's future was one of the reasons Mary had felt unable to accompany O'Hara to Gibraltar. There was an engagement, but when and for how long is not known; all that is certain is that Agnes was engaged in 1804. [63] In 1807 the 7th Earl of Elgin was divorcing his wife, Mary Countess of Elgin, by an Act of Parliament, and Lady Harriet Cavendish writing to her sister in November of that year observed that Mary Berry was 'at the height of worry about Mr Ferguson's affairs',[64] and a few weeks later to the same correspondent, 'she must be in terrible distress about Mr Ferguson who does appear from the trial to have been about as wicked as it is possible to be... the treachery and act was so great that was proved against him'.[65] He married Lady Elgin in 1808.

The sisters (Blackberry and Gooseberry, the nicknames given by the malicious)[66] were always on the move, frequently abroad, chiefly in Paris, or country visits at home. When in London in North Audley Street and later in Mayfair at 8 Curzon Street, they established a *salon* which was eagerly frequented by their vast acquaintanceship.

When in 1819 the Berrys relinquished Little Strawberry Hill, their father having died in 1817, it was with slight feeling of loss on Mary's part; her twenty-two years there, she wrote, had not been happy ones. Had her constant attentions upon Walpole to whom the whole family were under obligation been too much of a burden; her youth gone attending upon an old man? Had the weakness of her father's character, the lack of financial advantages, her own disastrous love affair, and all responsibilities falling upon herself, contributed in casting a shadow on her life? She had many friends through virtue of her association with Strawberry Hill but in after years did she ever regret not having gained a position in the world as the wife of Lord Orford?

As their lives reached into the mid-century they in turn were survivors of another age. Agnes died in January 1852 and Mary followed ten months later on 10 November 1852. They are buried in the same grave at Petersham Church but their consequence reposes within the embrace of Strawberry Hill.

> Farewell, dear Ladies! in your loss
> We feel the past recede,
> The gap, our hands could almost cross,
> Is now a gulf indeed.

Ye, and the days in which your claims
And charms were early known,
Lose substance, and ye stand as names
That Hist'ry makes its own.[67]

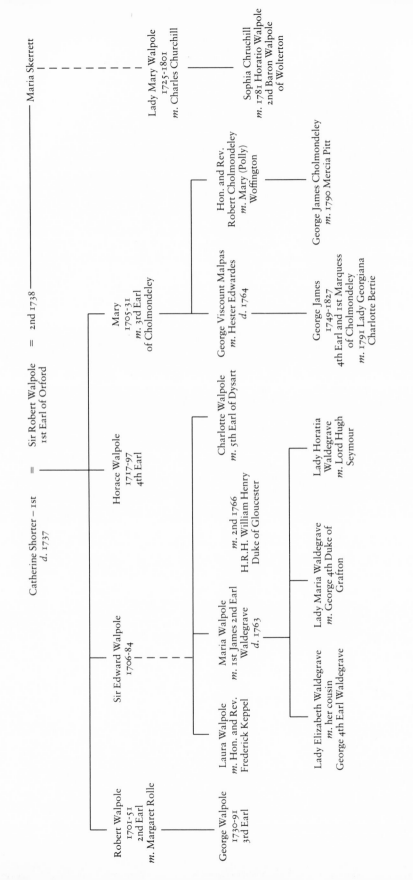

SIMPLIFIED FAMILY TREE SHOWING MOST OF HORACE WALPOLE'S RELATIONS MENTIONED IN THE TEXT

Notes

1   'Miss Berry gave me today the print of the late Lord Orford engraved from a sketch by Lawrence a very short time before his death. It is a head, a mere outline, but the most striking likeness I ever saw, for the features and expression.' Francis Bickley, *The Glenbervie Diaries*, i, 140. See final illustration.

2   Visits to Strawberry Hill, and Professor J. Mordaunt Crook's contribution to *Country Life*, June 1973, 'Strawberry Hill Revisited', have been the basis of this description of Walpole's domain.

3   Houghton, Lord, *Monographs*, 157.

4   The child's name was Charlotte Williams, known as Louchee, D.M. Stuart, *Dearest Bess*, 9.

5   The Brinsley Ford Archive, The Paul Mellon Centre for Studies in British Art.

6   Houghton, 159.

7   Romilly, S.H., *Letters to 'Ivy'*, 118-19.

8   Hemlow, Joyce, *The History of Fanny Burney*, i, 193.

9   On 25 June the whole Court set out for Weymouth, the Queen's two grehounds, Badine and Phillis, accompanying them. The latter, 'un petit Chef-d'Oeuvre de la Nature', had belonged to Frederick the Great and was small, timid and beautiful. The King's first essay of the waters on 7 July was a success. Fanny Burney who was with her royal mistress described how 'a machine follows the Royal one into the sea, filled with fiddlers, who play "God save the King", as his Majesty takes his plunge!' Olwen Hedley, *Queen Charlotte*, 176.

10 According to Mr Cambridge, Walpole had proposed to make Mrs Pepys a third piece (a Tiers Etat) of fig leaves.

11 Fothergill, *Sir William Hamilton*, 117.

12 Bickley, F., *The Glenbervie Diaries*, i, 63.

13 Sichel, W., *The Glenbervie Journals*, 77.

14 Fanny Burney would write of Polly's '*light* though not *forfeited* character' as being 'gay, flighty, entertaining and frisky'. J. Hemlow, *Fanny Burney*, i, 58.

15 There was a variant to the Duchess of Gloucester's inquiry: 'When am I to call Miss Berry my aunt?', and the reply: 'Whenever Miss Berry pleases.' Houghton, 162.

16 Fothergill, *The Strawberry Hill Set*, 92.

17 Lewis, Lady Theresa, *Extracts and Journals*, i, 246.
18 ffrench, Yvonne, *Mrs Siddons*, 152-3.
19 *Glenbervie Journals*, 110.
20 ffrench, *Mrs Siddons*, 142.
21 Granville, Castalia Countess, *Lord Granville Leveson Gower*, ii, 411-12.
22 Parsons, Mrs Clement, *The Incomparable Siddons*, 1909, 172.
23 Walford, E., *Old and New London*, iii, 221.
24 Lady Elizabeth Waldegrave was said to be amiable, gentle and sensible but loving grandeur. It was thought that despite his age, Lord Cardigan's fondness and magnificence joined might obliterate in her consideration his roughness of manners. *Diary and Letters of Madame D'Arblay*, ed. by her niece, 1854, v. 155.
25 Fothergill, *The Cardinal King*, 234, 252.
26 Fothergill, *Mrs Jordan*, 160-1.
27 Fulford, Roger, *Royal Dukes*, 99.
28 Damer, Mrs, *The Berry Papers*, 74, 77.
29 *Letters to the Countess of Ossory*, 1903, iii, 258, 252, 287.
30 Lewis, T., i, 385.
31 Fothergill, *Strawberry Hill*, 257.
32 Bryant, Arthur, *The Years of Endurance*, 119.
33 While Mrs Damer's house-hunting took her to Upper Brook Street, Upper Grosvenor Street and finally to Grosvenor Square, she nevertheless recognized that Berkeley Square was the 'ne plus ultra'.
34 Information derived from *A Short Description of the Isle of Thanet*, 1796, and Murray's *Handbook for Kent*, 1863, 212-13.
35 *The Berry Papers*, 177.
36 Ibid., 177.
37 Ibid., 147.
38 Ibid., 149.
39 Ibid., 142.
40 Ibid., 149-50.
41 Ibid., 159.
42 Ibid., 155.
43 Ibid., 162.
44 Ibid., 166-7.
45 Ibid., 167-8.
46 Ibid., 170.
47 Ibid., 170-3.
48 Houghton, 166.
49 *Berry Papers*, 159.
50 Ibid., 194.
51 Ibid., 179-81.

52 Ibid., 182-3.
53 *Country Life*, J. Redmill, 'The Grange', 8 May 1975.
54 *Berry Papers*, 185-9.
55 Houghton, 171.
56 Public Record Office, London.
57 *Berry Papers*, 194-5.
58 Strachey, Lytton, *Portraits in Miniature*, 118-19.
59 *Glenbervie Diaries*, i, 74.
60 Warburton, E., *Memories of Walpole*, ii, 365.
61 *Glenbervie Diaries*, i, 116.
62 Inglis-Jones, E., *The Great Maria*, 152; Watkin, David, *Thomas Hope*,
    18. In 1813 Miss Edgeworth had found the Berrys' house and gatherings
    'without any comparison the most agreeable' she had seen in town:
    'quite like French society'. In 1819 she thought the sisters dashing and
    fashionable – 'the French *ton*, French gestures but not well bred low
    French voices – *Moi je dis* in every tone. We saw quite enough to know
    that we wished to see no more.' Colvin, C., ed. *Maria Edgeworth*, 61,
    184.
63 Leveson Gower, Sir G. and Palmer, I. edd., *Hary-O*, 220.
64 Ibid., 232.
65 Ibid., 276.
66 Strachey, L. 115.
67 Houghton, 222.

Bibliography

ALL BOOKS ARE PUBLISHED IN LONDON
UNLESS OTHERWISE STATED

Baker, H. Barton, *Our Old Actors*, 1881.
Bickley, Francis, ed., *The Diaries of Lord Glenbervie*, i, ii, 1928.
Bryant, Arthur, *The Years of Endurance*, 1944.
Chancellor, E. Beresford, *History and Antiquities of Richmond*, 1894.
Cheke, Sir Marcus, *Cardinal de Bernis*, 1958.
Cobbett, Revd R.S., *Memorials of Twickenham*, 1872.
Colvin, Christina, *Maria Edgeworth, Letters from England*, 1971.
Crook, Professor J. Mordaunt, 'Strawberry Hill Revisited', *Country Life*, June 1973.
Dunbar, Janet, *A Prospect of Richmond*, 1966.
Evans, John, *Richmond and Its Vicinity*, 1825.
ffrench, Yvonne, *Mrs Siddons*, 1954.
Fothergill, Brian, *The Strawberry Hill Set*, 1983.
Fothergill, Brian, *The Cardinal King*, 1958.
Fothergill, Brian, *Sir William Hamilton*, 1969.
Fothergill, Brian, *Dorothy Jordan*, 1965.
Fullford, Roger, *Royal Dukes*, 1949.
Granville, Castalia Countess, ed., *Lord Granville Leveson Gower*, ii, 1917.
Hedley, Olwen, *Queen Charlotte*, 1975.
Hemlow, Joyce, *Journals and Letters of Fanny Burney*, i, 1972.
Herold, J.C., *Mistress to an Age*, 1959.
Hodgson, F.C., *Thames-side in the Past*, 1913.
Home, Hon. J.A., ed., *Lady Louisa Stuart's Letters to Miss Louisa Clinton*, Edinburgh, 1901.
Houghton, Lord, *Monographs, Personal and Social*, 2nd ed., 1873.
Hyde, Mary, *The Thrales of Streatham Park*, Harvard U.P., 1977.
Ironside, E., *History and Antiquities of Twickenham*, 1797.
Ketton-Cremer, R.W., *Horace Walpole*, 1946.
Leveson Gower, Sir George and Iris Palmer, edd., *Hary-O*, 1940.
Lewis, Lady Theresa, ed., *Extracts from the Journals and Correspondence of Miss Berry*, i, ii, 1865.
Lewis, W.S., ed., *Horace Walpole's Correspondence*, Yale Edition, 11, 12, O.U.P., 1944.

Martineau, Harriet, *Biographical Sketches*, 1869.

Melville, Lewis, ed., *The Berry Papers*, 1914.

Romilly, S.H., ed., *Earl of Dudley's Letters to 'Ivy'*, 1905.

Sichel, Walter, ed., *The Glenbervie Journals*, 1910.

Strachey, Lytton, *Portraits in Miniature*, 1931.

Stuart, D.M., *Dearest Bess*, 1955.

Walford, Edward, *Old and New London*, iii, nd.

Warburton, Eliot, ed., *Memories of Horace Walpole and his Contemporaries* i, ii, 1851.

Watkin, David, *Thomas Hope, 1769-1831 and the Neo-Classicist Era*, 1968.

Index

HW's sympathy for, 90; at Cheltenham, 163; her romantic attachment, 187-8, 194, 223-4; Mrs Damer's pity for, 198; to Royal Academy, 209; completes letter to HW, 219; and domesticity, 220; death, 224

Berry, Mary, 1; acquaintance with HW, 2; admired by him, 2, 10; characteristics, 6, 7, 9-10, 73; birth, 6; at Chiswick, 6; education and accomplishments, 6; whinges over lost inheritance, 7, 130, 169, 176; her success in society, 8; in Italy, 8-9; acquaintance with O'Hara, 9; her appearance, 10, 221; verses by, 11, 12-13, 41; affection for Mrs Damer, 15; unwell, 41; desires to go to Italy, 43; aware of jealousies, 55; leaves for Italy, 55; in Paris, 55, 60-1; trunks searched, 62, 63, 65; disappointment at Turin, 64, 69, 70; attends a hunt, 64; decides for Pisa, 73; offers to sacrifice time abroad, 79, and acts thereon, 82; cuts her nose, 89; her diet, 89; her pencil sketches, 99; and Cicero's *Letters*, 106, her hurt pride, 131-3; possibility of marriage to HW, 2, 134; to Oxford, 162, 164; at Broadstairs, 166; denies HW's interpretation, 175-7; to Mr Barrett, 50, 180, and critical of, 182; at Cheltenham, 183; Mrs Damer's bust of, 183, 184; her love-affair, 183ff., engagement, 94; takes leave of O'Hara, 196; ensuing correspondence, 196-7, 204-7, 211-13; engagement broken, 200; disclosures to HW, 203, 208; to Royal Academy, 209; hears of O'Hara's death, 213; writes of love-affair and dream, 214-15; HW's death, 221-2; edits HW's papers, 223; *Fashionable Friends*, 223; her courtship of Thomas Hope, 223; distress for Ferguson, 224; establishes a salon, 224; death, 224

Travels to: Augsburg, 122; Basle,

7; Bognor, 215; Bologna, 8, 122; Broadstairs, 164; Brompton, 137; Caserta, 8; Chambery, 8; Chamonix, 7; Cheltenham, 183; Coblenz, 7; Florence, 8, 67; Geneva, 7; Innsbruck, 122; Lausanne, 9; Liège, 7; Lymington, 42; Maastricht, 7; Montpelier, 9; Naples, 8; Oxford, 162; Padua, 126; Paris, 9, 55, 60ff., 128; Parma, 64; Pisa, 73; Rome, 26; Rotterdam, 7; Terni, 9; Turin, 64; Venice, 126

Berry, Robert, his line of conduct, 4-5; appearance and character, 6, 69, 73, 194; death of financial prospects, 6; refuses to marry, 6; torpidity, 15, 16; seeks house at Twickenham, 16, 17; agrees to house at Teddington, 37; required to sign agreement, 40; leaves for Italy, 55; hints at extended time abroad, 70; provides money, 205; HW's bequest to, 223; and Mrs, 6

Berry, William, *see* Ferguson, William

Bertie, Lady Georgiana Charlotte (and *see* Cholmondeley, Countess of) as Lord Great Chamberlain, 91

Bianchi, M., *Serimaride*, 162; *Antigone*, 208

Bibiano, 7

Blandford, Marquess of, 117, 120

Blenheim Palace, 164, 216

Boscawen, Hon. Mrs Edward, 29, 30, 47, 48, 107, 216

Boswell, James, his characteristics, 102; his circular letter, 102; *Life of Samuel Johnson*, 100

Botanic Garden, The, 18, 19

Boufflers, Comte and Comtesse de, and Comtesse Amélie, 66, 68

Bouverie, Hon. Mrs, 70, 71, 117

Boyd, Major-General Sir Robert, 59

Boydell, Lord Mayor, 82, 83, 85, 99

Bransome, Anne, 23, 143

Breteuil, Baron de, 27, 28

British Museum, 18

Broglie, duc de, 23, 25
Bruce, Lord, 65
Brudenell, Robert, 91, 92
Brunswick, Caroline Princess of, *see* Wales, Caroline Princess of
Brunswick, Duke of, 159
Brunton, Ann, 119, 120, and Louisa, 119
Budé, General de, 137, 138
Buller, Mrs, 91, 92, 94; to Paris, 119, 152; and son, 92, 94
Burke, Edmund, 97, 102, 154; *Letter from Mr Burke to a Member of the National Assembly*, 101, 103; *Reflections on the French Revolution*, 100-1, 103
Burney, Dr Charles, 216-17
Burney, Fanny, *see* Arblay, Mme D'
Burrell, Sir Peter, Bt, 95
Bushy Gate, 30; House, 44; Park, 33, 119, 202
Bute, Marchioness of, 165, 172
Byrom, John, *Spectator, The*, 144

Calder, Major-General Sir Henry, 59
Calonne, Mme de, 27, 28
Cambridge, Revd G.O., 26, 58, 139, 140, 151
Cambridge, Mrs, 36, 37, 39, 183; and Miss, 46, 111, 140
Cambridge, Richard Owen (the 'Infallible'), 27, 140, 151, 202; his characteristics, 26; would effect a lease, 66; effected, 68
Camden, 1st Earl of, 105
Cardigan, 5th Earl of, 91, 92, 192
Carlisle, 5th Earl of, 85
Caroline, Queen of Naples, 8, 116
Cashel, Charles, Most Revd Archbishop of, 193-4
Castlecomer, Lord and Lady, 33-4, 172
Cathcart, Lord and Lady, 35
Catherine, Empress of Russia (Semiramis, Slayczar), 147, 149; her war with Turkey, 75, 76, 77, 85-6, 87, 88, 91, 92, 105; her acquisition of

Houghton pictures, 130, 210
Catherlogh, Lord, 37-8
Cavendish, Lady Harriet, 224
Chapuy, General, 163
Charles I, 67, 135
Charles II, 166
Charles X, King of France, 49
Charles Edward Stuart, Prince (Young Pretender), 96, 98, 99
Charlotte, Princess, 52
Charlotte, Queen, 26, 27, 28, 76, 91; at Pantheon, 80, 81; makes peace, 87; and Countess of Albany, 99, 100; to Mrs Montagu, 106, 107; cancels drawing-room, 145
Châtelet, duc de, 23, 24
Chatham, 2nd Earl of, 98
Chesterfield, Lord, 161
Child Bankers & Co., 152, 153
Chiswick, 6
Cholmely, Mrs Francis, 24, 25
Cholmondeley, Countess of (*see also* Bertie, Lady Georgiana Charlotte), her marriage, 91, 92, 94; her appointment at Court considered, 170, 177
Cholmondeley, George, 3rd Earl of, *see* Walpole, George, 3rd Earl of Orford
Cholmondeley, George, marriage of, 44, 46, 54, 91; hypochondriac, 91, 94
Cholmondeley, Mrs George, 44, 91, 92, 95, 101
Cholmondeley, 4th Earl of (later 1st Marquess), 44; his mistress, 47, 48; his illegitimate children, 54, 92; his bride, 91, 92; his marriage, 94, 95, and HW's waistcoat at, 138; as Lord Chamberlain, 166; and Prospect House, 166, 171, and his nearby house, 173, 177; his appointment by Prince of Wales, 170, 173, 177, but declined, 177
Cholmondeley, Hon. and Revd Robert, his marriage, 44; as heir presumptive, 54; excluded from wedding, 95
Cholmondeley, Hon. Mrs Robert (Polly), background and marriage,